CORPORATE STRATEGY

Tools for Analysis and Decision-Making

Many companies are not single businesses but a collection of businesses with one or more levels of corporate management. Corporate strategy refers to how they compete. Written for managers, advisors, and students aspiring to these roles, this book is a guide to decision making in the domain of corporate strategy. It arms readers with research-based tools needed to make good corporate strategy decisions and to assess the soundness of the corporate strategy decisions of others. Readers will learn how to do the analysis for answering questions such as "Should we pursue an alliance or an acquisition to grow?", "How much should we integrate this acquisition?" and "Should we divest this business?". The book draws on the authors' wealth of research and teaching experience at INSEAD, London Business School, and University College London. A range of learning aids, including easy-to-comprehend examples, decision templates, and FAQs, are provided in the book and on a rich companion website.

PHANISH PURANAM is the Roland Berger Chair Professor of Strategy and Organization Design, and Academic Director of the PhD programme at INSEAD. He was previously Chair of the PhD programme at London Business School. A leading researcher, teacher, and advisor in the areas of corporate strategy and organization design, Phanish has won several honours for his work. He received his PhD at the Wharton School (University of Pennsylvania).

BART VANNESTE is Associate Professor of Strategy at the UCL School of Management. He researches and teaches corporate strategy, with a focus on the design and management of inter-organizational relationships. He received his PhD at the London Business School.

CORPORATE STRATEGY

Tools for Analysis and Decision-Making

PHANISH PURANAM

AND

BART VANNESTE

CAMBRIDGE
UNIVERSITY PRESS

CAMBRIDGE
UNIVERSITY PRESS

University Printing House, Cambridge CB2 8BS, United Kingdom

Cambridge University Press is part of the University of Cambridge.

It furthers the University's mission by disseminating knowledge in the pursuit of
education, learning and research at the highest international levels of excellence.

www.cambridge.org
Information on this title: www.cambridge.org/9781107120914

© Phanish Puranam and Bart Vanneste 2016

First published 2016

A catalogue record for this publication is available from the British Library

Library of Congress Cataloguing in Publication data
Puranam, Phanish.
Corporate strategy: tools for analysis and decision-making / Phanish
Puranam and Bart Vanneste.
pages cm
Includes index.
ISBN 978-1-107-12091-4
1. Strategic planning.   2. Decision making.   3. Industrial
management.   I. Vanneste, Bart.   II. Title.
HD30.28.P856   2016
658.4′012–dc23
2015026751

ISBN 978-1-107-12091-4 Hardback

Additional resources for this publication at www.cambridge.org/corporatestrategy

Contents

Figures

Tables

Boxes

Acknowledgments

We would like to acknowledge our teachers and co-authors, who have taught us a lot of what we know about corporate strategy. They are Laurence Capron (INSEAD), Ravee Chittoor (Indian School of Business), Ranjay Gulati (Harvard University), Prashant Kale (Rice University), Tobias Kretschmer (Ludwig Maximilian University of Munich), Marlo Raveendran (University of California), Harbir Singh (University of Pennsylvania), Kannan Srikanth (Singapore Management University), and Maurizio Zollo (Bocconi University).

We also acknowledge the invaluable input of our colleagues on early drafts of the book: Markus Becker (University of Southern Denmark), Laurence Capron (INSEAD), Ravee Chittoor (Indian School of Business), Felipe Csaszar (University of Michigan), Donal Crilly (London Business School), Emilie Feldman (University of Pennsylvania), Nirmalya Kumar (Tata Sons), Zdenek Necas (Ivey), Caterina Moschieri (IE Business School), Urs Peyer (INSEAD), Marlo Raveendran (University of California), Evan Rawley (Columbia University), Astrid Schornick (INSEAD), Metin Sengul (Boston University), Kannan Srikanth (Singapore Management University), and Brian Wu (University of Michigan). We are grateful to our many MBA, EMBA, MSc, and executive students at INSEAD, London Business School, and University College London, in particular Arnaud Bonnet (Imperial Innovations), Kimchi Hoang (INSEAD), Santosh Kumar (Facebook), Viren Lall (ChangeSchool.org), Elise Lee (Merck), Zan Li (University College London), Edwin Meyers (Capitales Cuestamoras), Mateen Poonawala (McKinsey), and Niels Christian Wedell-Wedellsborg (London Business School), who very generously read drafts of our chapters and provided excellent suggestions to improve them. We thank Caroline Koekkoek and Krithiga Sankaran for research assistance. We are grateful to Jan Vanneste (HBMEO) for the cover's artwork.

Introduction: what this book is about and how to use it

We wrote this book to help you make **good corporate strategy decisions** and perform sound analysis of the corporate strategy decisions of others, on the basis of knowledge obtained from **research**. Since this is the goal of the book, it is useful to be clear about the key terms in the statement above.

Corporate strategy refers to the strategy that multi-business corporations use to compete as a collection of multiple businesses. These businesses may each constitute a division within the corporation (or be bundled together with very similar businesses into a division), or may each be a legally distinct company, whose shares are held by a parent company. This book and its contents are applicable to all of these types of firms.

By **good decisions** we mean something quite specific. In the world of management, it is tempting but incorrect to define good decisions solely in terms of good outcomes. Because decisions are made with limited information and are not easy to reverse even after better information comes along, it is better to think about good decisions as those that (1) are the best given current information (and also feature a recognition that current information may not be complete), and (2) can be explained and defended to others. The first criterion is a straightforward one and requires little explanation. The second comes from the organizational context in which corporate strategy decisions are made. They must ultimately be evaluated and implemented by others who must be convinced and motivated by them.

Relatedly, this book is about **decisions**, not topics. It is written to provide an active guide for decision-making. This goes beyond a passive understanding of what corporate strategy is (which is the focus of a typical textbook). Rather, our goal is to help a reader with limited prior knowledge to (a) make a good decision on a concrete corporate strategy issue (e.g., should we pursue organic or inorganic growth, should we acquire or ally with this firm, or should we keep or divest this business) and (b) offer a well-reasoned justification for this decision, that is rigorous and clear. Thus, the emphasis is on concepts and how to use them to reach a decision, not on description.

Finally, this book is designed to provide tools for analyses and decisions about corporate strategy that are based on **research**. This means that the concepts, heuristics, ideas, and frameworks that together make up these tools are either directly or indirectly based on ideas and evidence that have passed the test of academic peer review. The linkage in some cases will be very proximate and we will give references to relevant research where this is the case.

At the same time, we also recognize the limits to exclusive reliance on the existing research base. We therefore also include ideas in this book whose connection to the research (and to rigorously validated ideas and evidence) is less proximate. While we strive to make these ideas always internally consistent, the evidence base may not always exist yet. The reader is warned to recognize these ideas by the absence of direct references (and is advised to exercise appropriate caution in adopting them).

The reasons we rely on the research base (even when we do so indirectly) in developing this material can be traced to our experiences teaching corporate strategy concepts to thousands of MBA, EMBA, and MSc students as well as senior managers and CEOs for over a decade at INSEAD, London Business School, and University College London. Through these experiences, we have come to realize two things. First, corporate strategy is an extremely complex topic. As we will explain, a lot of the complexity comes from the difficulty of separating out the components of a decision. Second, it is precisely in such situations of complexity that abstraction is valuable. In particular, our experience suggests that the abstractions and simplifications that researchers typically employ to study the complexities of corporate strategy can in fact be useful to practitioners, too. We believe that it should not be any more difficult for practicing managers to explain and defend decisions based on research, as it is to do so based on judgment and received wisdom. Of course, this book does not aim to be a comprehensive summary of the academic literature in corporate strategy; we are quite selective in picking what we need and know best (which, unsurprisingly, is often our own research) for the particular decisions we are interested in.

A final caveat to note is that the corporate strategy tools and frameworks we present, like all strategy frameworks, try to provide internally consistent representations that abstract from detail, assume some structure even for ill-defined problems, and simplify ambiguity into uncertainty, while still aspiring to be useful. We are keenly aware of the trade-offs on each of these dimensions.[1] An analogy may be useful here: a map, to be of any use at all, cannot possibly be of a scale of 1:1! It necessarily ignores, reduces, and simplifies and that's what makes it useful, both on individual journeys as well as in team efforts where all must agree and understand how to get to a destination. However, no one should or would make the mistake of confusing the map with the real thing. In much the same way, the frameworks and models we present are simplifications, which aim to be useful. They do not pretend to be "real." They offer a way to comprehend reality, and a basis for discussion. Thus the reader is forewarned that the ideas in this book must be complemented with a healthy dose of industry and company specific knowledge, and perhaps even skepticism about the ideas themselves, to be used in a creative and insightful manner.

In particular, we believe that the frameworks we propose can anchor useful debates around important decisions. A good way in which to use the frameworks in this book to make decisions is to have competing teams perform analyses to justify different alternatives. For instance, one group may perform the analysis about a diversification decision with the goal of minimizing the chance of an error of commission (i.e., the mistake of diversifying when one should not have) whereas another group may do so to minimize the chance of an error of omission (i.e., the mistake of missing a good diversification opportunity). As long as both teams use the same structured approach, such as that we describe in this book, the resulting debate will involve real communication and be enormously insightful, even when the teams reach opposing conclusions. We believe such an approach can be useful for almost any major corporate strategy decision – e.g., partner selection, valuation, and post-merger integration (PMI) in mergers and acquisitions (M&As).

How this book is organized: key decisions in corporate strategy

To make this book as useful as possible to corporate strategists, we have organized the material in terms of the critical decisions they face, and these make up the bulk of the book. Before we tackle these decisions, Part I (*Foundations*) of the book (Chapters 1, 2, and 3) introduce three theoretical pillars for the analysis of corporate strategy: corporate advantage, synergies, and governance costs.

Part I: Foundations
Chapter 1 (*Corporate advantage*) introduces and defines the concept of corporate advantage, and explains how it is different from competitive advantage, the key concept in business strategy. The chapter also explains why synergies are critical to sustaining corporate advantage when investors can easily replicate the same portfolio of investments as a corporation, albeit without the decision rights that the managers of a corporation enjoy.

Chapter 2 (*Synergies: benefits to collaboration*) develops a novel approach to analyze synergies between any two businesses at the level of their underlying value chain segments. If synergies are the potential gains from collaboration across different businesses, governance costs are the "tax" that eats into these potential benefits.

Chapter 3 (*Governance costs: impediments to collaboration*) introduces heuristic frameworks to assess the conditions under which these costs are likely to be significant impediments to the realization of synergy. A key insight for corporate strategists is that these costs can be controlled through the appropriate choice of a governance structure (e.g., contract, equity–alliance, joint venture, or full ownership). The optimal governance structure is thus one that takes into account the benefits of as well as the impediments to collaboration.

The frameworks in these three chapters lie at the heart of all the corporate strategy decisions that we discuss in the rest of the book, including diversification, divestiture, valuation, PMI, selection of strategic alliance partners, re-organizing the structure of the corporation, outsourcing, and offshoring. They are thus essential reading for getting the most out of any part of the rest of the book.

Parts II and III: Decisions about portfolio composition
In this part of the book, we examine decisions that pertain to which businesses should be in the portfolio of the corporate strategist, and how to assemble such a portfolio. The implicit assumption is that once these businesses are brought into the portfolio, synergies across businesses can be realized through administrative control. Chapters 4, 5, and 6 look at increasing the scope of the organization. Chapters 7 and 8 consider decreasing the scope of the organization.

Part II: Increasing the scope of the organization Chapter 4 (*Diversification*) introduces a basic test to consider when and where diversification, the entry into a new business, is useful. This brings together ideas about corporate advantage (why should *you* diversify rather than your shareholders), synergies (which business should you diversify into), and governance costs (what is the best governance structure to exploit synergies). We discuss vertical integration as a special case of diversification.

Chapter 5 (*Ally or acquire?*) covers the choice between strategic alliance and acquisition, two of the fundamental mechanisms of inorganic growth. A key distinction is that in an alliance the partners remain independent, whereas in an M&A one party gives up control. Because the associated benefits and costs differ, we discuss when an alliance is to be preferred over an acquisition, and vice versa.

Chapter 6 (*Organic or inorganic growth?*) considers whether to enter a new business organically (do it on your own) or inorganically (through alliances or acquisitions). We discuss the factors that favor organic growth and those that favor inorganic growth.

Part III: Decreasing the scope of the organization Chapter 7 (*Divestiture: stay or exit*) covers the divestiture decision, in particular the choice between different modes of exit from a business. Divestiture can be seen as a horizontal scope decision, in which the organization reduces the number of businesses it is active in. We focus on divestiture through sell-off or spin-off.

Chapter 8 (*Outsourcing: make or buy*) covers vertical scope decisions where there is a reduction in the number of value chain segments the corporation is active in while the number of businesses remains constant. We consider the conditions under which outsourcing is appropriate, and when to consider offshoring.

Part IV: Decisions about portfolio organization
In this last part of the book, we take the portfolio composition as given. The focus is on managing the portfolio to extract synergies across the businesses through administrative control.

Chapter 9 (*Designing the multi-business corporation*) covers organizational structure decisions. We analyze when pure, hybrid, and matrix structures are appropriate, and contrast the legal and organizational structure of multi-business corporations. We also discuss when it is time to re-organize.

Chapter 10 (*Designing the corporate HQ*) covers "corporate parenting" decisions: how to select the appropriate role for the headquarters (HQ) in a multi-business firm. We highlight three key dimensions: standalone vs. linkage based approaches to synergy across businesses, directive vs. non-directive approaches to managing each business, and resource allocation across businesses to balance growth and profits while exploiting synergies.

Chapter 11 (*Managing the M&A process*) examines the key choices when conducting an M&A. Given that a decision to undertake an M&A has been made, several steps need to be taken to successfully conduct it. We focus on the critical aspects: valuation, negotiations, and post-merger integration.

Chapter 12 (*Managing the alliance process*) analyzes the key choices when structuring an alliance. In an alliance, the goal is for the partners to collaborate but without either side gaining full control over the other. We discuss how partner selection, valuation, negotiation, and integration can help you to succeed with an alliance.

While Parts II and III separate the decisions around which businesses belong in the portfolio from how they are managed once the portfolio decision is made, this is an analytical convenience and in practice both aspects must be considered simultaneously. Therefore, the structure of the book is such that it allows the reader to selectively combine a set of chapters to get what she is after efficiently.

For instance, those interested only in M&A should read Chapters 1, 2, and 3 (as these provide the foundations), and then go on to Chapters 5 and 11. To consider the design of the corporate HQ, Chapters 1, 2, 3, and 10 would suffice. Table 0.1 illustrates how the

TABLE 0.1 *How the chapters build on each other*

Part	Chapter		Builds on Chapter											
			1	2	3	4	5	6	7	8	9	10	11	12
I Foundations	1	Corporate advantage												
	2	Synergies: benefits to collaboration	1											
	3	Governance costs: impediments to collaboration	1	2										
II Portfolio composition: increasing scope	4	Diversification	1	2	3									
	5	Ally or acquire?	1	2	3	4								
	6	Organic or inorganic growth?	1	2	3	4	5							
III Portfolio composition: reducing scope	7	Divestiture: stay or exit	1	2	3									
	8	Outsourcing: make or buy	1	2	3				7					
IV Portfolio organization	9	Designing the multi-business corporation	1	2	3									
	10	Designing the corporate HQ	1	2	3									
	11	Managing the M&A process	1	2	3		5							
	12	Managing the alliance process	1	2	3		5							

chapters are related. We do not have a separate chapter on international business because we view international aspects as increasingly being quite inter-mingled with corporate strategy decisions. For instance, foreign market entry is an instance of diversification, and a cross-border merger or joint venture is, first and foremost, an acquisition or an alliance, respectively. Where relevant, we mention how decisions may differ between a national and an international context.

Each chapter ends with a list of Frequently asked questions (FAQs) on aspects of corporate strategy, and some Further reading around the topic of the chapter.

Note

1. See for instance the insightful discussion on these issues in Levinthal, D. A. (2011). A behavioral approach to strategy – what's the alternative? *Strategic Management Journal*, *32*(13), 1517–1523.

PART I

Foundations

Corporate advantage

Mario had worked hard to become CEO of MoveIt, a large diversified producer of planes, trains, and tractors. Since he took over three years ago, things have gone well: revenues increased every year by at least 15 percent and profits are at an all-time high. But he has this nagging feeling that more is possible. At the same time, he does not know what that is. What should Mario strive for, and how can he know if he is doing a good job as CEO?

Corporate strategy refers to the strategy that multi-business corporations use to compete as a collection of multiple businesses. It is qualitatively different from strategy for a single business firm, or "business strategy." The number of businesses, goals, the nature of competition, and, consequently, the concepts used in analysis, all differ between business and corporate strategy.

Difference 1: Single vs. multi-businesses

Business strategy involves a **single business**, whereas corporate strategy involves **multiple businesses**. For instance, a corporation could have multiple businesses that make appliances, software, mining instruments, turbines, jet engines, and healthcare products. Each business has its own business strategy. The corporate strategy of the corporation cuts across and affects all these businesses.

The questions "what is a business?" and "how do we distinguish businesses from each other?" are inescapable if we think of corporate strategy as the strategy of multi-business firms. We find it useful to think of a business as uniquely identified in terms of its **business model**. A business model comprises the set of choices about customers, products, and value chain activities that every business must make.[1] These choices are also sometimes referred to as the "who/what/how" choices: who are the customers, what are we selling them, and how do we produce what we are selling and get it into the hands of the customers? Two businesses are different if their business models differ from each other on at least one of these dimensions. Thus, a business selling furniture out of local warehouses to customers in the UK is a different business than one selling to customers in India (different "who"). A business offering sushi for lunch from a small restaurant to busy professionals is a different business than one offering hamburgers (different "what"). An online only bank is a different business than one that serves customers exclusively through its branch network (different "how").

Industries, in contrast, are usually distinguished from each other in terms of low cross-price elasticity of demand – a price change within one industry has negligible effects on the demand for goods in the other industry. For example, sushi and hamburgers belong to the same industry if a price increase for hamburgers leads to more sushi being sold. Thus a corporation may have multiple businesses within the same industry. Airlines that operate both a full service and a budget carrier are an instance of this. On the other hand, being in a different industry necessarily means being in a distinct business. To be "in" a business means owning at least some of the assets needed for the activities involved in that business.

Difference 2: Competitive advantage vs. corporate advantage

The goal of business strategy is to maximize the net present value (NPV) of a business, i.e., its future cash flows appropriately discounted for their timing and riskiness (for a brief explanation of NPV see the appendix to this chapter). At the most basic level, this is achieved by ensuring that your buyers are willing to pay more for the outputs of a business than what your suppliers are willing to sell the inputs to you for. Willingness-to-pay (WTP) is the most that buyers will pay for a firm's product. The actual price (i.e., what the buyers pay the firm) will be equal to or less than the WTP, or a firm will sell nothing. Willingness-to-sell (WTS) is the least price for which suppliers will provide all inputs for a firm's product, including raw materials, capital, and labor. The firm's actual cost (i.e., what the firm pays its suppliers) will be at least as high (see Figure 1.1).

You have a **competitive advantage** over a competitor when your difference between buyers' WTP and suppliers' WTS sell is greater than your competitor's difference (between their buyers' WTP and

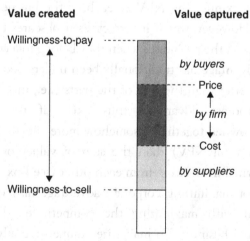

Figure 1.1 Willingness-to-pay and willingness-to-sell

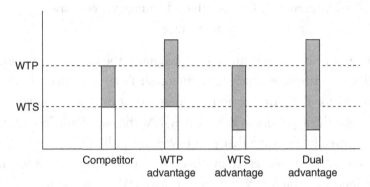

Figure 1.2 Different types of competitive advantage

their suppliers' WTS). There are thus two ways of increasing competitive advantage (see Figure 1.2): by raising the price the customers are willing to pay you (pursuing a differentiation advantage) and/or by lowering the price suppliers are willing to sell to you for (pursuing a cost advantage).[2] It follows that which one you should pursue will depend on the alternatives available to your customers and suppliers (i.e., their bargaining power with you).

One might think that the goal of corporate strategy is to individually maximize the NPV of each of the businesses in the corporation. However, this is incorrect, as it obscures the possible linkages between the businesses when they belong to a corporation. **Corporate advantage** has traditionally been understood as in some sense doing better than the sum of the parts (i.e., individual businesses). Corporate advantage thus exists if the collection of businesses **owned together** is somehow more valuable (i.e., generates higher total NPV) than the sum of values of individual businesses owned in isolation from each other (see Box 1.1).

The goal of maximizing corporate advantage may or may not be consistent with maximizing the competitive advantage of each individual business. To maximize competitive advantage for each business, each business must outdo its rivals in creating a wedge

> **Box 1.1 The corporate advantage test**
>
> The corporate advantage test can be written as:
>
> $$V[AB] > V(A) + V(B)$$
>
> V(A) is the standalone NPV of business A and V(B) that of business B. This is the value when each is **owned separately**. V[AB] is the NPV of business A and business B when they are **owned jointly**.

between their customers' WTP and their suppliers' WTS. However, some businesses could give up competitive advantage in their business in order to enhance the competitive advantage of other businesses in the portfolio; there may optimally be winners and losers within a portfolio if the winners win more than the losers lose.

Various studies have decomposed the profitability of businesses into factors that arise from the business unit, corporate parent, or industry level. The results show that business unit level factors (such as the management or capabilities underlying the business) explain a big part of the variance in the returns of businesses, but that additionally the corporate level explains a substantial part (ahead of industry level factors). Furthermore, it is also understood that the impact of the business level is at least in part due to decisions taken at the corporate level (such as which businesses to enter).[3] The implication is clear: corporate strategy matters, over and above business strategy, and matters at least as much as the analysis of industry competition. No business within a multi-business corporation can consider its strategic analysis complete without understanding its role within the overall corporate strategy of the parent.

Difference 3: Who is the competition?

The competition for a corporate strategist is different from that for a business strategist. For a business strategist, the competition is **anyone who can influence a business' cost or revenues adversely**. This includes direct rivals, but also buyers, suppliers, potential entrants, and companies that sell substitutes (famously captured in Michael Porter's "five forces" framework).[4]

For a corporate strategist, the competition is **anyone who can assemble a similar portfolio of businesses**. We distinguish between two types of such competitors: (1) investors (e.g., mutual funds) and (2) other corporate strategists (e.g., other multi-business corporations, their chief executive officers (CEOs), boards, internal and external advisors, chief strategy officers (CSOs), etc.).

Investors have cash flow rights over returns but typically no decision rights. They have only limited power to tell a corporation what corporate strategy decisions to take. On the other hand, corporate strategists have decision rights in the businesses through the administrative control exercised by corporate headquarters (HQ). Between these two groups is a grey zone. For example, activist shareholders can take a stake in a company and (publicly) pressure a CEO to divest a business. Private equity firms that traditionally focused on financial engineering and operational restructuring are now also engaged in exploiting linkages between businesses. A corporate strategist competes with all of them.

Identifying the competition helps the corporate strategist formulate an appropriate corporate strategy. Because investors have cash flow but no decision rights, their main strategy is **portfolio assembly**. In addition, corporate strategists can also use **business modification**. We discuss these next.

Corporate advantage from portfolio assembly: the "selection" approach

More corporate advantage is better, but how much is necessary? A natural, minimal benchmark for a corporate strategist is a passive investor. A corporate strategist should at least be doing better than someone who has no decision power over the individual businesses. But how can an investor create corporate advantage at all, without such power?

The answer lies in the definition of the NPV of a portfolio of businesses A and B: V[AB] = Future cash flows discounted at a discount rate. A discount rate is used to assign a present value (PV) to the cash flows that occur in the future. It follows that value can be created in two ways: influencing cash flows or decreasing the discount rate.

Recall that by our definition an investor cannot influence the cash flows of the businesses. However, an investor may be able to spot bargains: the usual mantra is to "buy low and sell high." In other words, buy a business for less than what it can be resold for later. If successful, an investor may capture value by getting a bargain: more cash comes in than goes out.

Further, an investor can decrease the discount rate. A discount rate depends on three factors. First, a discount rate depends on the timing of the cash flows. Cash flows in the near future are worth more than those in the far future. Getting $1,000 next week is more appealing than getting the same amount ten years from now. Second, a discount rate depends on the riskiness of the cash flows. Secure cash flows are worth more than risky cash flows. A $1,000 payment in ten years promised by the US government is more attractive than the same $1,000 payment in ten years promised by a stranger on a peer-to-peer (P2P) lending site. Third, a discount rate depends on who is the beneficiary of the cash flows. A diversified beneficiary might be willing to take on more risk than an undiversified beneficiary, so that the discount rate would be lower for a diversified than an undiversified beneficiary. For example, you may be unwilling to lend $1,000 to one stranger on a P2P lending site, but you might be willing to lend $100 each to ten different strangers.

In this last way, an investor can lower a discount rate through diversification. For instance, consider three equally valuable but different businesses, A, B, and C, each owned separately by Alexia, Barbara, and Charlie. Assume further that they have all their wealth invested in their own business and are passive investors (i.e., they don't interfere with their business). For each business, each year there's a 50 percent chance that the owner will get $300 and a 50 percent chance of $0. Thus, on average, each owner will get $150. One day they sit together and discuss combining their businesses into a single corporation ABC, with each obtaining a one-third stake. They are all in favor even though they agree that the businesses will be owned jointly but operated separately (the decision-making for each business is completely independent). The reason is that the risk has been lowered through diversification. Under the new structure, each owner will still get on average $150. But the annual payments are less likely to be as extreme as before (i.e., $300 or $0). In a given year, it is unlikely that all companies do well or all do poorly. Therefore the new investment is less risky than the old one. In other words, the discount rate is lower because the risk is diversified.

This logic underlies the classic investment advice: "don't put all your eggs in one basket." In fact, Alexia, Barbara, and Charlie favor this deal precisely because they had all their wealth tied up in a single business. They probably would not have done this deal had their wealth already been diversified into other assets.

In this example, the condition of corporate advantage is satisfied: $V[ABC] > V(A) + V(B) + V(C)$. This is entirely due to a reduction in discount rates because the cash flows are unaffected. If we take as a benchmark the performance of a passive investor, who can create corporate advantage merely through **selection** of a good portfolio of businesses, then a corporate strategist (with the same portfolio, but who administratively controls her selected portfolio of businesses) must in this example at least do better than the V[ABC] achieved by the three owners.

Corporate advantage from business modification: the "synergy" approach

It should be clear by now that a corporate strategist (i.e., a strategist in the corporate HQ of a multi-business firm, or anybody advising or assisting somebody playing that role) cannot rest content with the gains from risk diversification or bargain hunting if a typical investor can also access them. Rather, within the selected portfolio the corporate strategist must work on increasing the NPV of the portfolio of businesses. Unlike an investor, a corporate strategist can create value by changing the cash flows of the businesses (e.g., through increasing revenue or decreasing expenditures) as well as by decreasing the discount rates.

In Chapter 2, we will develop detailed frameworks for analyzing a central concept in corporate strategy: **synergy** between the businesses in a portfolio. For now, it suffices to note that we use synergy as an umbrella term to describe the various ways in which the cash flows and discount rates of businesses in a portfolio can be **modified through joint operation (i.e., collaboration and joint decision-making)** across them. Synergy is therefore the means through which corporate advantage is created relative to a typical investor who can **select** the same portfolio of investments (without exercising decision-making power over them, as she lacks the rights to do so).

In most mature capital markets, typical investors may be able to build the same or a more diversified portfolio than the corporate strategist, and typically with a lower cost of administrative overhead than that of a corporation. If the shareholders are already well diversified, then further diversification by the company will not reduce the discount rate. There are, however, situations in which the investor may simply not have access to the equivalent portfolio. She cannot buy shares in the relevant businesses or access mutual funds that do so, as has sometimes been the case in the emerging economies. In these situations, the corporate strategist may be able to get away with acting essentially as an investor with preferential access to investments, if she can merely select the portfolio and typical investors cannot. In other words, mere portfolio assembly may create sufficient corporate advantage in such cases, even if the returns and risks of the individual businesses are left unmodified.

So how much corporate advantage is enough for a corporate strategist? Ideally, a corporate strategist would maximize corporate advantage. But at a minimum, she should create no less value from the portfolio of businesses than any another actor would. What this minimum is varies by institutional context, and hence so does the appropriate path to achieve corporate advantage. When investors can replicate the portfolio of investments represented by a multi-business corporation, corporate advantage must necessarily rest on some form of synergy, which requires modification of the cash flows or the discount rates of businesses; otherwise assembling a portfolio of individually good but unlinked businesses may suffice. Thus corporate strategy in a developed and developing economy may look very different in the relative emphasis placed on portfolio assembly vs. modification, but we contend that both can be understood according to the same over-arching principles. Table 1.1 provides a summary of the different paths to corporate advantage.

To summarize, corporate strategy is the strategy of multi-business corporations and the goal is the pursuit of corporate advantage. Corporate advantage exists if joint ownership of businesses is more valuable than the same businesses owned separately. In Figure 1.3, this is the case if quadrant III and IV are more valuable than

TABLE 1.1 *Useful corporate strategies in different contexts*

	Modification of businesses: "synergy"		Assembly of portfolio: "selection"	
	Cash flows	Discount rate	Cash flows	Discount rate
Context	Increase cash flows (increase revenue or decrease expenses)	Reduce risk of business (systematic risk)	Buy under-valued businesses (unaltered cash flows are worth more than what is paid for them)	Reduce risk of portfolio (unsystematic risk)
Under-developed capital markets	✓	✓	✓	✓
Well-developed capital markets	✓	✓	X	X

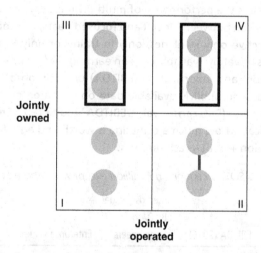

Figure 1.3 Investors can jointly own business, corporate strategists can additionally jointly operate them

quadrants I and II, respectively. If an investor can easily select and assemble a portfolio similar to a corporate strategist (i.e., compare quadrant I to III) then a corporate strategist potentially can only do better through modification of businesses (i.e., compare quadrant

III and IV). Figure 1.3 further clarifies that synergies may also exist between businesses that are owned separately (i.e., if quadrant II does better than quadrant I). An important question for corporate strategy, which we address in Part II on the scope of the organization (Chapters 4–6), is when common ownership is necessary to realize synergies.

Application: Movelt

Mario is CEO of Movelt, which is active in three businesses: planes, trains, and tractors, as we saw at the beginning of the chapter. To assess Mario's performance, we look at whether Movelt has corporate advantage, i.e., whether the business are worth more owned jointly than separately.

With the help of their investment bank, Mario prepares a sum-of-the-parts (SOTP) valuation (see Table 1.2). Such valuation is often done to assess the performance of multi-business organizations. It is a comparison between Movelt and **focused peers**, i.e., companies who are active only in planes, only in trains, or only in tractors. Mario uses privately available data on earnings before interest, tax, depreciation, and amortization (EBITDA) per division of his own corporation and publicly available data on valuation multiples of focused peers (Enterprise value/EBITDA multiples). **Enterprise value** indicates how much a company is worth and equals market capitalization + debt – cash reserves.

TABLE 1.2 *SOTP valuation (in £ million except where noted otherwise)*

Division	EBITDA (2016)	Enterprise value/ EBITDA of focused peers	Enterprise value	
			Total	£ per share
Planes	70	11	770	6.16
Trains	60	17	1020	8.16
Tractors	50	9	450	3.60

TABLE 1.2 (*cont.*)

Division	EBITDA (2016)	Enterprise value/ EBITDA of focused peers	Enterprise value	
			Total	£ per share
HQ		Costs	(67)	(0.54)
Total			2173	17.38
		Net debt	(869)	(6.95)
SOTP			1304 (market capitalization)	10.43 (share price)

From this, Mario infers an enterprise value per division for his own company. Taking into account the costs of HQ, net debt, and the fact that 125 million shares are outstanding, the SOTP valuation of Movelt suggests a price of £10.43 per share. This is an estimate of what the shares in a portfolio of investments in three standalone companies – 1 for planes, 1 for trains, and 1 for tractors – would be valued at if they had similar earnings to Movelt's divisions. Arguably the estimate is even conservative, as the cost of HQ in such a portfolio of pure investments (assuming there are no centralized functions at HQ) may not be as high as it is for Movelt. At the time of the analysis, the share price of Movelt is £9.40, i.e., lower than the SOTP valuation. Can we conclude that Movelt lacks corporate advantage because Movelt trades at a discount relative to its focused peers?

While it may be tempting to think so, in fact such a conclusion must be tempered with a lot of caution. If we use an SOTP valuation to assess corporate advantage, then we need to make two critical assumptions (see Table 1.3). First, that the focused peers

TABLE 1.3 *Assumptions when using SOTP valuation to infer corporate advantage (in £ million)*

Movelt	EBITDA	Enterprise value/ EBITDA	Enterprise value
Jointly owned	180	11.36	2044
Separately owned	180 (assumption 2: equal to jointly owned)	12.07 (assumption 1: equal to focused peers)	2173

whose multiples we use are truly comparable to Movelt's divisions. Second, that the earnings of Movelt's divisions would be unaffected if the divisions were split up and organized under separate rather than joint ownership. This assumption is particularly problematic. We want to know whether splitting up Movelt into three separately owned businesses would increase or decrease earnings. Using a technique in which we begin by assuming that the earnings are unaffected cannot provide a good answer.

So what is the discount calculated using SOTP good for? First, it does highlight the fact that the capital markets discount the earnings from Movelt relative to comparable earnings from standalone firms. Thus, a SOTP provides an insight into whether the capital markets appreciate a pound of earnings (or sales, cash flows, assets) of the multi-business firm more than those of standalone firms, but not into whether those earnings would be lower or higher. Perhaps Mario needs to explain to investors and analysts why the future prospects of his businesses are better than they think. Second, it gives us a **benchmark** rather than a measure. Mario must be confident that the EBITDA generated by the businesses in his portfolio are *at least* higher than the discount because they are in his portfolio, than when operated and owned independently. Obviously the larger the discount, the less plausible this argument is.

Corporate advantage is a goal, not a measure

Despite our ability to define corporate advantage clearly, in practice it remains very difficult to measure. The most important difficulty for all techniques is the same. The notion of corporate advantage requires a comparison between something we can observe – the performance of a multi-business corporation – and a counterfactual that we cannot – the aggregate performance of the individual businesses **if** they had been operating in isolation from each other (see Figure 1.4). By coming into existence, the multi-business firm in effect destroys its own best benchmark. In contrast, competitive advantage is easier to measure because it involves comparing observables – the performance of different businesses.

We therefore think of corporate advantage ultimately as an imperfectly measurable but nonetheless useful benchmark for corporate strategists, to use as a conceptual touchstone when contemplating strategic decisions.

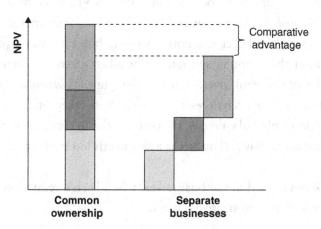

Figure 1.4 Corporate advantage involves a comparison between what is and what could have been

Frequently asked questions

1. The goal for corporate strategy is variously described in terms of "pursue synergies," "make sure your assets are not worth more to another buyer," or "seek corporate advantage." How do these three ideas relate to each other?

If an investor can replicate the portfolio of businesses that a corporate strategist controls, then corporate advantage exists relative to this investor only if the corporate strategist can extract synergies, i.e., modify the cash flows or discount rates of businesses. Therefore "seek corporate advantage" and "pursue synergies" mean the same thing if an investor can replicate the portfolio of businesses that a corporate strategist controls.

Different corporate strategists may generate different levels of corporate advantage for the same portfolio of businesses, so to compete with other potential controllers of the same portfolio; the goal of the corporate strategist is to maximize corporate advantage. However, even if you exploit such synergies in your portfolio to the fullest extent, this is not sufficient for you to be safe from being worth more to another buyer, because the assets they hold may generate large synergies with your assets. If the buyer is a non-synergistic buyer such as a private equity fund, then pursuing synergies to the fullest extent is sufficient for you to be safe from takeover. Note also that pursuing synergies to their full potential is not even necessary to be safe from takeover. Even if you have under-exploited synergies, the costs another player faces in taking over your assets may still make the assets worth less to them.

2. Given a portfolio of businesses, when is risk reduction by a corporate strategist useful?

Risk reduction is always useful for bondholders (because their loans become more secure) and for top managers and employees

TABLE 1.4 *Does risk reduction lead to a lower discount rate (and hence a higher NPV)?*

	Lowering unsystematic risk (i.e., business specific)	Lowering systematic risk (i.e., market risk)
Diversified shareholders	X	✓
Undiversified shareholders	✓	✓

(if their jobs become more secure). For shareholders, this depends on their alternatives. If the shareholders have no other investment opportunities, then any risk reduction by the strategist is beneficial. If the shareholder has unlimited other investment opportunities, then he can diversify away all the unsystematic risk (the risk that is unique to a business); then risk reduction by the strategist is only useful to the shareholder if it leads to lower systematic risk for the portfolio – the extent to which a company's returns vary with those of the broader capital market. In other words, whether risk diversification by a corporate strategist leads to a lower discount rate for shareholders depends on whether the shareholders themselves are diversified, and what sort of risk is being reduced (see Table 1.4).

3. Can diversification ever lead to lower systematic risk?

This would be the case if the combination of two businesses were less sensitive to the general economy than the same two businesses uncombined. Diversification by an investor does not lower systematic risk because this is defined as the risk that is undiversifiable (i.e., the risk that remains after diversifying). However, diversification by a corporate strategist with administrative control that allows the movement of cash between businesses can lower systematic risk if: (1) businesses have bankruptcy costs, i.e., the prospect of a near bankruptcy will discourage suppliers or customers from dealing with the organization (e.g. would you still buy a flight ticket if you suspected the airline might go bankrupt before you fly?) or will force the organization to forgo profitable investment opportunities (a product extension will be hugely profitable in two years but no funds are available for the upfront investments); (2) it is costly for businesses to hold enough financial slack to avoid all future bankruptcy costs; and (3) cash flows of businesses are imperfectly correlated (so that someone with administrative control can subsidize one business close to bankruptcy with funds from another business). Thus diversification by a corporate strategist can lower systematic risk for a portfolio containing businesses that face substantial bankruptcy costs, whose cash flows are not correlated, and in periods of financial downturn.[5]

4. What is the difference between "divisional," "holding," and "conglomerate" forms of multi-business corporations?

When the different businesses are **internal divisions** (as in the case of General Electric) the corporation is called a "multi-divisional corporation." This structure will typically have an integrated treasury function at corporate HQ that manages cash for the entire corporation. Another way to organize these different businesses is to structure each as a separate company, whose shares are held by a **"parent holding company."** For instance, Tata Sons is the parent holding company for the various businesses – software, steel, autos, and many others – that make up the companies in the Tata group. The term **"conglomerate"** is applied to either form when the collection of industries (and therefore businesses) the company is involved in appears so diverse as to show little coherence (at least in the eyes of the analyst covering the company). Thus BMW with two businesses – motorcycles and automobiles – is typically not described as a conglomerate, but General Electric is. Finally, the term "**business group**" is often used to describe a single family controlled conglomerate holding company structure; often some of the businesses in the portfolio will also be publicly listed, as is the case for instance in the Tata group in India or the Ayala group in the Philippines. More details about the structures of multi-business corporations can be found in Chapter 9.

5. With trends like "focus on the core" and outsourcing, aren't conglomerates a thing of the past?

No. Across the globe conglomerates defined as corporations with involvement in multiple industries (and therefore multiple businesses) are quite common.

In developed economies Rudolph and Schweltzer (2013) identified thousands of *publicly traded* conglomerates, which are defined as active in at least two out of 48 different industries, by region (Asia Pacific (Australia, Japan, Singapore, South Korea), Europe, and North America).[6] It is interesting that many conglomerates were identified even in the UK (1,588) and US (2,549), because in these countries, unlike in most other economies, inter-divisional dividends are taxed, making conglomerates less attractive.[7] The number of multi-business organizations in an economy must necessarily be at least as big as the number of multi-industry organizations. Basu (2010) found that in the US for the years 1999–2007, between 35 and 38 percent of the firms reported financial data for more than one industry they were operating in.[8]

In developing economies Khanna and Rivkin (2000) studied emerging economies (Argentina, Brazil, Chile, India, Indonesia, Israel, Mexico, Peru, the Philippines, South Africa, South Korea, Taiwan, Thailand, and Turkey). They found that for the firms for which data was available, a significant fraction in each country belonged to a business group (low: 23 percent, median: 48 percent, high: 64 percent).[9] A business group is "a set of firms which, though legally independent, are bound together by a constellation of formal and informal ties and are accustomed to taking coordinated action" (Khanna and Rivkin, 2000, 47–48). Typically, these business groups are highly diversified across multiple industries.

6. **How does strategy in multi-national corporations link to corporate strategy?**

We distinguish businesses in terms of their business models – their answers to the "who/what/how" (customers, products, activities) choices. By definition, multi-national corporations (MNCs) are active in multiple businesses because they serve customers across different countries (i.e., the "who"). Thus, MNCs are instances of multi-businesses organizations, and the frameworks developed in this book are applicable to them. There are of course additional complications because of differences in governance regimes and national cultures across businesses. We integrate the discussion of international aspects directly within the relevant chapters, rather than treating them in a separate chapter.

7. **Company A has two divisions B and C. Company A is listed. A SOTP valuation based on comparable focused firms suggests that it is trading at a 15 percent discount. You are senior partner in a private equity firm. Do you think you should take over A and unlock value by splitting it up into B and C? What else would you need to know?**

An SOTP valuation based on multiples makes two critical assumptions. First, that we have found truly comparable standalone listed firms for B and C (call them B′ and C′, respectively) in order to apply their Enterprise value to revenues/profits/assets multiple to B and C to impute a market value for them. Second, we assume that the profits or revenues of division B and C will not fall as a consequence of being unlocked from the current ownership structure, if we use multiples that use revenues or profits in the denominator. If either of these assumptions is not met, then we cannot be sure that we can create any value by breaking up the company. In addition, even if we could be sure that these assumptions were justified, the potential value unlocked must be compared to the costs of conducting the takeover and divestitures.

8. How does the corporate advantage test apply if the corporate strategist works in a privately held company rather than a listed one?

Whether the company is private or public should not in itself necessarily change the goal of the corporate strategist, which is to use the benefits of administrative control to maximize the value of the portfolio of businesses controlled.

However, the benchmark for how much corporate advantage is sufficient may vary with a few circumstances. First, wealthy owners may be content if the group realizes just risk diversification. Sound financial advice suggests that one should not put all one's eggs in one basket. Diversification of unsystematic risk can be easily done through a mutual fund if you have a $100,000 but might be harder if you have $75,000,000,000. Thus, the super-rich may treat their business group as their own mutual fund.

Second, the corporate advantage test focuses on economic value. The owners of private business groups may strive for additional goals besides purely financial ones, e.g., influence, status, power, and legacy.

Third, outside investors may sometimes not have access to the same investment opportunities as a corporation has (for example, the opportunity to invest in or buy a private company). In this case the benchmark for the corporate strategist may be lower.

> 9. Holding company A has two subsidiaries, B and C, in which it owns 90 percent shares each. Both the subsidiaries are listed, as is A, the holding company. The two subsidiaries have a market valuation of 60 million dollars each, whereas the holding company is valued at $100 million. Is this structure creating corporate advantage?

Based on its ownership of 90 percent of each of the companies, the holding company must be worth 0.9*60*2= $108 million if it simply transmits unchanged the value it derives from the two businesses to its shareholders. The fact that it is valued at $100 million suggests that there may be transmission losses and that shareholders may prefer to hold shares directly in the listed companies (rather than let the holding company act as a mutual fund manager).

However, this does not tell us anything about corporate advantage! Note that corporate advantage is based on a comparison between different ownership structures: common administrative control vs. separate autonomous entities. If both the business and the holding company are listed, we have information about the value of holding shares in the individual businesses and the value of holding shares in the holding company when those businesses are part of a holding company. We don't have information about the value of the businesses under separate ownership. Thus, in the example above, it may well be true that the two businesses would have been worth only $50 million each if they were not being managed by the holding company. (Incidentally, this kind of structure, with listing of both businesses and holding company, is rare but exists; the Ayala group in the Philippines is structured in this way.)

10. Is corporate strategy only relevant for a few big companies?

First of all, there are many big companies (see FAQ 5) and in many economies multi-business corporations are responsible for more than half of total output. However, corporate strategy is relevant even for single-business companies as they plan on new businesses to enter. The new businesses under consideration might be more or less related to the existing business.

11. I understand how business and corporate strategy are different. How are they related?

First, business strategy is about choosing a business model so that a company can generate competitive advantage in selling products and services to customers. By entering multiple businesses, a company may sacrifice profitability in one business but with the idea of making more in another business to compensate. So corporate strategy must reinforce business strategy for some (if not all) businesses, and increase the cumulative competitive advantage (i.e., the sum of competitive advantages for each business) of the portfolio. Second, competition for customers is affected if multi-business competitors meet in multiple markets. For instance, Siemens and General Electric sell both wind turbines and trains. They might compete less aggressively than if they met only in one market because the other could retaliate in multiple markets.[10]

Notes

1. Markides, C. C. (1999). *All the Right Moves: A Guide to Crafting Breakthrough Strategy*. Boston, MA: Harvard Business School Press.
2. Porter, M. E. (1985). *Competitive Advantage: Creating and Sustaining Superior Performance*. New York: The Free Press.

Brandenburger, A. M. and Stuart, H. W., Jr. (1996). Value-based business strategy. *Journal of Economics and Management Strategy*, 5(1), 5–24.

3. Bowman, E. H. and Helfat, C. E. (2001). Does corporate strategy matter? *Strategic Management Journal*, 22(1), 1–23.

McGahan, A. M. and Porter, M. E. (2002). What do we know about variance in accounting profitability? *Management Science*, 48(7), 834–851.

4. Porter, M. E. (1980). *Competitive Strategy*. New York: The Free Press.

5. Kuppuswamy, V. and Villalonga, B. (2010). Does diversification create value in the presence of external financing constraints? Evidence from the 2008–2009 financial crisis. *HBS Working Paper* No. 1569546. Retrieved from http://ssrn.com/abstract=1569546.

Hann, R. N., Ogneva, M., and Ozbas, O. (2013). Corporate diversification and the cost of capital. *Journal of Finance*, 68(5), 1961–1999.

6. Rudolph, C. and Schweltzer, B. (2013). Conglomerates on the rise again? A cross-regional study on the impact of the 2008–2009 financial crisis on the diversification discount. *Journal of Corporate Finance*, 22, 153–165.

7. Morck, D. (2005). How to eliminate pyramidal business groups: the double taxation of inter-corporate dividends and other incisive uses of tax policy. In J. M. Poterba (ed.), *Tax Policy and the Economy, Volume 19*. Cambridge, MA: MIT Press, 135–179.

8. Basu, N. (2010). Trends in corporate diversification. *Financial Markets and Portfolio Management*, 24(1), 87–102.

9. Khanna, T. and Rivkin, J. W. (2001). Estimating the performance effects of business groups in emerging markets. *Strategic Management Journal*, 22(1), 45–74.

10. Edwards, C. D. (1955). Conglomerate bigness as a source of power. In NBER Report, *Business Concentration and Price Policy*. Princeton University Press, 331–352.

Sengul, M. and Gimeno, J. (2013). Constrained delegation: limiting subsidiaries' decision rights and resources in firms that compete across multiple industries. *Administrative Science Quarterly*, 58(3), 420–471.

Further reading

For early thinking on corporate strategy, conceptualized as the strategy through which multi-business firms compete, see:

Andrews, K. R. (1971). *The Concept of Corporate Strategy*. Homewood, IL: Richard D. Irwin, Inc.

Ansoff, H. I. (1965). *Corporate Strategy*. New York: McGraw-Hill.

For the early work on diversification, and in particular the possible advantages of related diversification, see:

Chandler, A. D., Jr. (1962). *Strategy and Structure: Chapters in the History of the American Industrial Enterprise.* Cambridge, MA: MIT Press.

Rumelt, R. (1974). *Strategy, Structure and Economic Performance.* Cambridge, MA: Harvard University Press.

Wrigley, L. (1970). *Divisional Autonomy and Diversification (DBA thesis).* Boston, MA: Harvard Business School.

The argument for related diversification took its most popular form in the work of Prahalad and Hamel (1990), see:

Prahalad, C. K. and Hamel, G. (1990). The core competence of the corporation. *Harvard Business Review* 68(3), 79–91.

For other discussions of corporate advantage, see:

Collis, D. J. and Montgomery, C. A. (1997). *Corporate Strategy: Resources and the Scope of the Firm.* Chicago, IL: Irwin.

Goold, M., Campbell, A., and Alexander, M. (1994). *Corporate Level Strategy: Creating Value in the Multi-Business Company.* New York: John Wiley.

Porter, M. E. (1987). From competitive advantage to corporate strategy. *Harvard Business Review*, 65(3), 43–59.

Appendix: NPV

Net present value (NPV) is the sum of all future cash flows discounted to the present. The formula is:

$$\text{NPV} = \sum_0^t \frac{C_t}{(1+r)^t}$$

Where C is the net cash flow (inflows – outflows) in year t, and r is the yearly discount rate. Cash flows occurring in the far future will be discounted more than those occurring in the near future. Specifically, for a given year the cash flows will be multiplied by $1/(1+r)^t$, which is called the **discount factor**. Table A1.1 shows an example of a NPV calculation. The NPV is 15,510, which means that future cash flows are as valuable as receiving 15,510 immediately.

TABLE AI.I *NPV calculation with a discount rate of 7 percent*

Year	Incoming cash flows	Outgoing cash flows	Net cash flows	Discount factor	Discounted cash flows
0	0	10000	−10000	1.00	−10000
1	2000	5000	−3000	0.93	−2804
2	4000	3000	1000	0.87	873
3	6000	1000	5000	0.82	4081
4	8000	1000	7000	0.76	5340
5	10000	1000	9000	0.71	6417
6	10000	1000	9000	0.67	5997
7	10000	1000	9000	0.62	5605
				NPV	**15510**

Synergies: benefits to collaboration

> As an expert in corporate strategy, you are asked to advise the CEO
> of Very Good, Inc., a maker of children's toys. The company is
> considering acquiring one of three companies. With company A,
> a maker of plastic components, the goal is to share manufacturing
> facilities and therefore achieve better capacity utilization for both
> firms. With company B, another toy manufacturer, Very Good
> wants to work together to develop new products, as well as create
> a common procurement department that sources the components
> they need for their products in larger volumes. With company C,
> which owns a retail distribution network, the plan is for C to
> distribute Very Good's products and support them through in-
> store advertising. The CEO wants to know how the synergies differ
> and what the valuation and management challenges in each of
> these acquisitions are likely to be.

In Chapter 1, we stated that the goal of the corporate strategist
is to pursue **corporate advantage** – to create more value from
jointly owning a portfolio of businesses than the sum of their
values when they are owned independently. When investors
have equivalent investment opportunities, the threshold for
the extent of corporate advantage that a corporate strategist

must create is higher, and can only be met through **synergies**. In this chapter, we describe a systematic approach to analyzing synergies.

Despite their centrality to corporate strategy, synergies have remained hard to describe, value, and extract, and the word "synergy" itself is in great peril of becoming a mere buzzword. To a large extent, this is because we have lacked sophistication in being able to classify and distinguish different kinds of synergies, and their organizational implications. This chapter aims to rectify this.

What are synergies?

In its simplest form, an **operational synergy** potentially exists if two businesses *operated jointly are more valuable than the two businesses operated independently*. "Operated jointly" implies that decisions across the two businesses are coordinated with the aim of enhancing joint value. The degree of coordination required exceeds simple price-taking behavior such as in a market transaction.

In this book, when we say synergy, we will always mean operational synergy. Other forms of synergy that do not require joint operation (e.g., financial synergies or gains from trade) are also feasible. For instance, scale economies in financing may be a driver of alliances or acquisitions. Companies may sometimes be acquired to access a listing on a capital market, to move corporate domicile to a low tax location, to buy unused tax deductions, or to benefit from tax arbitrage and tax shields. These non-operational financial synergies are not the focus of this book. Our emphasis is on operational synergies, which arise from coordinated decisions about the operations of the two businesses – i.e., decisions about primary and supporting activities across the value chains of the businesses. See Box 2.1 for a test for the existence of potential synergies.

Box 2.1 The synergy test

The synergy test can be written as:

$$V(AB) > V(A) + V(B)$$

V(A) is the NPV of business A when operated independently and V(B) that of business B. V(AB) is the NPV of businesses A and B when they operate jointly.

The synergy test differs from the corporate advantage test in two ways. First, corporate advantage is defined in terms of jointly **owning** businesses and synergies in terms of jointly **operating** them. The ability to jointly operate and take coordinated decisions across the businesses can sometimes be achieved contractually (e.g., through strategic partnerships), but sometimes requires common ownership (e.g., by merging the two businesses, or by one business acquiring the other). Note that in this chapter we focus on understanding the conditions under which synergies *potentially* exist – i.e., when coordinated decision-making across businesses can improve their joint value. Chapter 3 (*Governance costs*) analyzes when ownership is necessary to *realize* value from synergies.

Further, as we know from Chapter 1, even with over two businesses it may still be feasible to create corporate advantage (through risk diversification). However, with decision rights it is also possible to realize synergies between two businesses. In other words, while an investor (e.g., a mutual fund manager) could create corporate advantage, an investor cannot extract synergies. This is why we emphasize joint operations and joint decision-making when defining synergies.

The second difference is that the corporate advantage test is about the portfolio of businesses; the synergy test is about any two businesses. Thus, for a corporate strategist to create corporate advantage over what an investor can achieve in efficient capital markets, there must at least be some form of synergy between, at a minimum, two businesses in the portfolio.

Our definition of synergy makes it easy to see why its existence is so important for corporate strategy. It is a basis for meeting the corporate advantage test when investors can diversify unsystematic risks; potential value capture from synergies brings partners to the table to negotiate strategic alliances or acquisitions; it enables acquirers to pay a premium and still make money (since synergies imply private value), and allows CEOs of publicly listed companies to justify their acquisitions and alliances to their shareholders. In fact, as we will see, the notion of synergy is also central to understanding organizational structures and relationships between units within a company (Chapter 9).

Where do synergies come from? Value chains and resources

Operational synergies between businesses entail coordinated decisions about the operations of each business. To classify the basic types of these decisions, we find it is useful to begin by representing the operations of each business through its **value chain**. A value chain represents the set of activities that must be performed to produce a product or a service and bring it to a customer. In an influential account, Porter (1985) distinguished between primary activities (such as in-bound logistics, production, out-bound logistics, marketing and sales, service), whose scale of activity varies directly with the level of production, and secondary activities (such as firm infrastructure, human resources (HR) management, technology development, procurement) whose scale does not depend directly on the level of production.

Using the example of the maker of children's toys, Very Good, we can draw a basic value chain as in Figure 2.1.

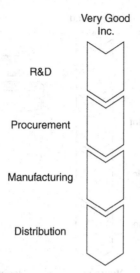

Very Good
Inc.

R&D

Procurement

Manufacturing

Distribution

Figure 2.1   Value chain of a toy maker

A value chain with three to seven steps provides a good starting point for many analyses. For some purposes, more detail may be required. Note also that in the example above we do not distinguish between primary and secondary activities. This is acceptable in many instances; some instances need a fuller distinction between the two. One important instance of the latter is when considering synergies between the corporate HQ and an individual business. While the HQ by definition does not produce anything, (a) it can be the location of centralized functions such as procurement or research and development (R&D), and (b) it can be the location of skills and brands that can generate value when linked to individual businesses.

Underlying each value chain activity are **resources**, which enable the performance of the activity. These can be thought of as the factors of production, classically defined as land, labor, and capital. Because of the importance of resources for competitive advantage and also for corporate advantage, a more fine

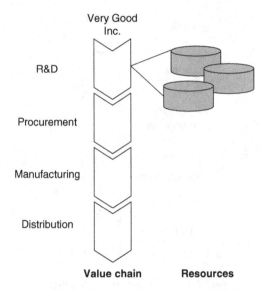

Figure 2.2   A value chain and the resources underlying value

grained definition is useful. Barney (1991) defined resources as all assets, capabilities, organizational processes, firm attributes, information, and knowledge that enables a firm to fulfill the activities in its value chain. Consider R&D as a supporting activity. The resources underlying this activity include physical infrastructure and equipment (i.e., labs) as well as the capabilities of teams of scientists and engineers (see Figure 2.2). Thus two pharmaceutical firms may both undertake R&D as an important activity in their value chain, but one firm may have an advantage over the other in this activity because of the superior quality of its resources.

Operational synergies between businesses ultimately must be traceable to links between the value chains of the respective businesses and the resources underlying them. When looking for operational synergies between businesses, we are in effect looking for valuable ways to coordinate decision-making across the value chain activities of the two businesses.

But which pairs of activities? What decisions do we coordinate, and how will that create value? To simplify the process of answering such questions, we have developed a structured approach to linking value chain activities across businesses that one might think of as "the algebra of value chains." Just as in algebra there are four basic operators that one uses on numbers (addition, subtraction, multiplication, and division), there are four basic operators that one uses on value chains in order to extract synergies.

What types of synergies are there?

The four synergy operators are obtained by crossing two dimensions: the similarity of the resources underlying the value chain activities being linked (low or high), and the extent of modification of the resources underlying these value chain activities that is necessary for value creation (low or high). These dimensions and the resulting four operators are summarized in Table 2.1.

We distinguish between these four different synergy operators that can be applied to the value chains of any two businesses resulting in operational synergies: *Consolidation, Combination,*

TABLE 2.1 *The four basic synergy operators*

	Involves similar resources	Involves dissimilar resources
High modification of resources required	Consolidation	Customization
Low modification of resources required	Combination	Connection

Connection, and *Customization*. We refer to these as the "4'C's." Each operator answers the following question: given two value chain activities, A and B, belonging to two distinct businesses, each operating independently, what are some ways in which operating decisions in these activities could be coordinated to create value? The answers in turn depend on whether we are linking similar or dissimilar resources across the two value chains, and how much modification the resources will require to produce value. Let's consider these two dimensions in some more detail.

First, the resources being linked may be more or less similar to each other. A classic distinction is between economies of *scale* and economies of *scope*. The first indicates that producing more of the same product leads to lower average cost. The second exists when producing different products together leads to lower average cost than if those products had been produced separately. This similar–dissimilar distinction is also useful when thinking about synergies. Linking similar resources produces qualitatively different effects than linking dissimilar resources. Broadly speaking, the former produces the advantages of scale, whereas the latter produces the advantages of scope.

The similarity of resources underlying different value chain activities is a matter of degree. Typically, for two businesses the resources underlying the same value chain activities are more similar than those underlying different value chain activities. For example, a pharmaceutical company's R&D resources could be more similar to those of a competitor than to its own manufacturing resources. However, even the same generic value chain activity does not imply the same resources. The pharmaceutical company may have strong R&D resources in cell biology, and a photo camera producer strong R&D resources in electronic imaging. Thus, similarity in resources is a matter of degree. For clarity, it is useful to remember that resources underlying different value chain activities are likely to be less like each other than resources underlying the same value chain activity.

Second, there can be variation in the extent to which the resources underlying value chains activities being linked must be modified. In certain cases, almost no modification is required. When a bank buys an insurance company in order to sell insurance policies through its retail branch network, neither the activities needed to create insurance policies, nor the activities needed to sell financial products through the branch network, change much. In other cases, resources must be modified significantly before value can be created. When a bank buys another bank in order to integrate and reduce the branch network, then the retail activities of (at least) one certainly need to be changed significantly. The extent of modification required is useful to understand the frictions that will eat into the value created by the synergies.

Next we describe the four synergy operators we obtain from crossing these two dimensions, in more detail.

1. Consolidation (involving similar resources and high modification)

This is the most intuitive synergy operator. It involves creating value by rationalization across *similar* resources (from similar value chain activities) by eliminating redundancies. This synergy operator affects mostly costs and invested capital. Figure 2.3 shows how the value chains across two companies might look after the consolidation operator has been applied to the first value chain activity in their respective value chains (e.g., procurement activity). Because the gains here come from elimination, the resources at one or both sides need to be trimmed and possibly adjusted. Hence, the modification to the resource base is substantial.

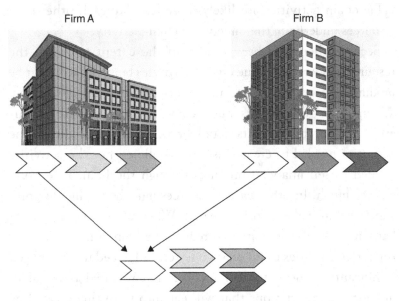

Figure 2.3 Consolidation (similar resources and high modification)

Examples of Consolidation

- Reduction in headcount by merging departments, where the same work is done by fewer people.
- Formation of shared services centers (e.g., finance, HR, treasury, legal, accounting) or intangible resources (e.g., brands, expertise) at the corporate level, which may require fewer people and lesser investment than if these were duplicated at the business unit level.
- Reduction in capital invested by closing factories. For example, four similar factories operate at 60 percent of full capacity. One is closed and the remaining operate at 80 percent.

2. Combination (involving similar resources and low modification)

This synergy operator entails creating value by pooling *similar* resources (from similar value chain activities). Two instances are combining purchasing to obtain volume discounts or acquiring a competitor and then raising prices for customers. These effects can impact either costs (e.g., bargaining power with suppliers) or revenues (e.g., bargaining power with customers). Regulators are typically wary of these gains derived from market power because they are associated with corresponding losses for either suppliers or customers. Acquisitions might be blocked based on anti-trust grounds if market power increases significantly. The extent of necessary modification of the resources in this case is, however, modest. Figure 2.4 shows how the integrated value chains across two

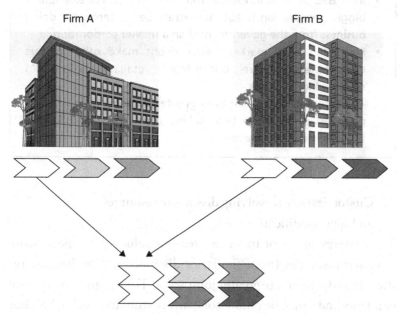

Figure 2.4 Combination (similar resources and low modification)

companies might look after the combination operator has been applied for the first activities in their respective value chains.

What is common to Consolidation and Combination is that on application of these operators, the initial value chain activities to which they have been applied disappear, as they are merged. The difference lies in whether the merged value chain activity is smaller than (Consolidation) or the same (Combination) as the combined size of the formerly independent activities; and whether modification of resources is necessary (Consolidation) or not (Combination).

Examples of Combination

- Volume discounts from increased procurement volume and the resulting increase in bargaining power with suppliers.
- Increased political influence from a larger size. For example, a bigger corporation is able to extract better terms for doing business from the government than a smaller corporation.
- Formation of a market leader might make other players compete less intensively out of fear of retaliation. This would result in higher prices.
- The corporate HQ might have greater bargaining power with providers of expertise (e.g., talent, consultants) and finance than individual businesses.

---

3. Customization (involving dissimilar resources and high modification)

This synergy operator involves creating value by co-specializing *dissimilar* resources (from similar or dissimilar value chain activities) in order to create greater joint value. For instance, a software company and a mobile phone company partner to develop handset hardware and operating software that work very well together because the technologies can be customized to each other;

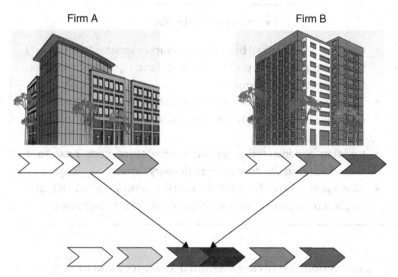

Figure 2.5 Customization (dissimilar resources and high modification)

company A allies with company B to provide an input or complementary technology/service that is customized to its requirements.
The key idea is that *Customization* of resources results in improved
value in production or consumption (either the final product works
better or costs less – producing either revenue or cost synergies).
This Customization implies investments idiosyncratic to the
pairing of value chain activities. By definition, Customization
involves modification of resources (on one or both sides).

For instance, the transfer of best practice – one company's
knowledge coupled with another's assets – can create unique
value. The second company will have to customize their assets to
the first's way of working. Figure 2.5 shows how the value chains
across two companies might look when linked through the
Customization operator – the second activity of both value chains
are the ones affected.

Examples of Customization

- Creating a customized bundle of product or services ("solutions") to meet the needs of particular clients (and significant modification of resources is required).
- Transferring intangible assets such as best practice, knowledge, or intellectual property (IP) from one business to another to improve operations.
- Building a dedicated warehouse with spare parts next to a manufacturing site to minimize delivery times.
- Management and functional expertise centralized at HQ, and applied to improve the operations of different businesses.

4. Connection (involving dissimilar resources and low modification)

This synergy operator generates value by simply pooling the outputs of *dissimilar* value chain activities, with little modification. For instance, customers may value being able to buy a bundle of different products or services together – in order to economize on the transaction costs of making separate purchases, for instance – then the sales and marketing teams for two different product teams may be connected so that they may jointly sell a product bundle, or cross-sell each other's products. In effect the product development of one business is being connected to the distribution channel of another.

Examples of Connection

- Provide a one-stop shop to reduce search and transaction costs for customers. The actual resource may require little change.
- Cross-selling of products to each others' customers: for example, a bank selling insurance products to its customers.
- Applying a common brand (of which the HQ might be the custodian) across different businesses, raising their revenues.

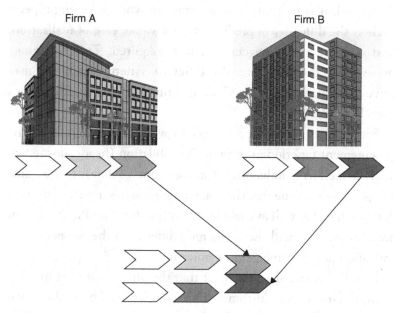

Figure 2.6 Connection (dissimilar resources and low modification)

Analyzing synergies using the **4C's** framework offers several benefits. First, it provides a structured approach to identifying synergy opportunities by analyzing the value chain. Given two businesses, the analyst can systematically explore the feasibility of each type of synergy. Starting with the resources underlying value chain activity 1 in business 1, for instance, one can first look for similar resources in the value chain of business 2, to find opportunities for Consolidation and Combination. Then one can look at dissimilar resources in business 2 to look for opportunities for Connection and Customization. Next, we can do the same for resources underlying value chain activity 2 in business 1. By the end of this process, you can be confident that you have not missed out any opportunities for extracting synergy.

Second, it is helpful in differentiating synergies along aspects such as the difficulty of predicting their value, ease of realization, and steady state management efforts required. This advantage arises from the fact that the different synergy operators may have distinctive "footprints" along a number of such dimensions (see Table 2.2).

For instance, consider a merger in which the synergies in the procurement function arise from Consolidation (headcount reduction) as well as Combination (procurement volume). In the same merger, let us assume that there are some synergies from Connection (cross-selling) as well as Customization (product bundling). In what meaningful ways will these synergies differ from the perspective of valuation and post-merger integration?

In this case, we should expect that the direct cost of extracting Consolidation and Customization synergies will be higher than the Combination and Connection synergies, respectively, because of the greater need for resource modification in the former. At the same time, the Consolidation synergies are perhaps the easiest to forecast because clarity about the extent of redundancy is usually easier to obtain; forecasting the effects of enhanced bargaining power may be relatively harder. Similarly it may be easier to estimate the impact of skill transfer on productivity than of product bundling on consumer's willingness-to-pay (WTP). Finally, given the nature of Consolidation and Customization synergies, once the initial process of removing redundancies or ensuring inter-operability is completed, there is little further need for ongoing management effort, whereas Connection and Combination may require a low but constant level of coordination of activity. These differences in the cost of implementation, managerial effort needed, and predictability should affect how synergies are valued, and how PMI is planned.

TABLE 2.2 Synergy operators and their attributes

	Consolidation	Combination	Customization	Connection
Involves linking	Similar resources	Similar resources	Dissimilar resources	Dissimilar resources
Degree of resource modification	High	Low	High	Low
Need for active collaboration between personnel from the different value chains involved	High initially, low eventually	Moderate, constant over time	Moderate, constant over time	Low, constant over time
Impact: one-sided or two-sided	One-sided	Two-sided	One-sided or two-sided	Two-sided
Key value driver	Modifying the value chain activities by disposal/better utilization of underutilized resources or excess capacity	Increasing bargaining power by pooling the unmodified activities of the value chain activities	Modifying the value chain activities through specializing them to each other to increase their combined value	Pooling the outputs of unmodified value chain activities to increase their value

TABLE 2.2 (cont.)

	Consolidation	Combination	Customization	Connection
Value drivers affected	Cost/Assets	Cost/Revenues	Costs/Revenues/Assets	Revenues
Examples	Eliminate redundancy (or share excess capacity) in functions/operations/technology development projects/sales forces/plants/equipment (i.e., tangible assets)	Gain bargaining power relative to suppliers; market power; government	R&D customized to manufacturing; software customized to hardware; application of one partner's business model/knowledge on another's assets; "solution" selling; joint product development	Cross-selling; product bundling; linking product development of one company to distribution channels of another; sharing brands

Finally, and perhaps most important, the 4C's approach makes it easy to explain the sources of value to investors, managers, and customers.

That said, it is important to realize that synergy analysis begins, not ends with the 4C's. It is complete only when a financial forecast of synergy *realization* has been made. Quantification of synergy impact is critical, for at least three reasons. First, it forces you to make your assumptions explicit. Second, it guides you towards synergies that are really value enhancing – i.e., which have significant revenue, cost, or invested capital implications. We have found that our students were often very creative (and sometimes even entertaining) when coming up with synergies. While this is good and desirable early on in an analysis, eventually only those synergies with actual net benefits should be pursued. Third, it provides a ranking of which synergies to prioritize. In the appendix to this chapter we provide an illustration of how a qualitative 4C's assessment can be quantified, using value drivers (i.e., financial measures that are affected by synergies).

Who benefits from synergy? One-sided vs. two-sided effects

One important distinction to bear in mind when analyzing synergies is whether they are **one-sided or two-sided**. To see the difference, consider two firms, A and B, whose standalone value is V(A) and V(B), respectively, and whose value when jointly operated is V(AB). Assuming the synergy test introduced on p. 31 is met, let the synergies from linking their value chains be S (where S = V(AB)–V(A)–V(B)). Let's break down these synergies into S(A) and S(B) such that S = S(A) + S(B). Here, S(A) and S(B) represent the synergies experienced by firm A and firm B, respectively.

Passing the synergy test implies that $S(A) + S(B) > 0$. The synergies are two-sided if both businesses benefit – i.e., $S(A) > 0$ and $S(B) > 0$. They are one-sided if one business gains more than the other business loses, e.g. $S(A) > 0$ and $S(B) < 0$ (and $S(A) + S(B) > 0$). To make the pursuit of synergies worthwhile for both businesses in this case, they must reach an agreement on some form of side payment from one business to the other. Forms of these side payments include an acquisition premium, in which an acquirer may pass on some of the one-sided benefits it experiences to the target, or upfront payments in alliances by one partner with another.

An important implication of this distinction between one- and two-sided synergy effects is that it is necessary to estimate separately the impact of synergies on the value of each business involved.

Do negative synergies exist?

There are circumstances in which the value of two businesses under coordinated decision-making may actually be lower than the sum of their values when they operate independently. One common instance is brand dilution. Imagine a watch company with a brand known for luxury operating a budget jewelry store under the same brand; or a film studio with a brand known for its family values operating a film business with violent action movies as a subsidiary under the same brand.

A second instance of negative synergies arises from organizational complexity. Since actions have to be coordinated across businesses to extract operational synergies, this necessarily implies some loss of initiative, independence, and speed in decision-making. These can be ignored when the gains from coordinated decision-making across businesses are large; but when they are not, these costs still remain and can create a net negative synergy from joint operation. One of our students once described these as "Dilbert" costs, after Scott Adam's iconic cartoons about the costs of bureaucracy, and the name has stuck in our minds since.

Another situation of negative synergies can arise because of concerns about the independence of action of two businesses under the same corporate umbrella. If business A is an internal supplier to business B, it may be difficult for business A to find clients outside the corporation, who are likely to be rivals of business B, and will suspect collusion between business A and business B. Similarly, if business A and business B each have clients who are rivals, these clients will suspect possible leakage of valuable information through their respective vendors into the hands of their rivals. This is a significant concern in the advertising industry, where when two firms who serve rivals (say, Coke and Pepsi) merge, the chances of both keeping their clients is low.

More generally, in this chapter we have focused on the potential benefits from collaboration arising from joint decision-making. However, achieving collaboration is typically not easy but requires creating the conditions that allow people to work effectively together. In Chapter 3, we discuss impediments to collaboration, which generate governance costs.

Application: How to look for synergies for Very Good

Now we have all the elements in place to advise the CEO of Very Good. Recall that Very Good is considering acquiring one of three companies: company A (a maker of plastic components) for sharing manufacturing facilities, company B (another toy manufacturer) for joint R&D and procurement, and company C (a retailer) for enhanced distribution.

Begin by drawing the value chain of each business (see Figure 2.7).

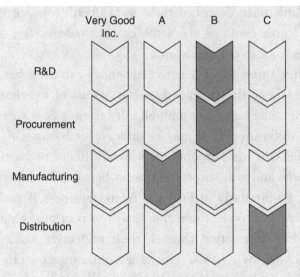

Figure 2.7 Value chain overview

The three acquisitions are different because the sources of potential synergy are distinct. Company A involves Consolidation, company B involves both Customization and Combination, while company C involves Connection synergies. These differences mean that the uncertainty about outcomes, the cost of implementation, and the linkages across value chains are likely to be different across the cases. These differences should be reflected in the valuation and management of these acquisitions.

Consolidation based synergies are easiest to predict and value, and may require a large upfront investment of managerial time and effort, but lower levels of steady state management efforts between partners. Customization synergies are harder to predict, and also require significant levels of ongoing collaboration between partners. Connection and Combination synergies require lesser resource modification, so will be relatively easier to extract than Consolidation and Customization. Thus, company C will be the cheapest acquisition to implement but perhaps the hardest to value precisely; company A will be the opposite, as it may be the easiest to value precisely, but expensive to implement. Company B will lie between both in terms of ease of valuation and cost of implementation.

Frequently asked questions

1. I am familiar with a synergy classification based on costs and revenues. Why do you suggest the 4C's framework?

A fairly common and intuitive way of thinking about synergies classifies them into cost and revenue synergies. *Cost synergies* exist between two businesses if their joint variable or fixed costs of production can somehow be lowered by linking the two businesses. *Revenue synergies* exist if their joint outputs can somehow be made more valuable by linking the businesses. For instance, cost synergies could arise from cutting redundant jobs; revenue synergies from cross-selling.

While this is a helpful first cut at classifying synergies, it is in fact quite crude. It offers little insights about the logic of value creation (for instance, cost synergies can arise either from Consolidation or Combination), valuation, or organizational implications. Apart from suggesting the vague intuition that cost synergies are somehow more "reliable" than revenue synergies, this distinction tells us very little about why this should be the case, the organizational implications of the two kinds of synergies, or the managerial efforts that will be required to extract the relevant synergies.

2. Does the nature of synergies differ in so-called "horizontal," "vertical," and conglomerate acquisitions?

Horizontal acquisitions are in the same business, vertical acquisitions are in subsequent businesses, and conglomerate acquisitions are in businesses that are neither horizontally nor vertically related. Since one dimension of the 4C's framework is similarity of resources (which depends on similarity in the value chain activities), the type of synergies will be different across the type of acquisition.

Conglomerate acquisitions may have few synergies between businesses (but may have some between the HQ and business); vertical acquisitions are less likely to rely on Consolidation and Combination synergies; horizontal acquisitions may have all four types of synergies.

3. Is buying out the competition a form of synergy?

Yes. By coordinating decision-making, two businesses operating as one may choose to raise prices and hence improve their value compared to the case when they operate independently as competitors. This is effectively a Combination synergy; the combined firm increases its bargaining power with its customers (and possibly its suppliers). Regulators typically do not like this, but when legally permitted because the increase in market power is below thresholds, such a form of synergy can be a justification for doing an acquisition.

4. Help! I keep mixing up the different C's. Is that a problem?

No. We occasionally do, too. The goal is not to classify a given synergy into one of the 4C's. Instead, the 4C's provide a search tool to look for synergy opportunities in a reliable and comprehensive manner. What we call a given synergy is of less importance.

5. Is relatedness a good measure of synergy potential?

Measures of relatedness are frequently used in studies that investigate how diversification influences a corporation's performance (see Palich, Cardinal, and Miller, 2000) for an overview of the empirical literature).[1] In these studies, an industry classification system (e.g., the standard industrial classification (SIC) codes in the US) is typically used to measure the extent and nature (related vs. unrelated) of diversification. Industry classifications are based on similarity of products and customers. These measures are not very useful indicators of operational synergy potential. Synergy potential derives from the value chain, not from the outputs of the value chain (i.e., products) or targets of the value chain (i.e., customers). In other words, if a business is defined in terms of who (customers), what (products), and how (value chain), then the synergies stem from the value chain.

That said, there are certain forms of synergy between businesses that are driven by similarity. When businesses are similar in terms of the sizes of capital investment projects, time spans of investment projects, sources of risk, stages in their industry life cycles, performance goals and measures, etc., then they create what is known as a "dominant general management logic" which binds the businesses together and makes it easier to administer them jointly.[2] One could view these as creating a form of synergy arising from consolidating the management expertise needed to administer each business.

6. **How do the mathematical definitions of corporate advantage and synergy differ?**

Corporate advantage concerns businesses that are jointly owned and synergy involves businesses that are jointly operated (see Figure 2.8). To distinguish between them, we have used "[ ]" for the corporate advantage test and "()" for the synergies test.

We represent the four quadrants as follows:

I: $V(A) + V(B)$: NPV of businesses owned and operated separately

II: $V(AB)$: NPV of businesses operated jointly

III: $V[AB]$: NPV of businesses owned jointly

IV: $V[(AB)]$: NPV of businesses owned and operated jointly

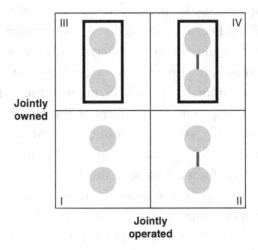

Figure 2.8   Investors can jointly own business, corporate strategists
can additionally jointly operate them

Thus the corporate advantage test compares quadrants III vs. I and IV vs. II; the synergy test compares quadrants IV vs. III and II vs. I.

7. Is an internal capital market a form of synergy?

An "internal capital market" refers to the fact that businesses get funding from the corporate HQ rather than directly from external sources (e.g., banks, bondholders, shareholders). While the empirical evidence on the average performance of internal capital markets is mixed, it appears especially helpful when external capital markets are under-developed (e.g., in some developing economies) or inaccessible (e.g., in a financial crisis). Because this is a form of financial (i.e., non-operational) synergy, this is not the focus of the book. However, we will discuss the organizational implications of internal resource allocation in Chapter 10 on the corporate HQ.

Notes

1. Palich, L E., Cardinal, L. B., and Miller, C. C. (2000). Curvilinearity in the diversification–performance linkage: an examination of over three decades of research. *Strategic Management Journal*, *21*, 155–174.
2. Prahalad, C. K. and Bettis, R. A. (1986). The dominant logic: a new linkage between diversity and performance. *Strategic Management Journal*, *7*(6), 485–501.

Further reading

Our synergies framework (the 4C's) builds on earlier work by Haspeslagh and Jemison (1991) and Dussauge and Garrette (1999), who discussed synergies in acquisitions and alliances, respectively:

Dussauge, P. and Garrette, B. (1999). *Cooperative Strategy: Competing Successfully Through Strategic Alliances*. Chichester: John Wiley.
Haspeslagh, P. C. and Jemison, D. B. (1991). *Understanding Different Integration Approaches*. New York: The Free Press.

To learn more about value chains, see:

Porter, M. E. (1985). *Competitive Advantage: Creating and Sustaining Superior Performance*. New York: The Free Press.

For a thorough treatment of resources and their importance for strategy, see:

Barney, J. (1991). Firm resources and sustained competitive advantage. *Journal of Management*, 17(1), 99–120.
Barney, J. B. and Clark, D. N. (2007). *Resource-Based Theory: Creating and Sustaining Competitive Advantage*. Oxford University Press.
Levinthal, D. A. and Wu, B. (2010). Opportunity costs and non-scale free capabilities: profit maximization, corporate scope, and profit margins. *Strategic Management Journal*, 31(7): 780–801.

On the importance of synergies, see:

Milgrom P. and Roberts, J. (1990). The economics of modern manufacturing: technology, strategy, and organization. *American Economic Review*, 80(3), 511–528.
Milgrom P. and Roberts, J. (1995). Complementarities and fit: strategy, structure, and organizational change in manufacturing. *Journal of Accounting and Economics*, 19(2–3), 179–208.

For an application of synergies in the context of M&As, see:
Ahern, K. R. and Weston, J. F. (2007). M&As: the good, the bad, and the ugly. *Journal of Applied Finance*, 17(1), 5–20.

Barney, J. (1988). Returns to bidding firms in mergers and acquisitions: reconsidering the relatedness hypothesis. *Strategic Management Journal*, 9, 71–78.

Capron, L. and Pistre, N. (2002). When do acquirers earn abnormal returns? Strategic Management *Journal*, 23(9), 781–794.

Appendix: valuing synergies

The best method to estimate the value of operating synergies between two businesses is through the computation of the net present value (NPV) of future cash flows of both the businesses after taking into account the effects of realized synergies between them (and the cost of realizing them).

The actual estimation of the NPV requires going from **synergy operators** (Consolidation, Combination, Connection and Customization – as outlined in this chapter) to **value drivers** (see Table A2.1).

Synergies can be converted into numbers through value drivers. There are five numbers that are the key value drivers for operational synergies:

1. Sales
2. Cost of goods sold (COGS)
3. Selling, general, and administrative expenses (SGA)
4. Capital expenditures (Capex)
5. Synergy extraction costs (i.e., the time and manpower needed to implement synergy projects); these can be seen as a component of SGA but it is useful to separate them for clarity.

In addition, there may be extraordinary (one-off) items such as profits from asset disposal/divestiture.

It is also possible that operational synergies may affect the costs of capital and therefore discount rates by altering the riskiness of cash flows. However, a well-developed description of this

TABLE A2.1 Synergy operators and value drivers

Synergy operator	Examples	Two-sided or one-sided	Value driver affected
Consolidation	• Reduction in headcount/capital invested by merging departments or factories/ sharing tangible resources • Sharing tangible assets such as a store location • Shared services: finance, HR, treasury, legal, accounting	One-sided – usually impact on target	SGA; Capex; COGS
Combination	• Volume discounts from consolidating procurement volume • Multi-market competition leading to less intensive competition • Size based political influence • Pre-empt rivals accessing the same resources	Two-sided	Revenue; COGS; SGA; Capex

TABLE A2.1 (cont.)

Synergy operator	Examples	Two-sided or one-sided	Value driver affected
Customization	• Creating customized bundle of product or services ("solutions") to meet the needs of particular clients • Joint R&D/new product development • Transferring intangible assets such as best practice, knowledge, or IP from one business to another to improve operations	One-sided or two-sided	Revenue; COGS; SGA; Capex
Connection	• Bundling products or services to reduce search and transaction costs for customers – one-stop shopping • Cross-selling of products to each other's customers • Linking different parts of the two value chains, such as distribution channels to production capabilities • Sharing intangible assets such as a common brand	Two-sided	Revenue

TABLE A2.2 *Estimated impact on business A*

Synergy operator	Comments	Value driver impacted	Assumption
Consolidation	Redundancy in operational staff can be eliminated by consolidating operations across business A and B	SG&A	Reduces from current level of 25 to 23 percent of sales
Combination	Increased bargaining power with suppliers	COGS	Reduces from current level of 50 to 48 percent of sales
Customization	Application of design expertise from business B improves A's products and consumer's WTP	Sales	Sales growth jumps from current 2 to 4 percent per year
Connection	Cross-selling business A and B's products	Sales	Sales growth jumps from current 2 to 5 percent per year (if done together with Customization, then the joint effect is 6)

mechanism does not yet exist. The usual practice therefore is to model the effects of synergies via operating cash flows, keeping discount rates unchanged.

Example: Let's consider a hypothetical example of valuing realizable synergies between two businesses, A and B. For simplicity, we assume that both businesses have identical cost of capital. We will assume that both businesses are commonly owned and operated. Finally, let's assume that a qualitative analysis of the synergies, translated into assumptions about the quantitative impact on value drivers, gives us Table A2.2 and Table A2.3.

TABLE A2.3 *Estimated impact on business B*

Synergy operator	Comments	Value driver impacted	Assumption
Consolidation	None		
Combination	Increased bargaining power with suppliers	COGS	Reduces from current level of 50 to 48 percent of sales
Customization	None		
Connection	Cross-selling business A and B's products	Sales	Sales growth jumps from current 2 to 4 percent per year

Note that Consolidation and Customization have one-sided effects (on business A only). As a consequence, the synergy extraction costs are assumed to be 10 percent of SGA in business A but only 8 percent in business B.

A summary of the remaining assumptions needed to compute the NPV of cash flows from the two businesses is as follows:

- Taxes: 40 percent
- Depreciation and Other deductions (including interest payments): 15 and 9 million dollars, respectively, for business A, and 5 and 3 for business B, every year
- Capex: at replacement level for B, and one-third for A
- Last year of operations: 2015
- Working capital requirements: 25 percent of revenues
- Terminal growth rate: 1 percent (terminal value is free cash flow in the next year divided by the difference between the cost of capital and the terminal growth rate)
- Cost of capital: 10 percent

The summary of the analysis is presented in Table A2.4. Detailed NPV computations can be found in Tables A2.5–A2.8.

TABLE A2.4 *Impact of synergies (in million dollars)*

	Business A	Business B	Total
NPV of cash flows without synergies	448.33	115.29	563.61
NPV of cash flows with synergies	503.67	139.82	643.49
Impact of synergy	55.35	24.53	79.88

This analysis shows that the impact of realized synergies could significantly increase the value of cash flows of the two businesses (from 563.61 to 643.49, i.e. +14 percent), but the absolute impact would be felt more on business A then on business B. A word of caution: ultimately these are still projections. In practice, more information comes to light as the synergy realization projects get underway, changing these forecasts considerably.

TABLE A2.5 *Business A standalone (in million dollars)*

	Notes on assumptions	2015	2016	2017	2018	2019	2020	2021
Net sales	2 percent yearly growth	300.00	306.00	312.12	318.36	324.73	331.22	334.54
Profit from asset disposal								167.27
COGS		150.00	153.00	156.06	159.18	162.36	165.61	167.27
SGA		75.00	76.50	78.03	79.59	81.18	82.81	83.63
Depreciation	Assumed constant	15.00	15.00	15.00	15.00	15.00	15.00	15.00
Other deductions	Assumed constant	9.00	9.00	9.00	9.00	9.00	9.00	9.00
Profits before taxes			52.50	54.03	55.59	57.18	58.81	59.63
Taxes	At 40 percent		21.00	21.61	22.24	22.87	23.52	23.85
Profits after taxes			31.50	32.42	33.35	34.31	35.28	35.78
Add back: depreciation			15.00	15.00	15.00	15.00	15.00	15.00

Cash flow from operations			46.50	47.42	48.35	49.31	50.28	50.78
Working capital	25 percent of sales	75.00	76.50	78.03	79.59	81.18	82.81	83.63
Change in working capital			1.50	1.53	1.56	1.59	1.62	0.83
Capex	Assume 1/3 replacement level for depreciation		5.00	5.00	5.00	5.00	5.00	5.00
Free cash flow			40.00	40.89	41.79	42.72	43.66	44.95
Terminal value Year 6	Terminal growth rate at 1 percent						499.47	
Synergy extraction costs			0.00	0.00	0.00	0.00	0.00	
Discount factor	Discount rate at 10 percent		0.90	0.81	0.73	0.66	0.59	
DCF			36.00	33.12	30.47	28.03	320.71	
NPV cash flows		448.33						

TABLE A2.6 *Business A with synergies (in million dollars)*

	Notes on assumptions	2015	2016	2017	2018	2019	2020	2021
Net sales	6 percent yearly growth from Connection and Customization	300.00	318.00	337.08	357.30	378.74	401.47	405.48
Profit from asset disposal								
COGS	One-step reduction from 50 to 48 percent of sales	150.00	152.64	161.80	171.51	181.80	192.70	194.63
SGA	Phased reduction from 25 to 23 percent of sales	75.00	77.91	80.90	125.77	87.11	92.34	93.26
Depreciation	Assumed constant	15.00	15.00	15.00	15.00	15.00	15.00	15.00
Other deductions	Assumed constant	9.00	9.00	9.00	9.00	9.00	9.00	9.00
Profits before taxes			63.45	70.38	36.03	85.84	92.43	93.59
Taxes	At 40 percent		25.38	28.15	14.41	34.33	36.97	37.44

Profits after taxes		38.07	42.23	21.62	51.50	55.46	56.15
Add back: depreciation		15.00	15.00	15.00	15.00	15.00	15.00
Cash flow from operations		53.07	57.23	36.62	66.50	70.46	71.15
Working capital	25 percent of sales	75.00	79.50	84.27	89.33	94.69	100.37	101.37
Change in working capital		4.50	4.77	5.06	5.36	5.68	1.00
Capex	Assume 1/3 replacement level for depreciation	5.00	5.00	5.00	5.00	5.00	5.00
Free cash flow		43.57	47.46	26.56	56.14	59.77	64.15
Terminal value Year 6	Terminal growth rate at 1 percent					623.93	
Synergy extraction costs	At 10 percent of SGA	7.79	8.09	12.58	8.71	9.23	9.33
Discount factor	Discount rate at 10 percent	0.90	0.81	0.73	0.66	0.59	
DCF		32.20	31.89	10.19	31.12	398.27	
NPV cash flows	503.67						

TABLE A2.7 *Business B standalone (in million dollars)*

	Notes on assumptions	2015	2016	2017	2018	2019	2020	2021
Net sales	2 percent yearly growth	100.00	102.00	104.04	106.12	108.24	110.41	111.51
Profit from asset disposal								
COGS		50.00	51.00	52.02	53.06	54.12	55.20	55.76
SGA		25.00	25.50	26.01	26.53	27.06	27.60	27.88
Depreciation	Assumed constant	5.00	5.00	5.00	5.00	5.00	5.00	5.00
Other deductions	Assumed constant	3.00	3.00	3.00	3.00	3.00	3.00	3.00
Profits before taxes			17.50	18.01	18.53	19.06	19.60	19.88
Taxes	At 40 percent		7.00	7.20	7.41	7.62	7.84	7.95
Profits after taxes			10.50	10.81	11.12	11.44	11.76	11.93
Add back: depreciation			5.00	5.00	5.00	5.00	5.00	5.00

Cash flow from operations		15.50	15.81	16.12	16.44	16.76	16.93
Working capital	25 percent of sales	25.00	25.50	26.01	26.53	27.06	27.60	27.88
Change in working capital		0.50	0.51	0.52	0.53	0.54	0.28
Capex	Assume replacement level for depreciation	5.00	5.00	5.00	5.00	5.00	5.00
Free cash flow		10.00	10.30	10.60	10.91	11.22	11.65
Terminal value Year 6	Terminal growth rate at 1 percent					129.45	
Synergy extraction costs		0.00	0.00	0.00	0.00	0.00	
Discount factor	Discount rate at 10 percent	0.90	0.81	0.73	0.66	0.59	
DCF		9.00	8.34	7.73	7.16	83.07	
NPV cash flows	115.29						

TABLE A2.8 *Business B with synergies (in million dollars)*

	Notes on assumptions	2015	2016	2017	2018	2019	2020	2021
Net sales	4 percent yearly growth from Connection	100.00	104.00	108.16	112.49	116.99	121.67	126.53
Profit from asset disposal								
COGS	One-step reduction from 50 to 48 percent of sales	50.00	49.92	51.92	53.99	56.15	58.40	60.74
SGA		25.00	26.00	27.04	28.12	29.25	30.42	31.63
Depreciation	Assumed constant	5.00	5.00	5.00	5.00	5.00	5.00	5.00
Other deductions	Assumed constant	3.00	3.00	3.00	3.00	3.00	3.00	3.00
Profits before taxes			20.08	21.20	22.37	23.59	24.85	26.16
Taxes	At 40 percent		8.03	8.48	8.95	9.43	9.94	10.47
Profits after taxes			12.05	12.72	13.42	14.15	14.91	15.70
Add back: depreciation			5.00	5.00	5.00	5.00	5.00	5.00
Cash flow from operations			17.05	17.72	18.42	19.15	19.91	20.70

Working capital	25.00	26.00	27.04	28.12	29.25	30.42	31.63	25 percent of sales
Change in working capital		1.00	1.04	1.08	1.12	1.17	1.22	
Capex		5.00	5.00	5.00	5.00	5.00	5.00	Assume replacement level for depreciation
Free cash flow		11.05	11.68	12.34	13.03	13.74	14.48	
Terminal value Year 6						174.42		Terminal growth rate at 1 percent
Synergy extraction costs		2.08	2.16	2.25	2.34	2.43		At 8 percent of SGA
Discount factor		0.90	0.81	0.73	0.66	0.59		Discount rate at 10 percent
DCF		8.07	7.71	7.36	7.01	109.67		
NPV cash flows	139.82							

3

Governance costs: impediments to collaboration

You are a Vice President of Strategic Alliances at WonderWorld, a producer of candy. You are contemplating entering into an alliance with one of two candidates. With company A, a producer of children's animation movies, the goal is to use the movie's main characters to promote the candy. With company B, a supplier of one of the main ingredients, the idea is to set up a just-in-time (JIT) supply relationship to lower inventories. Which alliance would be easier to manage?

When discussing the synergy operators in Chapter 2, we noted that these provide potential benefits from jointly operating two businesses. Yet, collaboration does not automatically arise if there are synergies. There are impediments to be overcome and these generate costs, which we refer to as **governance costs**. Governance costs are the frictions that prevent two businesses operating smoothly together to realize synergies. They act as "taxes" that eat into the potential benefits from synergies when they are attempted to be extracted.

Governance costs, along with synergies, constitute two of the most important concepts in corporate strategy. The reason is that together they determine **governance structure** – the choice about joint or separate ownership of businesses between which there are synergies. The fundamental idea linking these concepts can be stated very simply: **to exploit a potential synergy, pick a governance structure that unlocks the most value *net* of the costs of governance.** In Part II of this book (*Decisions about portfolio composition: increasing the scope of the corporation*, Chapters 4 through 6), we analyze in great detail how synergies and governance costs impact decisions on the ownership choices of the corporation (e.g., whether to diversify, to ally or acquire, or to grow inorganically or organically). In this chapter, we highlight the origins of governance costs.

Where do governance costs come from?

Governance costs are the costs of achieving effective collaboration, over and above the direct cost of what is being exchanged. The governance costs that arise under common ownership are referred to as the **ownership costs.**[1] The governance costs that arise in interactions between independent firms are referred to as **transaction costs.** In both cases, governance costs arise from impediments to cooperation and coordination (which are both necessary for successful collaboration) and the measures needed to control these (see Figure 3.1). The magnitude of governance costs typically differ by type of synergy.

Cooperation is the alignment of incentives to ensure that people are motivated to work together. When collaborating, businesses may care more about what is good for their own business rather than for the other business. Failures of cooperation are more likely if there is no shared future (e.g., two alliance partners know that the current joint R&D project is the last one), incentives are narrow (e.g., employees are rewarded on the basis of their own division's performance rather than on the performance of the company as a whole), or if synergies are one-sided (i.e., benefits to collaboration accrue to one party only). Examples of governance costs incurred to encourage cooperation between independent businesses include drafting contracts, monitoring suppliers, resolving price disputes, haggling about

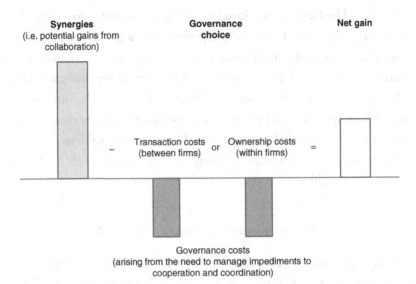

Figure 3.1 Governance costs and collaboration

product quality, and enforcing contracts through a court if necessary. The direct cost of cooperation failures include shirking, free-
riding, cheating, and misrepresentation.

The other source of governance costs lies in possible failures of
coordination. By **coordination** we mean the alignment of actions so
that people know how best to work together. Human problem solvers
often lack complete information, may not use the available information correctly, and more generally are imperfect at processing complex
information. Consequently, delays, mistakes, and miscommunication
can arise between people even if they are motivated to work together.

Failures of coordination are more likely if working across different geographical locations or time zones (e.g., an information
technology (IT) department that is offshored from France to the
Philippines), different professions (e.g., an alliance between two
IT companies vs. an alliance between an IT company and an
advertising company), or without a shared past (e.g., you may be
unfamiliar with the other party's standard procedures). Examples
of transaction costs incurred to facilitate coordination between

independent businesses are lengthy meetings, elaborate project manuals and documents, appointing coordinator roles such as key account managers, and of course rectifying mistakes when discovered. The direct costs of coordination failures are the costs of miscommunication, misunderstandings, and delays.

The link between governance costs and synergies

In Chapter 2 we distinguished between those synergies that require modification (Consolidation and Customization) and those that do not (Combination and Connection). A key premise in our approach to corporate strategy decisions is that **the governance costs of collaboration between independent businesses will typically be higher for synergies that need modification or are one-sided.** There is a robust body of evidence from carefully conducted research studies that supports this premise.[2]

To see the logic for this, consider the following: failures of cooperation (i.e., incentive misalignment) typically occur in situations in which one party comes to depend significantly on another. For instance:

- Business A agrees to share manufacturing facilities with business B and gets rid of its own factories, in order to generate synergies through Consolidation; subsequently business B does not provide access to its factories to business A.
- Business A relies on a single supplier, business B, for a key specialized input that generates synergies through Customization, with no ready alternative; business B then raises the price for providing inputs to business A.

In principle, one could create contractual agreements to prevent the problems noted above, but the costs of negotiating such an agreement (given that potentially one side could end up with a significant loss), or having to enforce it when there is a suspected breach, are governance costs.

Failures of coordination (e.g. misunderstandings, miscommunications, and delays) are typically situations of high interdependence in
which the parties involved need to interact and communicate in
order to make sure that their actions are aligned to each other. For
instance:

- Business A agrees to share manufacturing facilities with business
  B as between them they have excess capacity; business A and
  business B's production planning must be fully integrated and
  synchronized so that there are no delays or inventory problems,
  and they can exploit gains from Consolidation.
- Business A relies on business B to create a specialized input.
  Business B must understand the nuances of the unique requirements of business A in order to create synergies through
  Customization; alternately, business A and business B create a
  component each for a product, and the product quality improves
  enormously when both customize their components to each
  other. In each case business A and business B's employees must
  work closely together to achieve this.

It is because communication and interaction between individuals
from different businesses is fraught with difficulties that the situations above are likely to incur governance costs. It is not a coin-
cidence that both the synergy operators in the examples above,
Consolidation and Customization, feature significant need for modification and create greater benefits for one side than another,
because that is what creates the **dependency** and the **need for
interaction**.[3]

Thus while in principle two firms pursuing Combination or
Connection synergies may also find it difficult to agree on the extent
and distribution of value that will be created, since they incur
minimal costs of modifying their resources, at worst they are left
no better off if the agreement is breached. With Consolidation and
Customization, they could be left worse off. Similarly the need for
coordination, and consequently the danger of coordination failure,

is lower when neither firm needs to modify its current activities to a significant extent (as would be the case with Connection or Combination synergies).

Cooperation and especially coordination difficulties are naturally amplified when operating internationally. For example, misunderstandings, miscommunications, and delays are all more likely if your partner is in a different country, with a different language, with a different culture, and in a different time zone. Cooperation difficulties are also more likely if national boundaries create in- vs. out-group dynamics, or if misunderstandings get incorrectly attributed to cooperation failures, and these mistaken perceptions can become self-fulfilling, in that neither side wants to cooperate any more.

The link between governance costs and governance structure

Governance costs vary not only by synergy but also by governance form. In fact for a corporate strategist, differences in governance form primarily signal differences in their governance costs.

Let us consider more closely the two very basic (and polar opposite) governance structures to link two businesses with potential synergies between them: common ownership and arm's-length trade between separately owned businesses. In Chapter 5 we will introduce an entire continuum of governance structures between these two cases, but for present purposes a consideration of the two extreme ends of this continuum suffices. The optimal choice of governance structure depends on a comparison of the governance costs for each structure, for a given type of synergy. But why should the governance costs vary across these governance structures?

Common ownership for a group of businesses means that ultimately each business is administratively controlled by the group CEO and the assets are owned by the shareholders. In most legal regimes, courts do not interfere in disputes between the internal divisions of a corporation. It is up to the CEO (and his or her delegates) to resolve such disputes. Ultimately, decision rights (e.g., the right to decide what strategies to pursue or what synergies to exploit) lie in the hands of the CEO.

This administrative authority confers significant benefits when it comes to managing governance costs arising in collaboration between businesses within the same corporation (i.e., to control ownership costs). Once the businesses are brought under common authority, the scope for non-cooperative practice in transactions between the divisions is reduced, because the CEO can hire and fire, reward and punish, monitor, and manage. Incentives can thus be aligned though formal reward and promotion systems, but also through the shared culture that develops over time. The potential for misunderstanding and miscommunication between divisions is reduced because the CEO can design an organization, i.e. put in place communication channels, standards, business processes and procedures, that enable the effective coordination of activities. Coordination problems can thus be avoided through centralized decision-making, information channels, common language, terminology, and culture.

Yet every possible opportunity to exploit synergies through collaboration is **not** optimally organized within a corporation instead of between two autonomous businesses through arm's-length trade. This is because of the governance costs under common ownership (also known as ownership costs): when an autonomous business becomes a division within another, the incentives of the owner and managers are necessarily diluted. Each was earlier dependent on the profits of his own division; now each can to some extent free-ride on the other to produce an overall group profit. If one division sells to another, then less effort is required to keep the internal customer than if the customer is external.[4] Further, decision-making typically becomes slower and more bureaucratic as (at least) a layer of hierarchy has now been added (i.e., the infamous "Dilbert" costs). Considerations of equity and fairness perceptions begin to matter as social comparisons between employees arise, so that they must be rewarded and budgets allocated more equally than they would be if considered independent of each other. A unique feature of these ownership costs is that many of their components do not vary (or at least do not vary much) by type of synergy (whereas the transaction costs do). This property plays a crucial role in the choice of optimal governance structure, as shown below.

The optimal decision on how to organize a collaboration opportunity to exploit synergies between businesses – contractually between two autonomous firms or in one firm between two fully owned subsidiaries or divisions – turns on a comparison of the respective costs of governance for the type of synergy involved. These are, respectively, the transaction costs between independent businesses and the costs of ownership incurred in a jointly owned corporation, for a given type of synergy. It follows that when the synergies require significant modification or are mostly one-sided in their effects, the anticipated transaction costs are likely to be high, and controlling them through common ownership (even though costs of hierarchy will then be incurred), becomes relatively more attractive.

This is shown in Figure 3.2. For synergies that lie to the right of point "A," it is better to choose a governance structure that minimizes transaction costs rather than one which minimizes the costs of ownership.

All else being equal, synergies that are likely to generate significant transaction costs are less likely to be successfully realized in arm's-length relationships between independent firms than under common ownership. This result, which has a large body of empirical evidence and rests on the thinking of at least two Nobel laureates in economics, Ronald Coase (awarded in 1991) and Oliver Williamson (awarded in 2009), is an extremely useful heuristic for corporate strategists.

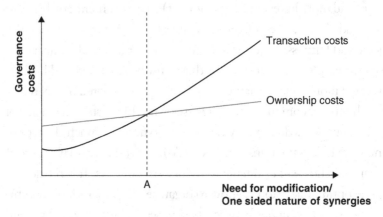

Figure 3.2 Governance structure and synergy characteristics

Application: WonderWorld

Let's turn to WonderWorld, our candy-maker from the beginning of the chapter. They face a choice between an alliance with company A (to co-brand candy) and an alliance with company B (to invest in JIT supply). Note that both have the same governance form (alliance) – a relationship between two independent firms. Leaving aside which one could generate more benefits (i.e., assuming that the magnitudes of potential gains from synergies are comparable), which one is easier to manage? This is akin to asking: where are the governance costs (in this case, since the businesses remain independent, transaction costs) higher?

It seems quite likely that the possible coordination and cooperation failures are greater with company B (JIT) than with company A (co-branding). First, for company B since production lines need to be adjusted, more modification is required than for company A (existing brands can be linked), and any modification is harder to unwind for company B than for A (i.e., the effects are one-sided). Second, the expected interdependence and need for interaction with company B is higher than with company A, resulting in a greater ongoing need for coordination. For these reasons, we should expect greater transaction costs in company B than in company A; perhaps the relationship with company B should be structured as an acquisition, which would bring the business under the common ownership with WonderWorld's other businesses (or abandoned).

The three conceptual pillars of corporate strategy

Figure 3.3 illustrates the link between the foundational concepts of corporate strategy: corporate advantage through joint owner-ship (Chapter 1), synergies through joint operations (Chapter 2), and governance costs and governance form (Chapter 3). In the absence of governance costs, collaboration between two busi-nesses would look the same under common ownership as under separate ownership; a corporate strategist would never outdo an investor, and synergies would always be pursued through joint operation, not joint ownership (II). It is precisely because of governance costs that choice of governance structure has

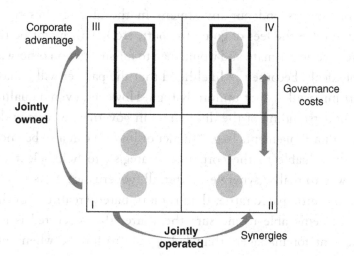

Figure 3.3   Corporate advantage, synergies, and governance costs

consequences, and sometimes joint ownership and operation of businesses (IV) can extract more value than an investor's portfolio of the same businesses (III), or the same businesses operated together but owned separately (II). We discuss these ownership choices in detail in Part II (*Decisions about portfolio composition: increasing the scope of the corporation*), which starts with Chapter 4.

Frequently asked question

1. Can governance costs be quantified?

Yes, sometimes they can. For instance, there is evidence that the cost saving from the offshoring of services to countries like India from the US or UK results in cost savings that are about 15–20 percent lower than the wage differences, and this difference can be ascribed to governance costs. For certain frequently occurring and fairly similar types of transactions, it may thus be possible to estimate governance costs. Another approach is to estimate the maximum damage that governance costs can inflict (e.g., our partner cheats and our investment in the alliance has to be written off + the fees of going to court, etc.). This might be too aggressive an estimate and would lead to missing out on otherwise viable deals, because the likelihood that the partner will behave oportunistically is not uniformly high. However, even a qualitative understanding of the differences in governance costs under different arrangements (e.g., "higher or lower") can also be enormously valuable to the corporate strategist, to help select the best way to realize synergies. After all, governance costs ideally are to be anticipated rather than (unfortunately) realized; for this reason, being able to measure them after they occurred is less important for managers than being able to foresee when they might be large.

Notes

1. These are also called hierarchy costs because of the hierarchical structure of firms.
2. David, R. J. and Han, S. K. (2004). A systematic assessment of the empirical support for transaction cost economics. *Strategic Management Journal*, 25(1), 39–58.

    Geyskins, I., Steenkamp, J. B. E. M., and Kuman, N. (2006). Make, but, or ally: a transaction cost theory meta-analysis. *Academy of Management Journal*, 49(3), 519–543.
3. Williamson, O. E. (1975). *Markets and Hierarchies: Analysis and Anti-Trust Implications*. New York: The Free Press.

    Williamson, O. E. (1985). *The Economic Institutions of Capitalism*. New York: The Free Press.

    Gulati, R., Lawrence, P. R., and Puranam, P. (2005). Adaptation in vertical relationships: beyond incentive conflict. *Strategic Management Journal*, 26(5), 415–440.
4. Vanneste, B. S. and Frank, D. H. (2014). Forgiveness in vertical relationships: incentive and termination effects. *Organization Science*, 25(6), 1807–1822.

Further reading

Much of our understanding of governance costs comes from a body of thinking that is known as the "The Theory of the Firm" in economics and management. The founding father of this theory was Ronald Coase, whose ideas have been extended by Oliver Williamson. Coase wrote a path-breaking paper in 1937 that raised a very significant question: why do firms exist at all instead of a series of contracts between individuals who do what they are each best at doing? After all, it was already well known since Adam Smith and David Ricardo that a division of labor based on specialization would increase total value. In the language of synergies, these "gains from specialization," where both parties are better off when each does what they are better at, would be a form of "Connection" coupled with "Consolidation" (as one of the parties ceases each activity). The question of interest was why contracts were not sufficient to harness these kinds of synergies between businesses. The answer proposed was that governance costs of joint ownership could sometimes be lower than those of managing through contracts (these were termed "transaction costs"). Coase (1937) and Williamson (1975) are useful background for a reader with a deeper interest in the intellectual foundations of corporate strategy.

Coase, R. H. (1937). The nature of the firm. *Economica*, 4(16), 386–405.
Williamson, O. E. (1975). *Markets and Hierarchies: Analysis and Anti-Trust Implications*. New York: The Free Press.

For more on the drivers of governance costs in an international context, see:

Ghemawat, P. (2007). *Redefining Global Strategy: Crossing Borders in a World where Differences still Matter*. Boston, MA: Harvard Business School Press.

PART II

Decisions about portfolio composition: increasing the scope of the corporation

4

Diversification

This chapter provides a framework to analyze the **corporate diversi-fication** decision: a firm trying to enter a new business starting from an existing one. "New" here means new to the firm, not necessarily new to the world. For example, a company that only made footballs may diversify and start producing and selling footwear (see Figure 4.1 for the value chains before and after diversification). In Chapter 1 we defined a business in terms of the "who" (customer), "what" (product or service), and "how" (value chain). Two businesses are different if they differ on at least one of these dimensions. Therefore, diversification implies a new choice on at least one of these dimen-sions. For example, a bank that traditionally only provided services to businesses starts targeting consumers (who), an accountancy that begins to offer consultancy advice to existing clients (what), or a university that starts selling courses online (how) are all diversifying. Internationalization – a company that begins selling in another country – is an instance of diversification in terms of the "who," e.g., a French champagne producer exporting to Russian clients.

"Entering" a business implies owning at least some of the resources and capabilities in the value chain underlying the new business, and accessing the rest, possibly through partners. It thus entails the process by which a firm accesses the resources and capabilities

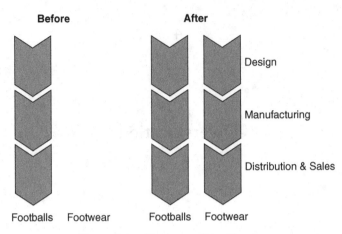

Figure 4.1 Corporate diversification

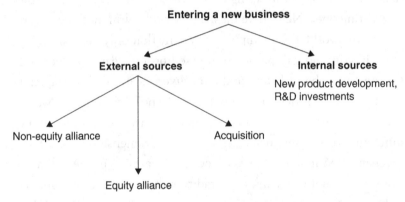

Figure 4.2 Growth tree: organic and inorganic growth

necessary to operate in a new business, through ownership and/or partnerships.

Choosing between modes of diversification

The basic modes available for a company to expand into a new business are captured in what we call the "Growth tree" (see Figure 4.2). At the first branch of the growth tree lies the choice between internal and external development. This has also been referred to as organic vs. inorganic growth. **Organic growth** is the process by which a company enters a new business on its own, including hiring, creation of a new project or business unit, or repurposing an existing business unit. If we think of the new business as possessing its own value chain, the goal of organic growth is to build up the resources and capabilities that this value chain entails on its own, without recourse to other firms.

Under **inorganic growth** we distinguish among three broad categories: non-equity alliances, equity alliances, and mergers and acquisitions (M&As). If a firm allies with another firm, both parties commit resource to joint activity – operate jointly – but remain independent. The relationship can exist without equity (such as a revenue sharing or licensing agreement) or with equity (including joint ventures). If a firm acquires another firm, the target firm ceases to exist and is now part of the acquiring firm (in a merger, both firms cease to exist and continue together in a new entity).

The goal for these relationships in the context of diversification (these may be conducted for other reasons) is to access ready-made resources and capabilities relevant to the value chain of the new business. These modes may differ widely in their costs and benefits. Ultimately, we must compare the four alternatives at the bottom of the branches of the growth tree to pick the best one.

The attractiveness of the new business in standalone terms is sometimes seen as the most important factor in the decision to diversify. However, in Chapter 1 we introduced a basic principle of corporate strategy: that the more mature and efficient the capital markets in which a company operates, the greater the pressure on the company to engage in diversification primarily on the basis of potential synergies between existing and new businesses. Put simply, the CEO should be spending the shareholder's money on entry into a new business *only* to extract value that the shareholder *could not* by investing directly in such a business on her own. Thus synergies from linking operations across the old and new business play a more important role in justifying diversification decisions. Finally, since there are many possible modes of entry into the new business, as captured in the growth tree, and the benefits and costs of each mode may be different, we need to think about the cost of entry and benefits created for each mode separately. The diversification test (see Box 4.1) captures the combined effects of these three considerations, namely the standalone attractiveness of the business (relative to cost of entering the business), the importance of synergies, as well as the costs and benefits of entry under different modes.

Box 4.1 The diversification test

Let's say your corporate portfolio currently comprises business A, and the question is whether you should also enter business B. The diversification test can be written as:

$$V_m(AB) - C_m(B) > V(A)$$

V(A) is the standalone NPV of business A. $V_m(AB)$ is the NPV of jointly operating both business A and B, under diversification mode m. $C_m(B)$ is the cost of entering business B through growth mode m. This leads to the combinations in the table below.

Growth mode (m)	Value of jointly operating business A and B ($V_m(AB)$)	Cost of entry ($C_m(B)$)
Internal development	Value of A and B when jointly operated and owned, taking into account governance (i.e., ownership) costs	Cost of building resources
Acquisition	Value of A and B when jointly operated and owned taking into account governance (i.e., ownership) costs	Cost of acquiring resources
Equity alliance	Value of A and part of B when jointly operated but only a share of B is owned, taking into account governance (i.e., ownership and transaction costs)	Cost of setting up alliance (including equity stake)

Non-equity alliance	Value of A and part of B when jointly operated but not jointly owned, taking into account governance (i.e., transaction) costs	Cost of setting up alliance

The diversification test is written from the perspective of one partner, but both parties to an alliance or acquisition will conduct their own analysis. Further if the diversification test is passed, it is also consistent with social value maximization. Ideally, you should diversify into the new business that generates the largest difference between the left and right hand sides of the inequality.

An important result for corporate strategists is that **to pass the diversification test, either bargains or synergies are required.** A bargain occurs when you pay less for a business than its standalone value, i.e., $C_m(B) < V_m(B)$. Under either acquisition or organic growth, you are entitled to 100 percent of the returns of business B so a bargain occurs at any price less than that. Under an alliance, you are entitled to only part of the returns from B and a bargain is said to occur whenever setting up the alliance costs less than that. The ability to "get a bargain" could arise from private information, an advantage created through regulation or political favor.

If it is unlikely you can "get a bargain" for any of these reasons, then the cost of entry will typically be at least as much as the value of the business (and usually more). In that case, diversification can only be justified through synergies. Recall the synergy test: potential synergies exist whenever jointly operating two businesses can create more value than the sum of their standalone values, i.e., $V(AB) > V(A) + V(B)$. Recall that the synergy test indicates potential value, and does not consider governance costs (which can be seen as a tax eating into the synergies). However, if it is not passed, then there can be no net value from synergies after accounting for governance costs, for any growth mode, m. If synergies cannot be achieved with joint operations free of any governance costs, then they cannot be achieved under any governance structure with their associated governance costs.

Thus if the synergy test fails, then it must also be true that $V_m(AB) < V(A) + V_m(B)$. Without bargains, as we noted, $C_m(B) > V_m(B)$. Therefore, if there are no bargains to be had, it is necessary that the synergy test be passed for the diversification test to be passed. Indeed if you get a great bargain, you may even be willing to tolerate some negative synergies. However even if the synergy test is passed, the governance costs associated with the mode of governance selected, and the costs of entry for this mode, may still be large enough to fail the diversification test. For instance in cross-border contexts, the costs of entry may be higher because of government regulations or lack of information about the true value of the assets being purchased. Therefore in the absence of bargains, passing the synergy test is *necessary but not sufficient* to pass the diversification test.

It also follows that a bargain by itself is neither necessary nor sufficient to diversify: you could diversify because of synergies (even if you have to pay more than the standalone value), and even if you can get a bargain negative synergies may stop you from diversifying. Similarly, synergies by themselves are neither necessary nor sufficient to diversify: if you can get a business for a bargain it might be worthwhile entering even if there are no synergies, or even with strong synergies you may be forced to pay too high a price to enter profitably.

Your best bet is when you can get both a bargain and extract value from synergies net of governance costs. Unfortunately, these clear cut cases are rare, so that the diversification decision must usually rest on a careful comparison of the cost of entry and realized synergies net of governance costs.

A five-step approach to the diversification decision

From the diversification test it follows that **a decision *whether* to diversify cannot be decoupled from the decision on *how* to diversify (i.e., choice of growth mode)**. The growth tree suggests a hierarchical structure to these choices: we can compare *within* the inorganic growth options and then compare the best inorganic growth option to the organic growth option. In Chapter 5, we will focus on choosing the best inorganic growth mode. In Chapter 6, we will compare the best inorganic growth mode to organic growth. Thus, the diversification decision involves comparing the best external with internal growth mode: if at least one of the options is better than the status quo (i.e., has a positive NPV), you would diversify using the best growth mode. If neither option is better than the status quo (i.e., NPV is zero or negative for both), you would not diversify.

Step I: Are there potential synergies between the old and new business?

In order to sharpen our thinking about the synergy test, rather than consider the new business in the abstract, assume that your goal is to understand if you can justify paying a premium for acquiring the best performing standalone firm in the new business under the assumption that the cost of implementing the merger is zero. If there are potential synergies, which you may use the 4C's framework from Chapter 2 to analyze, the answer will be a "yes" (assuming no costs of implementation is useful, otherwise you could only justify a premium if the synergies are larger than the governance cost). Even if the answer is "yes," this does not imply that you should acquire; this is just a test for the existence of synergies, which as we have seen above are necessary but not sufficient to justify entry when there are no bargains to be had.

On the other hand if the answer is "no," then you must simply ask if a diversification opportunity has arisen that really represents a bargain, and whether the size of the bargain is large enough to cover any negative synergies. If "yes," diversify, otherwise do not diversify.

Step II: Identify resource gaps

Assuming that the synergy test is being met, we must next identify the **resource gaps**: what the desired resources or capabilities needed to diversify into a new business are in order to operate in the new business. To do so, we must construct a hypothetical value chain for the new business, and identify the gaps: the resources and capabilities needed to operate in that value chain that we do not currently possess.

Step III: Identify candidates for resource acquisition through inorganic growth

Does any other company already possess the desired resources and capabilities identified as gaps in Step II? If the answer is "no," then organic growth is the only option, otherwise we need to do a full-fledged growth tree analysis (requiring both steps IV and V).

Two caveats are in order before we proceed: first, the choice between modes of growth is often a matter of emphasis rather than all or nothing. Companies diversifying into a new business may often use both organic and inorganic growth, indeed there may be complementarities between the two modes. This is because you may choose to build some of the resources needed to operate in the new business, but buy others. In fact, in our terminology, you need to own some resources to be "in a business." **Thus the growth tree analysis is ideally conducted at the level of individual value chain segments rather than at the level** of the entire value chain of the new business. Further, some internal capability is necessary to be able to assess potential partners from whom to buy resources and capabilities, and working with external partners may help direct and stimulate internal growth efforts. At the same time, the circumstances may dictate *primary* reliance on one of the modes of growth.

Second, regulatory requirements often block attempts by companies to grow purely organically. For instance, in some sectors in the Chinese and Indian economies, foreign direct investment (FDI) is restricted to constitute no more than (say) 50 percent ownership in a subsidiary. In such sectors, entry must necessarily be inorganic, and through partnerships.

Step IV: Optimal partner–mode combination for inorganic growth

For each identified potential candidate that can help fill resource gaps inorganically, we must consider different potential growth modes; non-equity alliance, alliance, acquisition. The value from each of these modes for each partner will differ and can be captured in what we call a "partner–mode" matrix (details in Chapter 5), identifying the best combination of partner and mode.

Step V: Compare with value from organic growth

We estimate the value of projects that organically build the resources needed to fill the resource gaps identified in Step II, and compare it to the value of the best partner–mode combination identified in Step IV. One can also work backwards, and see how much investment and time would be needed to generate an organic growth NPV that matches what we obtained for the best partner–mode combination in Step IV (details in Chapter 6).

Basic facts about diversification

The basic facts about diversification to emerge from meta-analyses of the existing research relate to three areas.

1. Diversification is an important economic phenomenon

Diversification is how multi-business firms are created. It is the norm among large companies. Diversified companies account for typically more than 50 percent of national economies, across the globe. The majority of firms in global rankings like the Fortune 500 are diversified multi-business firms, as are the business groups that dominate emerging economies.

2. Related diversifiers do better than single-business firms and unrelated diversifiers

Relatedness is broadly understood to mean the possibility of finding synergies across businesses. This finding holds for both accounting-based measures (e.g., growth, profitability, and return on equity (ROE)) and market-based measures (e.g., stock market returns and market-to-book values). Common explanations include that related diversifiers can extracts synergies that are, by definition, absent in single-business firms. In addition, the realization of synergies might be easier for related than for unrelated businesses (because of differences in business models). In line with this, M&As between related companies create more value when announced than between unrelated companies (i.e., the combined share price of acquirer and target go up more).

3. The existence of a diversification discount

It is often suggested that highly diversified firms trade at a discount. But a discount relative to what? One interpretation is that a diversified firm is worth less than a collection of single-business firms that operate in the same businesses as the diversified firm. The evidence indicates that this is indeed the case: diversified firms tend to have a discount of 10–15 percent relative to a similar portfolio of focused firms. So in this sense, there is a **diversification**

> **discount.** But we cannot interpret this as *causal*. If the diversified firms differ from the focused firms in respects other than degree of diversification, then we are comparing apples with oranges, and it does not follow that diversification is what caused these firms to suffer a discount. Comparing a diversified firm with itself over time (when it was more vs. less diversified) or using statistical tests that attempt to account for any difference between diversified and focused firms, the results show that the diversification discount when it exists is less than 10 percent and in some case disappears completely. Based on these findings, a strategy of diversification is not bad *per se*. Rather, some corporations diversify inappropriately leading to a discount, whereas others diversify without such a discount, and possibly with a premium.

To summarize, we give an overview of the five steps involved in the diversification decision:

- **Step I: Are there synergies to being in new + old businesses?**
  - Hint: could you justify paying a premium for acquiring the best performing standalone firm in the new business? (This is to distinguish the value from improving a standalone business from the synergies between businesses; it's the latter we are after here.)
- **Step II: Resource gap**
  - What resources needed for the new business value chain do we already have? What do we lack?
- **Step III: Identify best inorganic growth candidates who can fill the gap.**
- **Step IV: Identify combination of best mode for best inorganic growth candidates** and estimate value from this.
- **Step V: Estimate organic growth value,** and compare to the result of Step IV.

Steps III and IV are covered in Chapter 5; Chapter 6 covers Step V.

Common mistakes to avoid in diversification

Diversification for the wrong reasons: As we noted in Chapter 1, diversifying to manage unsystematic risks is only valuable if shareholders cannot do it. As the diversification test in this chapter makes clear, diversifying into a business just because it is attractive is also a mistake: there have to be synergies between the new and existing business.

Don't assume a blanket diversification discount: Investment banks and equity analysts often apply a diversification discount (i.e., a conglomerate or holding company discount). Discounts of 15 percent are common. We advise against arbitrarily applying such a discount. First, the existence of a discount is questionable once the correct apples-to-apples comparison is done (see above). Second, and perhaps more importantly, the calculation of any discount is about an *average* discount. As with any average, some diversified firms are above and some below so it may not give a good estimate for your diversified firm. Thus while applying a diversification discount as a bargaining tactic may be OK, this is unlikely to be a good valuation technique.

Consider relatedness is terms of the value chain, not in products or customers: Most of the studies rely on an industry classification, which is based on some similarities in products and/or customers. As we have seen in Chapter 2, the correct approach to a synergy based diversification decision is to consider the value chain. Any operational synergies come from linking value chain segments.

Use the growth tree iteratively: Even if organic growth seems limitedly attractive, do not rule it out immediately as it might be more attractive than either the ally or acquire option. Consider all branches of the tree.

Frequently asked questions

1. **In the diversification test, why is the standalone value of B (V(B)) not included on the right hand side?**

The standalone value of B ($V(B)$) does not feature explicitly, but it does so implicitly through the cost of entry ($C_m(B)$).

In the absence of bargains, the other side is unwilling to sell business B for less than the money it could generate on a standalone basis. Hence, the synergy and diversification tests are closely linked.

2. **Research has shown that failure rates for alliances, acquisition, and organic growth are high and their magnitude roughly comparable. Can we conclude that a CEO should be indifferent between these options?**

No. It would only make sense to be indifferent between these modes of growth if they could be interchangeably applied to the same business situation. This is far from the case. Alliances, acquisitions, and organic growth are alternative means by which a CEO can achieve business growth and they each have different strengths and weaknesses. The apparent similarity of failure rates masks the fact that each mode of growth is usually selected for different kinds of business growth situations; in fact, choosing the inappropriate model of growth may itself be a cause of failure.

3. **My business is doing poorly. Is this a good enough reason to diversify into a new business?**

No. You must still pass the diversification test, which is possible if the costs of bankruptcy are high and the costs of redeploying your current assets into the new business are low.

4. **Is vertical integration a form of diversification?**

Vertical integration may be seen as a particular form of "within business" diversification. For instance, suppose the footwear business shown at the beginning of the chapter formerly did just design but now enters manufacturing as well (forward integration) or the converse (backward integration). Technically, just the manufacturing of footwear or its design can be seen as a business by itself, since it has its own business model (i.e., distinct answers to the question of who is the customer, what is the value proposition, and how is this delivered). Thus the movement to integrate upstream or downstream value chain activities can be conceptualized and analyzed using the same basic tools we use to understand across diversification in general.

Further reading

For more on growth modes, see:

Capron, L. and Mitchell, W. (2012). *Build, Borrow, or Buy: Solving the Growth Dilemma*. Boston, MA: Harvard Business Press.

For meta-analyses of the empirical literature on diversification, see:

Capon, N., Farley, J. U., and Hoenig, S. (1990). Determinants of financial performance: a meta-analysis. *Management Science*, 36(10), 1143–1159.

Datta, D. K., Pinches, G. E., and Narayanan, V. K. (1992). Factors influencing wealth creation from mergers and acquisitions: a meta-analysis. *Strategic Management Journal*, 13(1), 67–84.

Palich, L. E., Cardinal, L. B., and Miller, C. C. (2000). Curvilinearity in the diversification–performance linkage: an examination of over three decades of research. *Strategic Management Journal*, 21(2), 155–174.

For estimates of the diversification discount taking into account firm differences, see:

Campa, J. M. and Kedia, S. (2002). Explaining the diversification discount. *Journal of Finance*, 57(4), 1731–1762.

Villalonga, B. (2004). Does diversification cause the 'diversification discount'? *Financial Management*, 33(2), 5–27.

For further reading on the costs of diversification, see:

Rawley, E. (2010). Diversification, coordination costs, and organizational rigidity: evidence from microdata. *Strategic Management Journal*, 31(8), 873–981.

Wu, B. (2013). Opportunity costs, industry dynamics, and corporate diversification: evidence from the cardiovascular medical device industry, 1976–2004. *Strategic Management Journal*, 34(11), 1256–1287.

Zhou, Y. M. (2011). Synergy, coordination costs, and diversification choices. *Strategic Management Journal*, 32(6), 624–639.

5

Ally or acquire?

Burger Behemoth Plc is a successful chain of fast-food restaurants, with a large network of restaurants around the country, some of which are franchised and others fully owned. Its brand has come to stand for standard, tasty, convenient, and quick meals, and it has enormous customer loyalty among families with young children below 12, and also among busy executives on the road. However, growth is slowing, and greater health awareness among consumers has led to a general disenchantment with fast food. The CEO of Burger Behemoth is contemplating some new businesses that they might enter. A candidate has emerged from internal discussion: the children's theme park business.

During the same discussion it was suggested that Mighty Monkey, Inc., an experienced player in the theme park business, might be a good partner to collaborate with. If Burger Behemoth were to decide to enter the theme park business through a collaboration with Mighty Monkey, which mode should they choose: non-equity alliance, equity alliance, or acquisition?

Inorganic growth: the costs and benefits of equity ownership in strategic partnerships

Broadly speaking, there are three modes of inorganic growth: non-equity alliances, equity alliances, and outright acquisition. Note that these forms of strategic relationship may also occur for reasons other than entering a new business – for instance, growth within a business or to help exit a business through outsourcing. However, most of what we know about choosing between these modes of growth will still apply.

It is useful to think about all strategic relationships as **relationships between firms that cannot be managed by a contract alone.** Non-equity alliances typically rely on contracts. However, they constitute alliances (rather than, say, simple procurement agreements) if the contract alone is insufficient, and a close working relationship is also needed between partners to adapt to changing circumstances and issues not specified in the contract.

Equity ownership can serve as an important supplement to contracts in alliances. Equity alliances involve one party taking an equity ownership stake in the other, and this could be reciprocal. When the equity stake of one party exceeds a threshold of around 25 percent in the other (this level varies across countries), then a right to veto is created. If a party's stake exceeds 50 percent in the other, then in effect it has gained control over it. An **acquisition** has taken place, and a contract may no longer be necessary (except for the employment contracts that bind the employees of the acquired company to the acquiring company). We can therefore view non-equity and equity alliances and acquisitions as different points on a line of increasing equity ownership, ranging from "Ally" (on the left) to "Acquire" (on the right), see Figure 5.1.

The choice of mode for inorganic growth is therefore a choice about where to locate the structure of the relationship on this line. This is determined by the costs and benefits of increasing equity ownership. In other words, **choosing the optimal governance structure is equivalent to picking the right level of equity.** Our focus is on the strategic considerations for selecting the right level of equity. There are also relevant accounting considerations (such as whether one can or must consolidate the

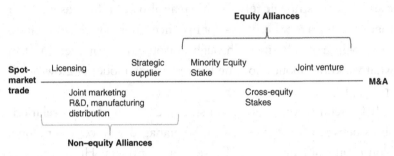

Figure 5.1 A continuum of governance structures

accounts of entities in which a parent has an equity stake; this varies significantly across countries).

Recall that the diversification test we discussed in Chapter 4 required that $V_m(AB) - C_m(B) > V(A)$, where $V(A)$ is the standalone (net present) value of business A, $V_m(AB)$ is the value of jointly operating both business A and B, under diversification mode m, and $C_m(B)$ is the cost of entering business B through mode m. In this chapter we describe a framework that is useful for assessing, in a qualitative sense, how $V_m(AB)$ and $C_m(B)$ vary for the different governance structures used for inorganic growth.[1]

The benefits of increasing equity ownership in strategic relationships

1. Exclusivity

Even at low levels of equity ownership, rivals are unlikely to consider creating relationships with the focal firm's partner. To take a hypothetical example, if company A were to take a 15 percent equity stake in company B, rivals of company A would be discouraged from forming a partnership with company B because of the role that company A may play through its equity ownership (and possibly concomitant board membership) to further its own interests at their expense. Full exclusivity can be achieved through complete ownership so that company A can exclude potential rivals. This factor is important for all the four basic synergy operators – Consolidation, Combination, Customization, and Connection. It highlights an increasing benefit from joint operation $V_m(AB)$ that is enabled by increasing levels of equity.

2. Cooperation

Equity ownership aligns the incentives and interests of the two partners. If firm A has an ownership stake in firm B, how well firm A does depends to some degree on how well firm B does. Thus, firm A would be less inclined to harm firm B's interests, or shirk from doing things that benefit firm B. While minority equity ownership is a partial step toward the alignment of interests, complete ownership through acquisition provides the greatest level of interest alignment and ability to monitor and control behavior. This factor is most important when the synergies require significant modification of underlying resources, i.e., in Consolidation and Customization (see Chapter 3). This highlights an increasing benefit from joint operation $V_m(AB)$ that is enabled by increasing levels of equity.

3. Coordination

In order to meet the objectives of a strategic partnership, knowledge flows and coordination between the partnering firms may be critical. Hence, managers in these firms may need to create inter-organizational linkages to enhance inter-partner coordination and knowledge flows. Greater equity ownership gives a firm the authority to implement more elaborate coordination mechanisms and stronger organizational linkages.[2] For instance, a minority equity position, under some legal regimes, suffices to provide a board seat that acts as a limited coordination mechanism between the partner firms. Ownership of a significant equity stake, on the other hand, may be necessary for undertaking deeper organizational integration between partners, by creating dedicated integration managers or permanent liaison committees. An acquisition through complete ownership further extends the ability to create organizational linkages, as full ownership makes it possible (though not necessary) to reconfigure organizational boundaries and units across partners if necessary. This factor is also most important when the synergies require significant modification of underlying resources, i.e., in Consolidation and Customization. This highlights another increasing benefit from joint operation $V_m(AB)$ that is enabled by increasing levels of equity.

In sum, increasing levels of equity ownership generate greater benefits from the control of governance costs arising from conflicting incentives and difficulties of coordination (see Chapter 3). Both the level of synergies that can be exploited as well as the portion that one gains of these synergies therefore increase in the level of equity; in the language of the diversification test, $V_m(AB)$ increases more rapidly with the level of equity when the three factors highlighted above are relevant. Note that larger equity stakes increase the possibility, but not the necessity, for using more complex and elaborate integration mechanisms (see Figure 5.2).

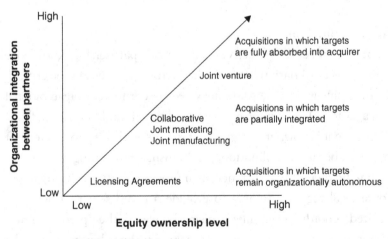

Figure 5.2 Possible organizational integration across governance structures

Note that we implicitly presume no prior relationship or trust between the potential partners. *Trust* refers to a willingness to be vulnerable in a relationship based on the expectations of what the partner will do. If trust exists, then the benefits of equity may be muted; either no equity or lesser equity may suffice under certain conditions, as trust is an alternative to equity to manage transaction concerns. Trust implies confidence in the motives and competence of the partner; low confidence in these factors is a source of transaction costs. Therefore either trust or equity ownership can serve to manage these transaction costs.

The costs of increasing equity ownership in strategic relationships

1. Lowered motivation

When company A takes an equity stake in company B, two mechanisms weaken motivation for individuals in company B. First, the owners and stock-owning employees of company B give up a certain portion of their rights to future gains. Consequently, they are less motivated to put in the desired level or quality of effort since they stand to get a smaller proportion of any gains that might be derived from it. Full acquisition can exacerbate the problem. Second, a company gets the right to direct the actions of its partner's employees when it takes high levels of equity in the partner. Roughly speaking, the greater the equity ownership, the stronger is the right to direct the partner.

For instance, a minority equity position allows for board representation, which is a weak form of control over the strategic direction of the partner firm. Full ownership, on the other hand, allows for much greater control and consequently the ability to implement even a major strategic redirection. An increase in control for the partner taking the equity ownership position, however, corresponds to a proportionate decrease in control for the other partner. As a result, both owners and employees of the latter partner have less autonomy to guide the future course of their actions and to decide how and where to put their effort. This loss of autonomy may result in lower motivation and reduced effort, besides possibly missing out on their valuable insights.[3] These are instances of the negative synergies from organizational complexity we discussed in Chapter 2, and referred to as "Dilbert" costs. They will likely be larger when there are significant changes to the working conditions of individuals in the organizations. This highlights a decrease in the benefit from joint operation $V_m(AB)$ that is created by increasing levels of equity.

2. Uncertainty and commitment

Viewing equity stakes as "real options" provides some very valuable qualitative insights into determining the desirable level of equity ownership in strategic relationships. A real (call) option, in simple terms, provides a company the future right (but not the obligation) to increase its level of equity ownership in its partners. By taking a minority equity position in the partner, a company creates the option to acquire it later. More importantly, this option becomes more valuable as uncertainty about the value of the partner increases, because uncertainty means that both the upside and downside increase. However the option but not the obligation implies that one only need acquire if the upside materializes. The lesser the equity one has to take upfront in order to gain this option to acquire later, the better. Stated differently, the more the equity ownership at a given point in time, the greater the opportunity cost in terms of forgone option value. This factor is likely to be most important when the uncertainty in synergy value is relatively high (i.e., in Connection and Customization synergies). This highlights a source of increase in the cost of entry $C_m(B)$ with increasing levels of equity.

3. Cost of control

What kind of premium over current valuation will we have to pay in order to induce the partner to cede (even partial) control? In the case of acquisition, this would correspond to the acquisition premium. But even in a minority equity investment, a control premium is implicit in the valuation of the stake. In a non-equity contract, one may still have to pay licensing or franchising fees. This cost of gaining control depends on the alternatives available to the potential collaborators, and not directly on the type of synergy involved. It is thus relevant for all four synergies: Consolidation, Combination, Connection, and Customization. This factor highlights an increase in the cost of entry $C_m(B)$ that increases with levels of equity.

4. Synergy independent cost of integration

At high levels of equity, control over the entire set of assets of one partner passes into the hands of the other. Yet not all of these assets may be of value to the new owner. The costs of disentangling the wanted from the unwanted assets, and disposing of the latter, are the costs of restructuring. These are larger when it is difficult to separate the wanted from the unwanted assets of the partner, and when it is difficult to find purchasers for the latter in the divestiture market. Further, all else being equal, larger and older organizations, regardless of the nature of the synergies involved in the deal, will require greater integration efforts to convert their systems and processes to be compatible with the acquirer. These are *synergy independent* costs of integration, that indicate an increase in the cost of entry $C_m(B)$ that rises with levels of equity.

In sum, increasing levels of equity increase both the synergy independent cost of entry (e.g., cost of control, loss of flexibility, integration costs) but also indirectly reduce the value from joint operations through suppressing motivation.

The checklist in Table 5.1 helps us to see when the benefits and costs of equity stakes are likely to be higher or lower.

TABLE 5.1 *Preferred equity level*

Benefits of equity ownership	Key questions	If the answer is "Yes," then level of equity should be	Relevant for synergy type	Effect
Exclusivity	Is there a benefit from excluding rivals from access to the resources of this partner?	High	Consolidation Combination Customization Connection	Increases value from joint operation
Cooperation	Is there a need for relationship specific investments by one or both partners that may potentially create a hold-up situation? Are the gains from synergy one-sided between partners? Is the prospect of future business an insufficient motivator for cooperation?	High	Consolidation Customization	Increases value from joint operation
Coordination	Is there a need for extensive knowledge sharing and coordination between partner firms?	High	Consolidation Customization	Increases value from joint operation

Costs of equity ownership

Motivation	Is employee motivation in the partner firm likely to drop as a consequence of changed work conditions (e.g., incentives, nature of work) after implementing the partnership?	Low	Consolidation Customization	Decreases value from joint operation
Uncertainty and commitment	Is there significant uncertainty regarding the quality/value of the assets being accessed from the partner?	Low	Combination Connection	Increases cost of entry
Control premium	Will it be expensive to induce partner to give up control?	Low	Consolidation Combination Customization Connection	Increases cost of entry
Cost of synergy independent integration	Will it be expensive to separate out and dispose of unwanted assets in the partner?	Low	Consolidation Combination Customization Connection	Increases cost of entry

The questions about the benefits of ownership are meant to high-light when managing by a contract may be particularly difficult because of transaction costs, making equity ownership more useful in such circumstances. Similarly, some questions focus on the conditions that make equity ownership more costly. These can be seen as parameters that influence the benefits and costs of any given level of equity ownership, and therefore the optimal equity ownership levels.

Which benefits are most important in a given situation, and how should you weigh the relative benefits and costs? To address this issue, we recommend that you first consider the extent of equity suggested by each of the three benefit criteria independently (exclusivity, alignment of incentives, and need for organizational linkages), and then pick the level of equity suggested by the *most important* of the three criteria. Thus, if the gains from aligning interests and the need for achieving coordination both seem moderate, but the exclusivity criterion is the most important, then choose full ownership. This approach clarifies and emphasizes what the primary motivation for taking the equity stake is. This is very important in managing the partnership, as well as in evaluating its success. Similarly, managers should consider the equity levels suggested by the cost criteria (motivation, uncertainty, premium, and synergy independent integration costs), and pick the level of equity indicated by the most important criterion. For instance, if motivation problems appear to be relatively unimportant, but uncertainty about the value of the partner is significant, then managers should choose low levels of ownership.

When the benefit and cost criteria lead to similar conclusions, there is little difficulty in choosing the level of equity. More complicated situations arise, however, when the benefit and cost criteria point to different levels of equity. A solution might involve taking a level of equity between those suggested by the benefit and cost criteria.

TABLE 5.2 *Identifying the best combination of inorganic growth mode and candidate firm*

NPV estimates	Firm 1	Firm 2	Firm 3	Firm 4
Non-equity alliance	15	10	26	22
Equity partnership	50	**65**	54	47
Acquisition	60	45	60	55

To obtain a quantitative estimate for the value of the best inorganic growth mode, one could use an NPV estimation with synergies between the existing and new businesses, which accounts for the estimated cash flows based on the level of ownership, cost of entry, and discount rate relevant to that mode (see the appendix to Chapter 2 for a discussion of how to value synergies). If there is more than one possible firm that is a candidate for an alliance or an acquisition, the results of this analysis can be expressed as a matrix of modes and candidates and firms (see Table 5.2).

It may be intuitive to estimate the numbers in the matrix above for acquisitions: compare the value of synergies to the control premium to be paid. But how about the case of an equity partnership? The approach is similar, where we compare the portion of the synergies our equity stake or strategic partnership allows us to capture, and the premium over valuation of the portion of the equity purchased.

Note however, that the synergies we would obtain with a 25 percent equity stake are not necessarily 25 percent of what we would obtain with 100 percent ownership – because of the governance costs (in this case, transaction costs) we have discussed in Chapter 3 as well as in this chapter. Indeed, as we have noted, the benefit of increasing ownership stakes is precisely to control these transaction hazards. To make this concrete, imagine that the realizable synergies with firm 2 are valued at 65, and that the control premium needed to acquire is 20, leaving an NPV of 45 for the acquisition (see Table 5.2). If we instead considered a strategic alliance with a 20 percent equity stake, the value of the realized synergies is not necessarily 20 percent of 65 = 13; it may be much lower because of the tax that transaction costs impose, which cannot be controlled in a strategic alliance to the same degree as they could be controlled in a full acquisition. On the other hand, it may even be higher if the costs of motivation and flexibility loss are high under an acquisition. In the case of a non-equity contractual agreement, the ability to control transaction hazards as well as the costs of lowered motivation and loss of flexibility are lower; but the cost of setting up such relationships is also much lower, and may involve things like the fee of the contract, licensing fees, etc.

The partner–mode matrix thus involves a fair burden of computation, but the qualitative guidelines in Table 5.1 should help to guide the analysis and act as a sanity check.

The case of vertical integration

A particular instance of the choice between ally and acquire arises in buyer–supplier relationships, and is referred to as the "vertical integration" decision. The choice is between defining a contractual agreement with a supplier for an input vs. acquiring the supplier in order to gain full control over it. This is typically because of synergies from Customization between the buyer and supplier – the supplier or buyer have to customize their own resources to benefit the most from the efforts of the other. For instance, the supplier may have to retool their manufacturing line, or the buyer may have to redesign their product to use the supplier's outputs. Customization synergies require significant modification and can be one-sided, leading to an increased need for alignment of interests and coordination between partners. The factors identified in Table 5.1 are all relevant in this choice, which can be treated as any other form of the ally vs. acquire choice. One could also conduct vertical integration by setting up an internal supplier through organic growth. The factors relating to the choice between inorganic and organic growth are covered in Chapter 6.

Application: Burger Behemoth

Suppose you are the CEO of Burger Behemoth, whose diversification problem was described at the beginning of this chapter. If you were to work with Mighty Monkey to enter the theme park business, how would you conduct your analysis for the optimal governance mode?

Step I: The synergy test

Whatever the mode of diversification, synergies with the existing business are necessary, unless one can be assured of bargains. The first step therefore is to understand whether the existing fast-food restaurant business could generate any synergies with theme parks conditional on being in the business (i.e., ignore for now the process of entering these businesses). The following thought expriment may help: Suppose you were to acquire a standalone, well performing publicly listed company in the theme parks business today (e.g., Mighty Monkey), how would you justify paying a premium above its market cap (assuming the integration costs were zero)? If you can think of synergies that would justify paying a premium in this case, then in principle you have passed the synergy test with these businesses.

To make sure that you are considering all the possible ways in which synergies might exist between the businesses, you may find it useful to use the 4C's approach outlined in Chapter 2. Recall from Chapter 2 that operational synergies come in four types: Consolidation, Combination, Customization, and Connection. Further, these operational synergies derive from the value chain (and its underlying resources). So you could begin by constructing a generic value chain for the children's theme park business or a specific one (if you have a candidate firm in mind, e.g., Mighty Monkey). Consult industry experts to make sure you are not missing anything. Also consider carefully the possibility of dis-synergies (e.g., the possibility of losing business in concessions operated by within other theme park chains).

In this instance, it is likely that you may see some Connection synergies (e.g., applying the Burger Behemoth brand and related customer knowledge, which we are told has a strong appeal among families with young children) and possibly some customization synergies (e.g., expertise in real estate sourcing, which is at the heart of a franchising business like Burger Behemoth's).

Let's assume the theme park business passes the synergy test.

Step II: Identify the resource and capability gaps in the value chains of the target businesses

Using the value chain for the children's theme park business, identify which of your existing resources and capabilities in the fast-food restaurant has excess capacity (or is of an intangible nature with low costs of re-use) that can be repurposed to this industry. Whatever is left represents the gaps in the value chains you will need to fill – through inorganic or organic growth.

In the case of theme parks, assuming that Burger Behemoth uses its brand to target families with young kids, the gaps in resources and capabilities may include physical infrastructure, content generation (to keep coming up with new rides), and service delivery (the training of staff, the management of crowds and rides).

Step III: Selecting inorganic growth modes

For theme parks, you will have to generate a set of possible candidate firms that have the necessary capabilities you identified in the gap analysis in Step II. You can get your investment bankers to help you screen for target firms, much as they would do for an acquisition, based on the criteria you identified (e.g., an ailing theme park chain). For each candidate firm, the question you have to ask is about the optimal level of equity ownership in this firm that would get you the most value from entry for each mode of entry m, $(V_m(AB) - C_m(B))$. Start with a non-equity alliance as a base case, and see if you can do significantly better with higher levels of equity.

Let's assume that the qualitative analysis based on the checklist in Table 5.1 suggests that in the case of theme parks, value is maximized through a non-equity revenue sharing strategic alliance, in which Burger Behemoth co-brands and co-promotes with a theme park company, and helps in their expansion plans by lending them its real estate selection capabilities. You should consider at least two candidates, so that you have a back-up alternative and a reservation price for your negotiations with the first alternative.

From this analysis we would conclude that **if we enter theme parks with an external partner it would be through a non-equity alliance.** In Chapter 6 we compare this alternative to organic growth.

Basic facts about the choice between alliance and acquisition

- There are well documented instances of all four operational synergy operators (Consolidation, Combination, Connection, Customization) in alliances as well as acquisitions. In principle, these are alternate governance structures that enable pursuit of the same objective.
- Managers may recognize that alliances and acquisitions are different governance modes for achieving the same basic objective, and yet they systematically fail to consider the alternative when actually engaging in an alliance or an acquisition.[4]
- Meta-analyses show that as expected transaction costs increase, relationships between firms are more likely to contain hierarchical elements (including greater levels of equity stakes). As technological uncertainty increases, the likelihood of equity ownership declines.[5]
- Experimental studies of managerial choice of governance structures confirm that managers do indeed prefer higher levels of equity when either the value of partner's resources or the expected transaction costs in the relationship increases; however, their choices are more sensitive to the former than the latter.[6]

Common mistakes to avoid

Underestimating control difficulties in alliances: Strategic alliances are temporary organizations between peers; consequently the interests of partners cannot be assumed to be aligned. While alliances are easier to set up and exit than acquisitions, this also means that they may be harder to manage on an ongoing basis, because no partner has absolute authority over the other, but must instead engage in a series of negotiations. For the same reasons, differences in culture may matter more in alliances than in acquisitions as impediments to synergy realization.

Underestimating integration costs in M&A: The costs of integration in an acquisition are both synergy dependent and synergy independent. Even if no synergies are being actively pursued (because the target was a bargain), it is still true that there might be costs of restructuring, standardization, and alignment of systems. Note that these costs are distinct from governance costs – the reduction in value from joint operation that can occur with increasing equity levels (such as the effect on lowered motivation).

Becoming fixated on a single alternative: As the growth tree makes clear, the choice of mode of growth is a hierarchical and iterative process. One must consider all branches of the tree as well as multiple partners. Beginning with "Let's see if we should acquire company X" is dangerous, as it can blind us to the alternatives that may be superior as both modes and partners. Relatedly, it is useful to have a second best alternative always in mind when one approaches another firm either as an alliance partner or a potential target in an acquisition, so that a clear walk-away price can be established. Finally, the practice of separating the teams that focus on M&A and alliances is a dangerous one because it gives rise precisely to this kind of fixation on particular alternatives rather than a consideration of the entire growth tree.

Frequently asked questions

1. **Why do we not consider direct cost of purchase? Aren't acquisitions more costly because they always involve larger sums of money than alliances?**

Yes, acquisitions involve larger sums than alliances. However, what's relevant for acquisitions is only the premium you pay on top of the standalone value. If you pay simply the standalone value, the NPV is zero because what you pay is equal to the cash flows that you get back. Similarly the benefit of the acquisition is really in the synergy value (above the standalone value). Table 5.1 may thus be seen as comparing how these synergy benefits and costs of control change at different levels of equity ownership. Relatedly, the total costs of integration in an acquisition will be typically higher than for an alliance. However, in a comparison of these modes, it is the synergy independent costs of integration that matter (e.g., of restructuring and alignment of systems). The costs of integration that are a fraction of the synergies only increase with the degree of integration; an acquirer can choose the level of integration (see Figure 5.2) and therefore a sensible acquirer would only incur higher levels of these costs if the gains from synergies offset them sufficiently. Hence they drop out of consideration in the choice between alliance and acquisition.

2. **Bank Two, a French commercial bank, wants to expand rapidly into an Asian country. Internal analysis suggests that building its own branch network will take too long, and Bank Two has identified a potential acquisition target that has a sizeable branch network. Which of the following factors would make it less important for Bank Two to find significant synergies with this potential target, and why?**

(a) Bank Two is a privately held company.
(b) There are unlikely to be any potential acquirers for the target company.

If Bank Two is a privately held company, acquiring a target with few synergies will be less of a problem compared to the problems it would have with its shareholders (and stock price) if it was publicly traded – however, an acquisition with fewer synergies creates less value, thus the effect of an acquisition with low synergies will affect the bottom line of a privately held or publicly traded company in the same way. The fact that there are no other potential acquirers might indicate that Bank Two values the target's assets higher than other firms, and this is a first indicator that there are indeed synergies (we assume no private information). Further, if there are few other bidders, then the premium need not be too high, in which case the magnitude of synergies can be lower.

3. **I identified a partner that I want to work with and I need to decide whether to ally or acquire. Even though the partner is in the same business I am active in, can I still use the inorganic branches of the growth tree?**

Yes. Even though you have the necessary resources and capabilities, the trade-offs you face in deciding between ally or acquire are the same. You can use the same set of questions from Table 5.1.

4. **Is it always better to acquire when expanding abroad?**

No. It is true a full acquisition can give you more control, but the synergy independent costs of integration, costs of uncertainty, as well as lowered motivation because of cultural differences, can be significant. Indeed regulation around limits to FDI may make acquisitions impossible, and you may have to expand in partnership with a local player.

Notes

1. Kale, P. and Puranam, P. (2004). Choosing equity stakes in technology-sourcing relationships: an integrative framework. *California Management Review*, 46(3), 77–99.
2. Gulati, R. and Singh, H. (1998). The architecture of cooperation: managing coordination costs and appropriation concerns in strategic alliances. *Administrative Science Quarterly*, 43(4), 781–814.
3. Hackman, J. R. and Oldham, G. R. (1975). Development of the job diagnostic survey. *Journal of Applied Psychology*, 60(2), 159–170.
4. Dyer, J. H., Kale, P., and Singh, H. (2004). When to ally and when to acquire. *Harvard Business Review*, 82(7–8), 108–115.
5. Geyskens, I., Steenkamp, J. B. E. M., and Kumar, N. (2006). Make, buy, or ally: a transaction cost theory meta-analysis. *Academy of Management Journal*, 49(3), 519–543.
6. Puranam, P. and Kale, P. (2013). The design of equity ownership structure in inter-firm relationships: do managers choose according to theory? *Journal of Organization Design*, 2(2), 15–30.

Further reading

For more on trade-offs between governance modes, see:

Geyskens, I., Steenkamp, J. B. E. M., and Kumar, N. (2006). Make, buy, or ally: a transaction cost theory meta-analysis. *Academy of Management Journal*, 49(3), 519–543.
Kale, P. and Puranam, P. (2004). Choosing equity stakes in technology sourcing relationships: an integrative framework. *California Management Review*, 46(3), 77–99.
Puranam, P. and Kale, P. (2013). The design of equity ownership structure in inter-firm relationships: do managers choose according to theory? *Journal of Organization Design*, 2(2), 15–30.

For more on how the choice between an alliance and an acquisition is influenced by trust and pre-existing relationships, see:

Gulati, R. and Nickerson, J. A. (2008). Interorganizational trust, governance choice, and exchange performance. *Organization Science*, 19(5), 688–708.
Puranam, P. and Vanneste, B. S. (2009). Trust and governance: untangling a tangled web. *Academy of Management Review*, 34(1), 11–31.
Vanneste, B. S., Puranam, P., and Kretschmer, T. (2014). Trust over time in exchange relationships: meta-analysis and theory. *Strategic Management Journal*, 35(12), 1891–1902.

6

Organic or inorganic growth?

Burger Behemoth Plc is a successful chain of fast-food restaurants, with a large network of restaurants around the country, some of which are franchised, and others fully owned. Its brand has come to stand for standard, tasty, convenient and quick meals, and it has enormous customer loyalty among families with young children below 12, and also among busy executives on the road. However, growth is slowing, and greater health awareness among consumers has led to a general disenchantment with fast food. The CEO of Burger Behemoth is contemplating some new businesses that they might enter. A candidate has emerged from internal discussion: the children's theme park business.

After examining possible modes of inorganic growth into these businesses, one candidate has emerged for non-equity partnership – Mighty Monkey, Inc., an established player in the theme parks business. Should Burger Behemoth go for this non-equity partnership or should it instead go on its own?

Recall that the basic modes available for a company to expand into a new business are captured in what we call the "growth tree" (see Chapter 4). At the first branch of the growth tree lies the choice between organic (internal) and inorganic (external) growth. Under inorganic growth the choice lies between non-equity alliances,

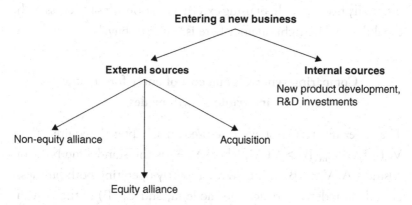

Figure 6.1 Growth tree: organic and inorganic growth

equity alliances (including joint ventures), and acquisitions. These were the focus of Chapter 5. In this chapter we focus on comparing organic growth to these inorganic growth modes (see Figure 6.1).

What is organic growth?

We refer to **organic growth** as the process by which a company enters a new business on its own – hiring, creation of a new project or business unit, repurposing an existing business unit, etc. If we think of the new business as possessing its own value chain, the goal of organic growth is to build up the resources and capabilities that this value chain entails, without recourse to other firms.

The choice of organic vs. inorganic growth is distinct from the traditional "make or buy" analysis, which refers to a choice between making a product or service internally (and assumes that you have the capability to do this) or procuring it from an external supplier (who is also capable of producing the product or service, but at a different cost). This depends on a comparison of transaction costs and production cost differences (Chapter 9). Organic vs. inorganic growth refers to the choice between developing the resources and capabilities needed to deliver a product or service to customers internally from scratch, or using external relationships to access such capabilities. The right analogy here is "build or buy."

Comparing synergies and cost of entry for organic vs. inorganic growth modes

The diversification test we discussed in Chapter 4 required that $V_m(AB) - C_m(B) > V(A)$, where $V(A)$ is the standalone NPV of business A, $V_m(AB)$ is the NPV of jointly operating both business A and B, under diversification mode m, and $C_m(B)$ is the cost of entering business B through diversification mode m. In Chapter 5 we discussed how $V_m(AB)$ and $C_m(B)$ vary for different inorganic growth modes. Here we analyze the conditions under which $V_m(AB)$ and $C_m(B)$ will increase or decrease for organic growth, relative to that for external growth modes.

Synergies under organic growth are similar to those under M&A

The benefits of organic growth – which involves total control over the newly created, possibly synergistic resources and capabilities – can be *approximated* by the NPV that would accrue from acquiring the same assets inorganically, assuming **zero** cost of control (so that there is no premium for acquisition) and **zero** synergy independent costs of integration (i.e., the costs of restructuring and divesting unwanted assets, the costs of converting the acquired organization's systems and processes to be compatible with the acquirer). This approach assumes that the synergy dependent costs of integration (e.g., governance costs, which act like a marginal "tax" on the gains from synergies) are the same in organic growth and acquisition. This may not be a valid assumption if the prospective partner has a different culture, and cultural difference matters for synergy extraction. Regardless, assuming no differences in the realized gain from synergies might be a useful first approximation, and one that we follow here. If the initial approximation is known to be inaccurate, then a second approximation can be made (based on the first) with an allowance in favor of organic growth.

For instance, the benefits from entry through building a new 100 unit production line in business B should be similar to the benefits from acquiring an existing 100 unit production line in the same business at its standalone value, with no cost of synergy independent integration, assuming minimal cultural differences. The appendix to Chapter 2 provides the tools needed to value synergies.

Cost of entry under organic growth differs from that under inorganic growth

The costs of entry under organic growth are qualitatively different from those of inorganic growth. The costs of entry under organic growth can be estimated as they would be for any internal project for the company, with estimates of the investment required and time periods involved, appropriately discounted for the risks of the project. However, before we embark on this quantification exercise, it may be useful to do a qualitative check on whether we face conditions under which the entry costs of organic growth are particularly cheaper than those of inorganic growth.

The starting point is to have clarity on the **resource gap** – i.e., those resources that are necessary to enter the new business but currently not present in the company. If no potential partner has them, you have no choice but to build them yourself. Assuming a potential partner has them, you face the choice of either inorganic or organic growth. Three factors influence this choice (see Figure 6.2).

First, can you copy the resource? This will be harder if there are legal barriers (e.g., patents or protected technologies), the resource is present in people rather than codified (e.g., it may be difficult to

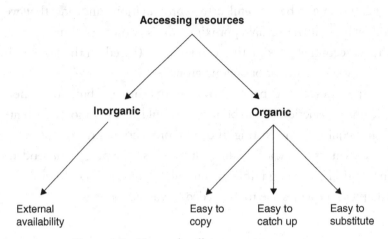

Figure 6.2 Key trade-offs in accessing resources

copy customer friendliness), or prone to causal ambiguity (i.e., it is difficult to understand how to build the resource, for example, how to be innovative). To expand on the latter, there may be large uncertainties involved in building a resource. It may be impossible to fully specify which factors play a role in their accumulation process, e.g., if a large element of luck is involved. This is often true for knowledge based (e.g., IP arising from R&D) and other intangible assets (e.g., brands or management skills). For instance, volumes have been written about Toyota's production system, yet few have been able to replicate it.

Second, even if in principle it is possible to copy the resource, it may be difficult to catch up with the potential partner, who has begun building before you. This is referred to as **first mover advantage** (for them) or **second mover disadvantage** (for you). To expand on the drivers of second mover disadvantage, we can think of the resources and capabilities that underlie value chain activities in terms of their levels ("stocks") and in terms of their flows ("investments"). The levels of a resource may be relatively hard to change in the short run. Examples include reputation, loyalty, R&D capability,

brand image, and organizational culture. Flows represent investments in each period that add up to the stock of the resource (e.g.,
R&D spending, advertising budget, or training of employees). In
financial statement terms, loosely speaking the income statement
shows details of flows, while the balance sheet shows (some, but not
all) resource stocks.

To compete, what one ultimately needs is the stock of resources,
not the flow (think of brand vs. advertising expenditure). However,
how easily others can recreate the stock through a flow of investments matters a lot for how sustainable the competitive advantage
based on a stock of resources is. **The characteristics of the process
by which flows are converted into stocks determine if there is
second mover disadvantage in resource accumulation.** If competitors can easily convert their flows (investments) into stocks
(resources and capabilities), then it is hard to sustain competitive
advantage by being the first to begin building the resource.
Conversely, if you are a later entrant, you cannot hope to **build**
(i.e., organic growth) if there are strong first mover advantages in
resource accumulation created by the characteristics of the process;
then you should explore options to **buy (i.e., rely on inorganic
growth)** instead.

Dierickx and Cool (1989) set out several important properties
of the resource accumulation process that affect this trade-off. The
three properties listed below all describe conditions under which the
conversion of investments (flows) into assets (stock) is faster, slower,
or uncertain. These are:

1. **Inter-connectedness of asset stocks:** The rate at which investment in asset 1 converts into the stock of asset 1 increases with
   the stock of asset 2. Thus the rate of accumulating increments in
   an existing stock may depend not just on the level of that stock,
   but also on the level of other stocks. If a company has a strong
   brand, for instance, investments in building a sales force might
   bear fruit more rapidly. If a company has a strong R&D capability

in making internet switches, investments in R&D for internet routers may generate returns more rapidly.

2. **Asset mass efficiencies**: This indicates there are increasing returns to investing in the flows – the rate at which the flows get converted into stocks increases with the level of the stock. The phenomenon of "success breeds success" and network externalities are instances of this property. For instance, a lab with good scientists finds it easier to attract even more good scientists.

3. **Time compression diseconomies**: This implies that over and above the quantity of investment flows (investments), the time periods over which they are accumulated has a positive effect on asset stocks. This creates an "economy" for the first mover, and a "diseconomy" for the second mover. Thus a second mover who spends $10 million in the tenth year cannot catch up with a first mover who has been spending $1 million a year for ten years. Imagine going on a crash training program, where you work out ten hours a day for three months, hoping to become as fit as another who has spent one hour a day in the gym for the last two-and-a-half years!

Discussions of the organic growth vs. inorganic growth decision often emphasize the notion that "if speed is important, organic growth is ruled out." However, as we have pointed out here, the issue is not really speed but second mover disadvantage. If others have the relevant assets, it is difficult for you to replicate them, and there is a strong second mover disadvantage for you to try to build similar resources, then in effect you are forced to consider inorganic growth. You must, however, still consider the costs and benefits of inorganic growth set out in Chapter 5.

The third dimension when considering building a resource is whether you can substitute the potential partner's resources for a different resource. The basic idea is that an external partner has a resource that facilitates new business entry. You may find that it is hard to copy or hard to catch up. A remaining possibility is for you to build a resource that differs from that of the potential partner but is functionally equivalent for entering the new business. Imagine, for example, that you want to enter the minivan market. The market leader uses an advanced technology of composite materials to produce the chassis. You find it impossible to replicate this technology. Instead you consider producing the chassis based on a more easily adoptable technology of steel stamping. Thus, instead of replicating the resource you aim to invent around it. The potential partner's resource provides a useful template as to what to look for.

Combining these factors, the checklist in Table 6.1 gives a qualitative indication of the conditions under which the costs of organic growth may be higher or lower. Note this gives an indication of the

TABLE 6.1 *Deciding between inorganic and organic growth*

Issue	If the answer is "yes," then favored growth mode is	Key questions
External availability	Inorganic	Are partners available who have the resource?
Easy to copy	Organic	Are legal hurdles to copy the resource absent (e.g., patents)?
		Has the resource been codified or is it independent of people?
		Is it clear how to build the resource?
Easy to catch up	Organic	Do you own related resources and capabilities that can help in building the desired resources?
		Are increasing returns absent when investing in these resources?
		Are "crash investment programs" (e.g., trying to match $1 million/year over ten years with $10 million in one year) likely to succeed?

TABLE 6.1 (*cont.*)

Issue	If the answer is "yes," then favored growth mode is	Key questions
Easy to substitute	Organic	Can you substitute the potential partner's resource with a different resource?

relative costs of organic vs. inorganic options for deciding between these alternatives, not the absolute cost of organic growth.

When comparing organic growth with inorganic growth modes of different levels of equity (see Table 5.1), note that organic growth enjoys all the benefits of high equity levels but does not suffer many of the costs (e.g., no loss of motivation, control premium, or synergy independent integration costs). The magnitude of second mover disadvantages relative to the costs of control, motivation losses, and integration thus often determine this choice between "build" and "buy."

Application: Burger Behemoth and Mighty Monkey

Suppose you are the CEO of Burger Behemoth, whose diversification problem was described at the beginning of this chapter. How would you conduct your analysis to decide between organic and inorganic growth?

The analysis continues from Chapter 5. We assume that (a) the synergy test has been passed, (b) the resource gaps have been identified, and (c) the best inorganic growth mode has been selected (i.e., non-equity alliance).

Step IV: Comparing with organic growth mode

For theme parks, the benefits of organic growth would be proxied by the benefits of a hypothetical full acquisition (with zero premium and no synergy independent integration costs) of one of the theme park chains considered in Step III (p. 114–15) (which may or may not be the theme park chain chosen for strategic alliance). However, the qualitative analysis of the resources needed to operate in this business (physical infrastructure, content development, and service delivery capabilities) is very likely to suggest that even if you could possibly replicate them there are strong second mover disadvantages. You have few related assets to leverage, there are increasing returns to investing in these assets, and crash programs will not work. Thus, organic growth is not really an option for Burger Behemoth. Thus, let's say you conclude that net benefit inorganic >net benefit organic for theme parks. If Burger Behemoth enters theme parks, it will be through inorganic growth – specifically a non-equity alliance with an existing theme park chain.

Basic facts about the choice between organic and inorganic growth

- When entering new markets, companies are more likely to rely on organic growth the more related that market is to the companies' existing markets.[1] Having related resources makes it easier to replicate the necessary resources (see Table 6.1).

Common mistakes to avoid

- **Do not ignore organic growth**: True, few things create as much excitement in the corporate boardroom as an M&A. Organic growth does not have the same glamor but can be a viable alternative. Considering organic growth is useful even if only to create a better M&A deal by developing a strong reference point for bargaining.
- **Do not assume that organic growth is easier than inorganic growth** (because, for instance, there is no control premium or synergy independent integration): In fact, evidence suggests that failure rates of organic growth initiatives are comparable to those of M&As and alliances.[2] A selective approach to the usage of each to match the resource gap being filled is most likely to succeed.

Frequently asked questions

1. **Discussions of the "organic vs. inorganic growth" decision often emphasize the notion that "if speed is important, one should use inorganic growth":**

   (a) Explain why this should be the case: why would inorganic growth necessarily be faster?
   (b) Even if it were faster, would inorganic growth automatically be preferable to organic growth?

(a) In general, it will take more time to replicate internally what somebody has already developed externally. This is because the external resources are ready and the internal resources need to be developed to get to the same level. While acquiring a company for its external resources might take some time to get the financial and legal issues dealt with, allying with a company can be done quickly.

(b) However, the issue is not speed but the extent of "second mover disadvantage" – i.e., how hard it is for a later mover to copy an earlier mover's competencies. In other words, even if organic growth were rapid, it can hardly beat acquiring a firm that already has the capabilities you need in terms of speed. The cost of this difference in time needed to catch up has to be balanced against the cost of inorganic growth (e.g., control premium, post-merger integration, motivation loss).

2. **How should I decide how to enter a foreign market?**

The mode of foreign entry (e.g., greenfield investment vs. joint venture) relies on the same criteria as above: external availability of partners who can fill the resource gap, ease of replication, and ease of catching up. It might be cheaper to build for some countries than others (e.g., those that are geographically or culturally close). FDI policies may rule out organic growth into others. Consequently, a company's entry mode varies by host country.

Notes

1. Helfat, C. E. and Lieberman, M. B. (2002). The birth of capabilities: market entry and the importance of pre-history. *Industrial & Corporate Change, 11*(4), 725–760.
   Brice, D. J. and Winter, S. G. (2009). A general interindustry relatedness index. *Management Science, 55*(9), 1570–1585.
   Lee, G. K. and Lieberman, M. B. (2010). Acquisition vs. internal development as modes of market entry. *Strategic Management Journal, 31*(2), 140–158.
2. On organic growth: Day, G. S. (2007). Is it real? Can we win? Is it worth doing? *Harvard Business Review, 85*(12), 110–120.
   Van der Panne, G., Van Beers, C., and Kleinknecht, A. (2003). Success and failure of innovation: a literature review. *International Journal of Innovation Management, 7*(03), 309–338.
   On alliances: Kale, P., Dyer, J. H., and Singh, H. (2002). Alliance capability, stock market response, and long term alliance success: the role of the alliance function. *Strategic Management Journal, 23*(8), 747–767.
   Kale, P. and Singh, H. (2009). Managing strategic alliances: what do we know now, and where do we go from here? *Academy of Management Perspectives, 23*(3), 45–62.
   On M&As: Pautler, P. A. (2003). Evidence on mergers and acquisitions. *Antitrust Bulletin, 48*, 119–221.
   King, D. R., Dalton, D. R., Daily, C. M., and Covin, J. G. (2004). Meta-analyses of post-acquisition performance: indications of unidentified moderators. *Strategic Management Journal, 25*(2), 187–200.

Further reading

For more on resources and their accumulation process, see:
Barney, J. (1991). Firm resources and sustained competitive advantage. *Journal of Management, 17*(1), 99–120.
Dierickx, I. and Cool, K. (1989). Asset stock accumulation and sustainability of competitive advantage. *Management Science, 35*(12), 1504–1511.
Helfat, C. E. and Peteraf, M. A. (2003). The dynamic resource-based view: capability lifecycles. *Strategic Management Journal, 24*(10), 997–1010.

For more on the choice between organic and inorganic growth, see:
Capron, L. and Mitchell, W. (2009). Selection capability: how capability gaps and internal social frictions affect internal and external strategic renewal. *Organization Science, 20*(2), 294–312.

Capron, L. and Mitchel, W. (2012). *Build, Borrow, or Buy: Solving the Growth Dilemma*. Boston, MA: Harvard Business Review Press.

Moatti, V., Ren, C. R., Anand, J., and Dussauge, P. (2015). Disentangling the performance effects of efficiency and bargaining power in horizontal growth strategies: an empirical investigation in the global retail industry. *Strategic Management Journal*, 36(5), 745–757.

PART III

Decisions about portfolio composition: reducing the scope of the corporation

7

Divestiture: stay or exit

Let's say you are the CEO of ABC Sports, which began its corporate life making footballs. It now has a leading brand in this product line. A few years ago, the management decided to leverage their strengths in the football business to enter footwear. The experiment has not been deemed successful, as your shareholders kindly pointed out to you during the most recent annual shareholder meeting. You are thinking of getting out of the footwear business and of refocusing on making footballs. Should you exit the footwear business and, if so, in what manner?

Divestiture refers to the process of reducing the portfolio of the businesses a firm owns. It is one of the two important ways in which a corporation reduces its scope. The other is outsourcing (the subject of Chapter 8). Divestiture occurs when the firm reduces the number of businesses it is active in by completely pulling out of the value chain and ceasing to offer the products from that value chain to the relevant customers. Consider ABC Sports, which is active in two businesses: footballs and footwear. If ABC Sports decides to *divest* the footwear business, this implies that it will no longer offer footwear. Alternatively, it may decide to *outsource* the manufacturing of the footwear, while

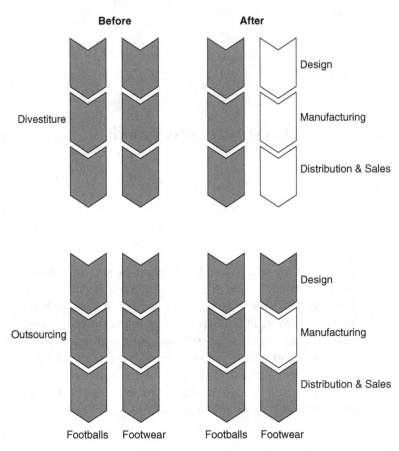

Figure 7.1 The difference between divestiture and outsourcing

still designing them and distributing them. The difference can be visualized as in Figure 7.1.

The two basic modes of divestiture are sell-offs and spin-offs. In a **sell-off**, the divested business is *sold to another company*. When the other company uses a significant amount of debt to finance its purchase, the transaction is called a leveraged buy-out (LBO). A special case of this is when the incumbent management of a business unit takes over the ownership of the business (again typically using debt finance); this is called a management buy-out (MBO). In a

spin-off, the shares of the divested business B are *distributed to the shareholders* (of the parent business A) and business B is listed on the capital market. Thus, the shareholders can choose whether they want to hold both shares or sell their stakes in business B. The parent business A may also choose to hold some residual stake in business B. This can be a tax free event, if the parent divests a minimum threshold of shares. In contrast, the corporate parent is liable to capital gains tax in the event of a sell-off.

Two other modes of divestitures are equity carve outs and split-ups. In an **equity carve out**, the parent sells a fraction of business B's stock to the general public and keeps the rest. This is also called an initial public offering (IPO). Typically, parents keep initially around 80 percent of business B's shares. As such, they keep control, can consolidate the earnings of business B with the parent's other business, and avoid paying taxes on the money raised from the sale of shares (taxes are due if the fraction sold is above a threshold). Under a **split-up,** shares are created in the underlying businesses, while those in the former parent are discontinued. In Table 7.1 (p. 138), we summarize the differences between these modes of divestiture. In Figure 7.2, we highlight the ownership differences.

It is only in the case of an equity carve out that the parent firms continue to control and exert influence on the business. Yet, within a few years of an equity carve out, the vast majority of parents will have reduced their stake to only a minority or no stake at all by selling more to the general public, by distributing shares to the parent's shareholders (spin-off), or by selling to another company (sell-off). This raises an interesting question: if equity carve outs are temporary, why go through the trouble of doing one instead of opting directly for, say, a spin-off or sell-off? Staged transactions can offer certain benefits. A spin-off preceded by an equity carve out generates cash, whereas one without does not. This is handy for cash constrained companies. A sell-off preceded by an equity carve out

TABLE 7.1 *Modes of divestiture*

	Sell-off	Spin-off	Equity carve out	Split-up
Ownership passes to	Other company	Existing shareholders	Public	Existing shareholders and sometimes public
Generates cash	Yes	No	Yes	Yes if through equity carve outs; no if through spin-offs.
Parent remains in control	No	No	Generally (in the short term)	Parent ceases to exist
Tax free event	No	Yes, if percent of shares divested is above threshold	Yes, if percent of shares in the IPO is less than threshold	Yes

establishes a market price that companies can use in their negotiation for the sale of the business. This is useful when there is uncertainty about the value of the business.

In the remainder of this chapter we will focus on sell-offs and spin-offs. Split-ups are typically achieved through spin-offs and carve outs, and carve outs often end up as sell-offs and spin-offs.

The divestiture decision

Let us say your corporate portfolio comprises business A and business B. Whether you should keep or get rid of business B in the portfolio is the divestiture decision (see Box 7.1).

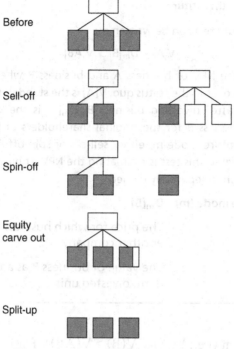

Figure 7.2   Ownership after divestiture

From the divestiture test it follows that a corporate parent should divest for one or both of the following reasons:

(a)   Failing the synergy test.

(b)   Another corporate parent is a better owner.

1. Failing the synergy test

In the absence of synergies, divestiture is a good option. Assuming $D_m[B] \geq V[B]$ (i.e., for a sell-off, the price of selling a business is at least the standalone value of that business; for a spin-off, $D_m[B]$ is the standalone value of that business), then a failure to pass the synergy test is sufficient to pass the divestiture test. The synergy test fails if separately operating two businesses is at least as good as jointly

---

Box 7.1 The divestiture test

The divestiture test can be written as:

$$V[A] + D_m[B] > V[AB]$$

V[AB] is the NPV of business A and business B when they are jointly owned, as in the status quo. V[A] is the standalone value of business A after divesting business B. $D_m[B]$ is the value from divesting business B for the original shareholders of the parent under divestiture mode m, either sell-off or spin-off. The key to operationalizing this test is estimating the NPV of business A and business B when separately owned.

Divestiture mode (m)	$D_m[B]$
Sell-off	The price for which business B is sold to another company
Spin-off	The value of business B as an independent, divested unit

---

operating them (i.e., $V(A) + V(B) \geq V(AB)$). For instance, there are no benefits from collaboration and each business would be better off making their own, independent decisions. The synergy test also fails if there are negative synergies. For instance, business B supplies business A and business B has difficulty attracting other customers as long as it is jointly operating with business A. Thus, failing the synergy test is grounds for a divestiture. It goes without saying that before proceeding to divest, we should also look at the possibility and feasibility of taking measures that will ensure that we pass the synergy test, such as restructuring, re-engineering, and synergy projects.

2. Another corporate parent is a better owner

If business B is better off with a different corporate parent than the current one, then it's time to divest business B. This might be the

	Synergy test: Pass	Synergy test: Fail
Is there a better parent? Yes	Situation 1: Sell-off	Situation 4: Sell-off (if high premium or low taxes) or Spin-off (if low fees)
Is there a better parent? No	Situation 2: Keep in portfolio (if full ownership is best), Equity carve out (if partial ownership is best), or Spin-off (if no ownership is best).	Situation 3: Spin-off

Figure 7.3 Choosing a divestiture mode

case even if business B is performing well and is benefiting from the presence of business A. Thus, it is not necessary to fail the synergy test; even if the synergy test is passed (i.e., $V(AB) > V(A) + V(B)$), as long as you can get a really good price for business B (i.e., $D[B] >> V[B]$) then you should still divest. This might happen, for instance, if some other corporate parent has even stronger synergies with business B than you do (or thinks that they do). This is one of the reasons that an active policy of looking for divestiture opportunities is sensible.

Whether the divestiture test is passed in one or both ways noted above has implications for the mode of divestiture. The joint implications are laid out in Figure 7.3. Suppose the synergy test is passed. If there is a better parent (Situation 1), i.e., the other parent can pay more for the business than that what it is worth to you, then a sell-off is an attractive option. If there is no better parent (Situation 2), this leaves several alternatives for how best to exploit synergies. Chapter 5 uses equity levels to distinguish governance structures, e.g., non-equity alliance, equity alliance, and full ownership. If full ownership is best to exploit synergies, then keeping the business in the portfolio is preferred. If partial ownership reduces the governance costs, then an equity carve out can be considered. If no ownership allows synergies to be exploited at the lowest cost, then a spin-off should be considered.

Suppose the synergy test is failed; then we have effectively ruled out the option of keeping the business in the portfolio, and we must still decide between spin-off and sell-out. If there is no better parent (Situation 3), then the option is clear: a spin-off. The case where you fail the synergy test and believe you can realize a gain from sale to another parent is an interesting one (Situation 4). You should consider a sell-off, especially if the other parent is willing to pay a high premium compared to what the business is worth to you. However, capital gains are typically taxed. So companies may still choose a spin-off, possibly preceded by an equity carve out. The choice between a sell-off and a spin-off will depend on considerations such as the expected valuation in each mode, the applicable tax rate, and the underwriting fees (for the equity carve out), see FAQ 6 (p. 150).

Basic facts about divestitures

The basic facts about divestiture to emerge from existing research relate to two areas.

1.   When does a divestiture occur?

(a) **Unrelated diversification:** Companies that are most diversified are more likely to divest a business, and they are most likely to divest the business that is unrelated to their other businesses. It could be that synergies are fewer (e.g., jointly operating value chains does not create value) or harder to exploit (e.g., top management time is limited).

(b) **Poor operating performance:** Companies that perform poorly (e.g., low earnings) are more likely to divest a business, and they are most likely to divest the business that does worst.

(c) **Poor stock market performance:** A company with a substantial diversification discount is more likely to divest, i.e., if it trades at a discount relative to non-diversified companies (see the SOTP analysis in Chapter 1 and also Chapter 4 on diversification). Such a discount arises if shareholders and analysts have difficulty in valuing the different businesses or appreciating the synergies between them (e.g., when the company has an unusual mix of businesses). Analysts are typically organized by industry, making it harder for them to appreciate value creating opportunities that span multiple industries. After a divestiture, the company might be easier to value (but possibly at the loss of synergy exploitation).

(d) **External pressure**: Activist investors often demand a divestiture, especially if a company is diversified into unrelated businesses, or has poor operating or stock market performance. Thus, external pressure amplifies the preceding conditions.

(e) **New CEO**: Divestitures often coincide with the appointment of a new CEO. A divestiture can be a transformative change for a company and a new person may find it easier to take and implement such a decision than a CEO who has been in the job for many years.

Other important, but somewhat idiosyncratic, reasons for divestiture include tax advantages, or anti-trust requirements following a merger to avoid excessive concentration of markets.

2. What is the outcome of a divestiture?

The consequence of a divestiture for the divesting parent is typically good for market returns. On average, a corporate parent that divests a business increases shareholder value. When measured in terms of a change in share price, this amounts to a low single-digit increase (typically around 2 percent) for the divesting parent. Likewise, accounting measures such return on assets (ROA), return on sales (ROS), and return on earnings (ROE) also improve for the parent.

Note that these findings do not, however, mean that a corporate parent should divest all its business, or that a strategy of divestiture will benefit every corporation that attempts it. This is because these results are mostly from a non-random sample of divested units – corporate parents divest precisely those businesses for which it makes sense and hold on to those for which it is better that they stay in the corporation.

Somewhat surprisingly, spin-offs and carve outs seem to do better than sell-offs in terms of value creation for the parent. One interpretation is that the destroying of standalone value is more of a problem (and therefore unleashes more value when solved) than missing out on the additional value a better parent can create. Alternatively, it could be that this reflects a sequential process. First there is a partial IPO and then a sell-off so that the market reactions to an IPO may already include expectations about a subsequent sell-off.

Application: ABC Sports

Lets say that you are appointed the CEO of ABC Sports, whose problem was described at the beginning of this chapter. You notice that various stakeholders are increasingly asking why ABC Sports entered footwear, and why it should continue to operate in that business. The more vocal critics ask for the footwear business to be divested. How would you reach a decision?

Step 1: The synergy test

The first step is to understand whether the footwear business is generating any synergies with the football business. (Note: we focus on operational synergies; you may also want to check for financial synergies.) The following two thought experiments may help. First, imagine that starting today, the two businesses would be moved into separate ownership and would be operated completely independently, with no communication or exchange of any kind between the two. How would the value of the businesses be affected? If there are indeed synergies between the two businesses, then the effect of such a separation should be an adverse one. Second, imagine that the ownership of the businesses would still be separated, but the business would be allowed to collaborate. In other words, if there are synergies, would those be best exploited under separate or common ownership?

To make sure that you are considering all the possible ways in which synergies might exist between the businesses, you may find it useful to use the 4C's approach outlined in Chapter 2. Recall from

Chapter 2 that operational synergies come in four types: Consolidation, Combination, Customization, and Connection. Further, these operational synergies derive from the value chain (and its underlying resources). So you could begin by drawing the value chain of the footwear business and that of the football business to make an assessment of the presence or absence of these different types of synergies.

You could also get some benchmarking data to compare how your footwear business is doing compared to other standalone footwear businesses, or those that are part of a larger corporate portfolio. But please note that you may still be passing the synergy test between football and footwear businesses even if the footwear business is doing poorly compared to its standalone peers.

If at the end of this exercise you conclude that significant synergies *do* exist between the businesses and those are hard to extract without (partial) ownership, then we have *ruled out* one option: spin-off. This is becaue a standalone valuation for the business cannot exceed what it is worth to you if there are synergies. You must still decide whether to keep footwear in your portfolio, or whether you can find a better corporate parent. If on the other hand you are *not* convinced that any synergies exist, then you have *ruled out* the option of keeping footwear in the portfolio: you must then decide between spin-off and sell-off. In other words, whether or not you pass the synergy test, you must consider the option of finding a better corporate parent.

Step 2: Finding a better corporate parent

Next, you should analyze whether other corporations are better corporate parents. You should distinguish between the following types of corporate parents:

(a) **Synergistic buyers**: Corporate parents active in the footwear business, or those who are not in footwear but who may see synergies with their existing businesses.

(b) **Financial buyers** (with limited operating synergies) who may be primarily interested in the footwear business to improve their financing structure.

Note that these are two ideal types of buyers, and in reality some kinds of buyers will fall somewhere in between; private equity firms, for instance, are sometimes seen as purely financial buyers, but this need not be true. To the extent they aim to improve the operations of their acquired companies by applying superior management skills, or by linking to the operations of other portfolio companies, then they are also synergistic buyers. You may also consider dividing up the business into pieces that are more likely to find better corporate parents. For instance there may be different takers for the manufacturing assets and for the brand and distribution assets of the footwear business.

With the help of your corporate development team, you can make a list of companies under each category. You could look at trade journals, or ask your investment bankers to quietly ask around and get a sense of what the market might be like. You could also look for private equity firms that have been active in the past in related sectors, and see if your footwear business fits the profile of the kinds of deals they have done – in terms of the operational performance relative to peers, or financing structure, for instance. For the synergistic buyers, you could use the same kind of analysis you did in Step I, to see if their value chains would generate stronger synergies with your footwear business than you do between footballs and footwear. In particular, you should look closely at those potential buyers that are in the footwear business, as they may have significant Consolidation/Combination synergies with your footwear business.

At the end of this exercise, you must be able to answer the following question: is it likely that you can realize a valuation from these other buyers that will leave you with a gain if you were to sell your footwear business to them? What you do next depends on combing this information with the results of your synergy test in Step I, as shown in Figure 7.3.

Step 3: Implement

If the analysis leads to an indication that sell-off or spin-off is indeed appropriate for the footwear division, then you now have a clear rationale for your decision. Consider also the possible dependencies between your retained business and the divested business, **particularly in the case of sell-off when you are still passing the synergy test** – one of the units may still need to provide some inputs or services to the other. This is equivalent to realizing $D_m[B]$ not at one time, but over a period of time in the divestiture test (see Box 7.1). These should be contractually specified and agreed upon with the buyer, and possible transactional hazards should be considered (see Chapter 3 and also Chapter 8 on outsourcing).

You will also need to prepare your footwear (and indeed football division) employees for the divestiture. The rationale for the divestiture, how it will ultimately create value for shareholders, and what guarantees you have obtained from the buyer about the care of your employees once transferred to them, all need to be communicated clearly to the relevant constituencies.

If, on the other hand, you choose to retain footwear in the portfolio, you now have a clear rationale for this – including a more detailed statement of synergies than you probably started with, and a sense of how other corporate parents might value the business. Next time you are asked why the footwear business is part of ABC Sports, you know what to respond: because ABC Sports can create more value from the footwear business than if it were standalone, and no one else can replicate it!

Common mistakes to avoid

Be proactive, not reactive: Divesting when you can, and not when you have to is usually preferable; distress sales rarely turn a profit. It's hard to let go of businesses, and it is something that does not come naturally to many corporate managers. Hence, for divestitures to happen management often seem to need to be pushed into action, e.g., by activist investors, bad performance, new incentive plans, or even replacement of the CEO. However, from the divestiture test, it is clear that divestitures might be sensible even if a business is doing well. In other words, a proactive attitude is useful, which is at the core of what a corporate strategist as the manager of a portfolio of businesses must cultivate.

Consider the consequences for the retained organization: Sometimes divesting a business might still mean that your remaining business are dependent on them, or vice versa – for inputs (as in the case of outsourcing) or to share infrastructure. Think about how these dependencies will be managed once ownership changes hands. Transaction service agreements (TSAs) are contractual means of recognizing such dependencies and stipulate how the buyer can continue to receive certain services from the seller for a period after the divestiture (and possibly the other way round). These should be part of the divestiture negotiations in the case of sell-offs, and may also influence the valuation of the assets. A more subtle form of dependency lies in the fact that your own employees will evaluate you as an employer based on how the divested employees fare in their new parent corporation. A transparent and fair process for transitioning employees to the new parent is therefore not just ethically important but it is also good business sense.

Frequently asked questions

1. **Another corporate parent wants to buy one of my businesses. We think the other parent is a better owner, but we can't agree on a price. What should we do?**

Here it appears that both sides see benefits from a deal. One possibility is to do a partial IPO (i.e., equity carve out), followed by a sell-off. The market price after the IPO then becomes a reference price for the negotiation. This is especially useful when it is difficult to value a business (e.g., uncertainty about future growth rates, intangible assets).

2. **I understand the importance of identifying the best corporate parent for divestiture decisions. Is this also relevant for the diversification decision when buying a company in a business in which you are currently not active?**

Yes and no. When you buy a company, it's important to understand if you can create more value than the current owner and other bidders, i.e., if you are a better parent. If you cannot create more value, you are unlikely to end up with the target company and if you do, you probably will have over-paid.

However, what matters is that you're a *better* parent than the companies involved (target, bidders, potential bidders), but not necessarily the *best* parent if the better parent is unaware of the target opportunity. In that case, you can go ahead and buy the target and then try to sell on to the best parent (by the divestiture test).

3. Can a SOTP valuation of my multi-business firm help me with divestiture decisions?

Recall that a SOTP (sum-of-the-parts) valuation using multiples from comparable standalone businesses makes two critical assumptions: first, that the comparable businesses are truly comparable and, second, that the profits of your divisions will remain the same even if unlocked from your structure. If these two assumptions are valid, then the SOTP valuation can tell us is the portfolio is indeed worth more than the sum of the parts – i.e., if the HQ is creating some value by controlling the businesses in the portfolio. If it is not, then we may conclude that a split-up is worth considering, but it is not possible to know which particular business should be divested. Of course a split-up and spin-off are the same if there are only two businesses in the portfolio.

4. What can a CEO do so that the market gets the company's synergy story?

Complicated or unusual portfolios of businesses are hard to understand for outsiders, which may lead to low analysts' valuations. This is a problem for a CEO, especially if his corporate strategy is based on synergies about which he needs to convince the market. A drastic solution is to divest a business. Not only is this decision hard to reverse, but also a CEO may sacrifice synergies that are hard to explain but valuable. There are other alternatives. Most importantly, be transparent and provide sufficient information to the investment community. Even though the financial reporting requirements on the individual businesses are lower than for the corporation as whole, sharing reliable data about the businesses is crucial for understanding how the portfolio could be worth more than the sum of the individual businesses. Make sure that analysts follow the company. Furthermore, an investor relations department is essential. If the market "does not get it" but the CEO is convinced about the synergies, then he can put his money where his mouth is: buy the under-valued shares of the company.

5. I have heard about a split-off and spin-out. What are these?

A split-off is like a spin-off: a business is divested as a standalone unit and no cash is generated. In a spin-off, shareholders get shares in the divested business and keep their shares in the parent (though they are free to sell either share). In a split-off, shareholders have to choose whether they keep their shares in the parent or instead take shares in the divested business.

A spin-out is a company founded by a former employee of the parent, possibly with its financial or technical support. This is not a divestiture because the business did not exist before. Confusingly, the term "spin-out" is sometimes used to mean "spin-off."

6. When the synergy test is failed and there is a better corporate parent, how do I choose between a sell-off and a spin-off?

Suppose we had to choose between a sell-off (subject to corporate tax) and a spin-off preceded by an equity carve out (let's assume that this is tax free) for the business, the choice would rest on a comparison of the following two numbers:

A. Value from IPO or spin-off: (expected share price * shares sold at IPO – underwriting fees) + (remaining shares * expected share price).
B. Value from sell-off: expected sale price of company – [(expected sale price – book value)*(tax rate)].

The acceptable expected sale price from the sell-off should be such that the second number is at least as large as the first.

> **7. The presence or absence of bargains features in the diversification decision (Chapter 4). Where does it feature in the divestiture decision?**

A bargain implies a good deal for one party and a bad deal for the other. For diversification, we are interested in buying a business for less than what it is worth. For divestitures, we are interested in selling a business for more than what it is worth. Hence, when considering bids of other corporate parents, some may over-pay, which is bad for them but good for your corporation.

Further reading

For a theoretical discussion of the reasons for divestiture, see:
Hoskisson, R. E. and Turk, T. A. (1990). Corporate restructuring: governance and control limits of the internal capital market. *Academy of Management Review*, 15(3), 459–477.

For a matched sample comparison of firms that divest and others that do not, to understand what might be driving divestiture behavior, see:
Berger, P. G. and Ofek, E. (1999). Causes and effects of corporate refocusing programs. *Review of Financial Studies*, 12(2), 311–345.

For meta-analyses of the empirical literature on divestitures, see:
Brauer, M. (2006). What have we acquired and what should we acquire in divestiture research? A review and research agenda. *Journal of Management*, 32(6), 751–785.

Lee, D. and Madhaven, R. (2010). Divestiture and firm performance: a meta-analysis. *Journal of Management*, 36(6), 1345–1371.

For recent studies on divestitures, see:

Feldman, E. R. (2014). Legacy divestitures: motives and implications. *Organization Science*, 25(3), 815–832.

Feldman, E. R., Amit, R., and Villalonga, B. (2014). Corporate divestitures and family control. *Strategic Management Journal*, in press.

Moschieri, C. (2011). The implementation and structuring of divestitures: the unit's perspective. *Strategic Management Journal*, 32(4), 368–401.

For the rationale behind equity carve outs, see:

Allen J. W. and McConnell J. J. (1998) Equity carve-outs and managerial discretion, *Journal of Finance*, 53(1): 163–186.

Vijh A. M. (2002) The positive announcement-period returns of equity carve-outs: asymmetric information or divestiture gains? *Journal of Business*, 75(1): 153–190.

8

Outsourcing: make or buy

Kappa Consulting is a boutique consulting firm, operating in London, UK. They employ a small team of five consultants and ten analysts who over the years have become very adept at working together; the analysts have become skilled at understanding the requirements of the consultants, and can prepare analyses and reports to their specifications. The firm has a small set of clients who value and trust the consultants. On a recent trip to Bengaluru in India, the CEO met up with a former MBA classmate who tells him that he runs a Knowledge Process Outsourcing outfit, that employs graduates with talents and skills comparable to Kappa's consultants, but with wages 40 percent lower than what Kappa pays its analysts. He recommends that Kappa offshore and out-source analytics work to his unit, and so cut costs in the London operations, and instead scale up its consultants. What should the CEO do?

Outsourcing occurs when an organization hands over part of the value chain it owns to a different firm, while maintaining the number of business it is active in. In contrast, a divestiture occurs when the firm reduces the number of businesses it is active in by completely pulling out of a value chain and ceasing to offer the products from that value chain to the relevant customers. In other

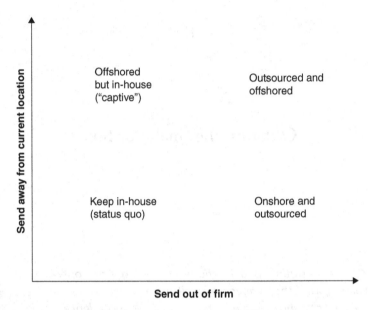

Figure 8.1 Outsourcing and offshoring

words, in outsourcing, the firm continues to offer the products and services based on inputs from the outsourced value chain activities to the relevant customers, but these parts of the value chain are no longer done in-house.

Offshoring occurs when part of a value chain moves to another geography, usually one with lower cost. Offshoring may or may not involve outsourcing. The same firm could merely relocate operations to a new location (see Figure 8.1). Thus decisions on whether to move the process out of the firm's boundary as well as out of the current geographical boundary occur together, if only implicitly (i.e., we may be implicitly choosing not to offshore, when we outsource to a local vendor).

The canonical outsourcing situation is one where before a company owned an entire value chain and, afterwards, only parts of it. For example, a company active in the footwear business can outsource manufacturing while continuing to do design and

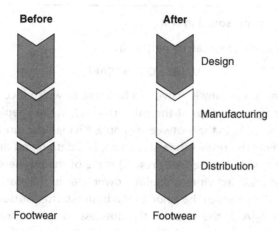

Figure 8.2 The company remains in the footwear business
after outsourcing manufacturing

distribution, see Figure 8.2. The key question therefore is whether manufacturing and design/distribution need to be owned in the same corporate portfolio. This is the outsourcing decision. It does not involve asking whether the company should get out of the footwear business, which is the divestiture decision. Note that just the manufacturing of footballs can be seen as a business by itself, since it has its own business model (i.e., answers to the question of who is the customer, what is the value proposition, and how is this delivered). But for clarity, in this book we will refer to it as a value chain activity as seen from the perspective of a firm that begins by owning the entire business (i.e., manufacturing, design, and distribution). Thus outsourcing involves refocusing by exiting value chain activities that are parts of the businesses in the portfolio, whereas divestiture involves refocusing by exiting the entire set of value chain activities that constitute a business in the portfolio.

A further distinction between divestiture and outsourcing is that under outsourcing there remains an ongoing dependency between the outsourced value chain activities and those that are kept in-house. Such ongoing dependency may or may not be the

---

Box 8.1 The outsourcing test

The outsourcing test can be written as:

$$V_O[A] + O[B] > V[AB]$$

Let's say a company is active in a business, of which it considers outsourcing some steps of the value chain (B) while keeping the rest in-house (A). In the footwear example, B is manufacturing, and A represents the rest of the value chain, i.e., design and distribution. Then, V[AB] is the (net present) value of the business when the value chain activities are jointly owned, as in the status quo. $V_O[A] + O[B]$ refers to the value of the business after outsourcing, in which $V_O[A]$ is the value of the business comprising retained value chain activities and O[B] is the value realized from the outsourced value chain activity B. O[B] is the value for the original owners, which may be realized over time through a contractual agreement with the vendor who takes B from the company.

---

case after divestiture. Despite these differences, we can analyze the outsourcing decision in a broadly similar way to divestiture, because both involve refocusing (see Box 8.1).

From the outsourcing test it follows that a corporate parent should outsource value chain activities B for one or both of two reasons.

1. Failing the synergy test

If value chain activity B no longer benefits from being jointly operated with value chain activity A, then it's time to outsource value chain activity B. Suppose that synergies are absent (i.e., $V(AB) \leq V(A) + V(B)$). Then as long as the change in ownership does not destroy value, then a failure to pass the synergy test (i.e. $V(AB) \leq V(A) + V(B)$) is sufficient to pass the outsourcing test. An ownership change could destroy value of the unit that is outsourced (i.e., $O[B] < V[B]$) if key people leave the unit or if the unit is transferred to the new owner without proper compensation to the original owners (e.g., an upfront payment or guaranteed lower prices for a fixed period). The remaining units could suffer (i.e., $V_O[A] < V[A]$) if the inputs received from B are worse than before.

The synergy test may fail even though it used to pass. For instance, the inputs provided by business B to business A have become standardized so that ongoing collaboration is no longer needed. The synergy test may also fail because of dis-synergies, for instance, missed opportunities for B to sell to A's rivals, or because of poor management of B by A's managers as it is not seen as important enough to merit attention.

2. A vendor can do better than the in-house unit

More typically in outsourcing situations, the synergy test is likely to be passed, possibly with Connection and/or Customization synergies. If value chain activity B is better off with a different corporate parent than the current one, then it's time to outsource this activity. This might be the case even if the synergy test is being passed. Thus, even if there are gains from jointly operating businesses A and B such that $V(AB) > V(A) + V(B)$ (and even if $V_O[A]) < V[A]$), as long as $O[B] >> V[B]$ (i.e., if you can get a lot of value out of outsourcing parts of the business to a vendor, because the vendor is a specialist, or can exploit synergies with her other businesses), then you should still outsource.

It should be clear that $O[B]$ – the value realized by handing over business B to a vendor – plays a critical role in this decision. The larger it is, the more likely it is that the outsourcing test will be passed. $O[B]$ itself depends on how much value the vendor creates when running the value chain activities that comprise B when B is under their portfolio, compared to the value from operating it as a separate standalone business $V[B]$.

A specialist vendor often will be able to create significant value when running business B as part of its portfolio, compared to when business B is standalone, because of advantages relating to efficiency, effectiveness, and flexibility (see Figure 8.2). Efficiency implies that the vendor can do it cheaper, and effectiveness implies they can generate higher WTP. Flexibility benefits for the client refers to the ability to convert fixed to variable costs, making the performance of the client firm less dependent on market conditions (i.e., lowering systematic risk). The vendor, on the other hand, can balance demand across multiple clients.

Put simply, while value chain activity B may not be one in which you can establish any competitive advantage (it's not "core" for you), it is one where a specialist vendor can do so (it is "core " for them). The value unlocked by passing on business B to an external specialist vendor (instead of doing it in-house) can be shared with the vendor through an agreement so that, all else being equal, the greater the value the vendor can create, the larger O[B] will be. This is the essence of the outsourcing decision, also known as the "make or buy" decision.

Motive for outsourcing	Advantages	Reasons
Efficiency	• Lower costs	• Wage differences across geographies • Economies of experience • Economies of scale • Specialisation of provider • True costing and sharper incentives • Employee professionalization
Effectiveness	• Greater willingness to pay of your own customers	• Access to better technology • Continual improvements
Flexibility	• Move assets off balance sheet • Meet changing market demands	• Convert fixed costs into variable costs • Scalability

Figure 8.3 Why a specialist vendor can create more value after taking over parts of your value chain

However, because outsourcing involves an ongoing contractual provision of inputs from B to A between two independent firms, we must also be particularly mindful of transaction costs. As we discussed in Chapter 3, real world contracting is inescapably incomplete: every eventuality cannot be foreseen, even the costs of trying to agree upfront on clauses to cover as many eventualities as possible are not small, and having the contract enforced in a court of law is not always easy or cheap. Honest misunderstandings and miscommunications are also likely. This creates potentially large transaction costs between the parties to a contract. These transaction costs can eat into the synergies between value chain steps A and B.

When outsourcing occurs despite the existence of synergies between A and B, we must therefore be concerned about any transactional hazards in the relationship. (If there are no synergies, then the impact of transaction costs will largely be restricted to the fixed cost of finding and negotiating with the vendor, as other transaction costs are a proportion of potential gains from synergies.) Thus a key issue in outsourcing is to verify whether the potential gains from outsourcing to a specialist vendor will be offset by the transaction costs of dealing with that vendor. These choices are summarized in Figure 8.4. Note that outsourcing may be appropriate even when the synergy test fails but no vendor is better at managing B, because of the principle of comparative advantage. Outsourcing here may allow the firm to focus on doing more of what it is better at (e.g., A).

	Synergy test (with retained value chain activities): Pass	Synergy test (with retained value chain activities): Fail
Can the vendor manage these value chain activities better? Yes	Outsource if transaction costs are not too high, else keep in-house	Outsource
Can the vendor manage these value chain activities better? No	Keep in-house	Outsource

Figure 8.4 When to outsource

When synergies exist between A and B, they are likely to be of the Customization and Connection variety, as these synergies are most relevant in the ongoing relationship between the distinct activities underlying A and B. The other two synergies, Consolidation and Combination, involve similar resources, which are unlikely to be relevant here because A and B are different value chain steps (see Chapter 2). Further, given our understanding of governance costs (see Chapter 3), we might reasonably expect that in general Customization based synergies between A and B would result in higher transactional hazards (because substantial modification is required, and can lead to "hold-up" by the vendor) than Connection synergies. This suggests caution in outsourcing when Customization synergies are involved, even if a specialist vendor promises a very high O[B]. In contrast, if the synergies are of the Connection type (which do not require modification), outsourcing should be easier.

To make the assessment of transaction costs more concrete, let us consider the case of outsourcing services, which may perhaps be the most complex form of outsourcing. Increasingly, the outsourcing of services goes hand in hand with offshoring. We can distinguish among three categories of transaction costs to consider in the out-sourcing (with or without offshoring) of services:

Contracting costs: These are the costs of selecting vendors, negotiating, and reaching agreement on contractual deliverables, designing and implementing monitoring, measurement, and dispute resolution mechanisms.

Because services are intangibles that are produced and consumed simultaneously, and depend on the human capital of producers, it is useful to consider separately two sub-categories of the transactional hazards associated with failures of coordination.

Transition costs: These are the costs of knowledge capture and transfer from one set of personnel to another, as well as the costs of severance, retraining, and employee relocation. Much knowledge is embedded in people and social relationships, and such knowledge is difficult to transfer to vendors or captive organizations. Transition costs involve incentivizing employees to share knowledge, transfer knowledge, create documentation, etc. While these may be always large (e.g., even when offshoring without outsourcing), they may be even larger when transition occurs to non-employees.

Interaction costs: These are the cost of managing the interactions between the outsourced (and offshored) processes and the processes remaining within the original location inside the firm. Once the process is moved it needs to function in-sync with the other related processes retained in-house, and costs arise from the need to manage interactions between the process and context. The outsourcing of business processes involves substantial coordination; the client and vendor employee may need to interact continuously during the "production" of the service. Interaction costs involve costs such as ongoing process mapping and interface design, travel and communication, and coordination mistakes. Again, while these may be always large (i.e., even with offshoring without outsourcing), they may be even larger when interactions occur with non-employees.

Suppose the assessment of transaction costs suggests that they are likely to be high, this does not mean that we must necessarily decide against outsourcing. Some other options to consider include:

Dealing with high contracting costs
- Define better service level agreements (SLAs) and metrics that are easier to verify and measure by both parties, and if necessary by a court
- Maintain partial ownership over the supplier, for instance through a minority equity stake, or a joint venture with the vendor
- Increase bargaining power over the vendor:
  - Be a significant customer for the vendor
  - "Multi-sourcing" – use multiple vendors

- "Plural sourcing/tapered integration" – keep some production in-house
- If all else fails, consider offshoring only instead of outsourcing

Dealing with high transition costs

- Modify what you want to outsource to make it easy to train new employees, e.g., better process documentation, standardize, codify
- Consider having the vendor take over key employees from clients – "re-badging"

Dealing with high interaction costs

- Modify what you want to outsource to reduce interdependencies with the processes left behind, e.g., modularize, simplify dependencies with other processes, black-box
- Ensure a vendor employee presence on client sites, *or*
- Build tacit coordination mechanisms – common language, terminology, virtual collaboration tools.

If one had a choice, for all three kinds of transaction costs, selective outsourcing may be the easiest solution. Select only those things for outsourcing that will generate small values of transaction costs.

Basic facts about outsourcing

The basic facts about outsourcing to emerge from various studies as well as meta-analyses of the existing research relate to two areas.

1. What can be outsourced? What can be offshored?

The variety of things that can be outsourced seems to be constantly growing, and spans very simple to very complex activities, in both manufacturing and services. Thus thinking along the lines of "Can R&D be outsourced?" may be the wrong question. The right question may be "When does it make sense to outsource R&D?" There will be some firms for whom it will make sense to find an R&D specialist to outsource to, and who can find ways to manage any related transaction costs (for instance, consider pharmaceutical firms that routinely outsource many kinds of R&D).

As regards to offshoring, research suggests that the ability to execute a task remotely may have little to do with how simple or standardized the task is. Rather what matters is whether the linkages between geographically distributed tasks can be managed easily. If work can be divided into chunks that can be executed more or less independently, whether the chunks involve creative or standardized work *per se* matters less. Some researchers have argued that this insight underlies the revolution in the offshoring of knowledge based services that took place after the late 1990s.

2. When are transaction costs anticipated to be high? What do firms do to manage them?

Meta-analyses show considerable support for the idea that transaction costs are anticipated to be high when there is (a) a high dependency of one partner on another, and (b) when the future business conditions are hard to predict. Note that these two just happen to be the most commonly studied antecedents to transaction costs, and these results do not imply that other sources of transaction costs do not exist, or are unimportant. Under such conditions of dependency and uncertainty, managers also seem to prefer not to "buy" (i.e., outsource using arm's-length contracts) but rather to manage the relationship within the same firm ("make"), or rely on strategic relationships ("ally") (i.e., those in which the parties are tied by more than the contract). Strategic alliances differ from contractual relationships in that, in addition to the contract, there is often a long-term implicit agreement, a statement of a shared purpose or goal, attempts to create shared norms of cooperation and trust, and channels for rich information exchange.

The research also shows that the decisions to make or ally (rather than buy) when transaction costs are expected to be high, are associated with superior performance. Thus, alliances are often an effective way to manage transaction costs in outsourcing without having to necessarily move production (back) in-house.

Application: Kappa Consulting

Let's say you have been appointed to advise the CEO of Kappa Consulting, whose problem was described at the beginning of this chapter. How would you advise the CEO about outsourcing and offshoring the analytics parts of the business (while still retaining the consulting part of the business in-house and onshore)?

Step I: The synergy test

The first question to address is whether there exist synergies between the work of the analysts (e.g., data gathering, analysis, preparing presentations) and the consultants (e.g., business development, client meetings, and problem formulation). Recall from Chapter 2 that the two synergy operators that link dissimilar resources are Customization and Connection. Since the analysts' and consultants' work seems highly *adapted* to each other, it seems reasonable to think there are synergies from Customization. As knowledge workers gather experience, they often develop specific ways of ways of working together, communication often becomes tacit so that many things can be left unsaid, and each side modifies its way of working to suit the strengths and weaknesses of the other. There also seems no evidence for dis-synergies, e.g., missed opportunities to serve other consulting firms by providing analytics services. There is thus no *prima facie* case for outsourcing based on failing the synergy test.

If on the other hand the synergy test had been failed, we would have actively investigated outsourcing. Since transaction costs are a tax on the gains from synergies, if there are no synergies, we should be less concerned about the impact of transaction costs that eat into potential value from synergy. Under such circumstances, given no synergies, we would have found it better to outsource even if external vendors are not necessarily better than our in-house unit, as we could then allocate our attention to other things that we do better.

Step II: Can a vendor do better?

Figure 8.3 lists several reasons for why a specialist vendor can do better than you at managing the business you outsource. Access to lower wage labor pools is the most salient in this story, but other reasons also potentially apply. Thus a case can be made for investigating the option to outsource, as the test for outsourcing could be passed on the strength of the significant cost savings by the vendor, some of which can be passed on to you.

Step III: Estimating the impact of transaction costs

Figure 8.5 summarizes the indicators of transaction costs and possible remedies in the case of services.[1]

Let's consider the transaction hazards and sources of transaction costs in this situation:

Key questions to ask about the process	If the answer is "yes":
• Is it difficult to measure the process' performance? • Is the process so unique that only a few vendors can perform it well?	**Contracting** costs will be high. Do thorough due diligence on vendors. As an alternative consider setting up a "captive" (i.e. fully owned) unit if offshoring.
• Is the performance of the process badly affected when there is employee turnover? • Does it take a long time to train employees to work on the process effectively?	**Transition** costs will be high. Invest in codifying knowledge underlying the processes. Don't allow the process to transition to a vendor until knowledge capture and transfer is complete.
• Does working on this process entail frequent interactions with people working on linked processes? • Will changes to this process lead to changes in several linked processes?	**Interaction** costs will be high. Re-engineer the process to make interactions with other processes as routinized and structured as possible. Make sure that formal communication channels between client and vendor organizations exist, and also encourage periodic face-to-face meetings to foster informal communication, develop relationships and build common understanding about how processes are linked.

Figure 8.5 Indicators of transaction costs in outsourcing and offshoring

First, *contracting costs*: You should consider the costs of negotiating and reaching agreement on contractual deliverables, designing and implementing, monitoring, measurement, and dispute resolution mechanisms. Data secrecy and the possibility that you are effectively training a potential competitor should also be considered.

Second, *transition costs*: These are the costs of knowledge capture and transfer from your analysts to the new set of personnel in Bengaluru who will take over these activities. Since your unit has been in existence for a while, it is very likely that the analysts have developed significant tacit knowledge about how they go about their work, and this may be difficult if not impossible to transfer.

Third, *interaction costs*: These are the cost of managing interactions between the consultants who will remain in London and the new analysts who will be working from Bengaluru. Indeed, these may need to interact continuously, and the question for you is whether electronic communication will be sufficient to replace the current face-to-face interaction arrangements; or would you perhaps need to modify the way both your consultants and the analysts will work so that they can do so remotely?

Step IV: Decision

As you will see, some of the costs above are of the nature of a large one-time investment (e.g., transfer and process modification), whereas others may be recurring; some are easier to forecast the impact of and others are very hard to quantify. To help you reach a decision, two factors might be useful to consider.

First, the scale of the savings from offshoring. If you intend to scale up your analytics team to well beyond ten people, then the gains from wage arbitrage will begin to outweigh the costs of transition and interaction. Second, how much does your CEO trust the former classmate? If you cannot be confident about the competence of his team, issues around data confidentiality or his intentions in terms of potentially becoming a competitor (all forms of contracting costs), then you should be very wary of outsourcing in this case. At larger scale, but with the same concerns about contracting costs, you might consider a captive unit – a wholly owned subsidiary of your company that will enable you to gain the benefits of wage arbitrage without exposing you so much to contracting costs.

Common mistakes to avoid

Ignoring transaction costs: Outsourcing often carries significant transaction costs, starting with finding a vendor and negotiating a contract. Then there's the expense of moving the operation from one location to another and subsequently keeping it in sync with the rest of the company. These hidden costs can eat significantly into the potential gains from transferring a formerly in-house activity into the hands of a specialist vendor. For instance, estimates suggest that close to 60–70 percent of wage differences are consumed in transaction costs when off-shoring. Misleading analogies may create blind spots in these transaction costs. For instance, procuring stationary or buying power supply are in fact *not* good examples of outsourcing. The difference arises because you (probably) never made stationary or produced power in-house. When you outsource, you must move from a state where you made something in-house to one where you now procure. This adds significant complexity.

Misunderstanding the purpose of contracts: Unlike divestitures, outsourcing is not a one-time transaction, but an exchange that evolves over time, as competitive conditions and technology change. One reaction to this is to attempt to write complex contracts that protect both parties in all possible circumstances. This could be futile, as it will typically be impossible to take all contingencies into account. This does not mean that contracts are irrelevant. Managers should write a contract that ensures that all parties understand their roles and responsibilities, and then put in place a process for negotiating changes when necessary. Indeed the process of negotiating a contract will enable the client and vendor to understand the risks, rewards, and interests for both sides.

Trying to outsource risk: Risk sharing between clients and vendors is one of the most contentious issues in outsourcing, leading to acrimonious negotiations and poor relationships. There is a very common – and reasonable – perception that vendors should bear greater liability for failure than regular, in-house, employees who do a job. The client can and should specify the standards that the vendor must meet, and the penalties for falling short. However, it is unrealistic for the client to ask the vendor to take on unlimited liabilities or unlimited indemnities for failure. Legally the client will be liable to end customers in most cases anyway. You can only completely outsource risk to insurance companies.

Frequently asked questions

1. For the same component, companies sometimes use multiple vendors or they simultaneously make internally and buy externally. For instance, a maker of TV sets sources 80 percent of its TV screens from three different suppliers, but they also make about 20 percent of the volume internally. Should this "inefficiency" be removed and should the company move to a single vendor, either internal or external?

It could be efficient for a company to make and buy the same product. The reasons include:

- Benchmarking with external suppliers to improve efficiency of an internal supplier; using an internal supplier to understand the external supplier's costs
- Retaining enough knowledge in-house to deal with vendors
- Posing a credible threat of in-sourcing in the case of unsatisfactory supplier performance; or outsourcing if the internal division under-performs
- Balancing fluctuations in demand.

These advantages have to be offset against the inefficient internal production which will be typically of lower scale and possibly also of lower competence. You should recommend stopping internal production only if the factors above are not important.

Likewise, a company can benefit from using multiple external vendors. The reasons typically invoked include:

- Lower risk by hedging against bankruptcy risk of any one supplier
- Increase competition between vendors as long as they can take on each other's volumes, you can shift between them easily, and the coordination across vendors is relatively easy for you as the client to execute.

2. It is sometimes argued that only standardized, commodity-like processes should ever be outsourced. Is this true?

No. It is important not to confuse non-standardized processes as necessarily being the same as a process at which you have a competitive advantage. Because your company performs a process differently it does not automatically mean that it performs it better. The process is core only if you do it differently and better in the sense that it gives you an advantage over competitors by enhancing customers' WTP or lowering suppliers' WTS.

In principle, any non-core activity (i.e., one at which you have no advantage) can be outsourced, subject to arrangements for managing transaction costs (i.e., interaction, transition, and contracting costs). Standardized commodity-like processes do typically generate lower transaction costs because (a) specifying contracts for them is easy and there are plenty of alternative vendors, leading to low contracting costs, (b) interactions costs are likely to be low as processes are standardized and generic, and (c) finally, transition costs are also likely to be low because standardized processes are likely to be well documented. However, if your organization has competence at managing contracting, interaction, and transition costs because of experience at selecting and contracting with vendors, at transitioning and relocating processes within the company, or at managing vendor relationships or remote coordination with subsidiaries successfully, then it might be feasible to outsource even non-standardized commodity-like processes, as long as specialist vendors can generate significant cost savings to offset these transaction costs.

Thus, what is feasible to outsource depends not only on the transaction costs, but also on the management competence of the outsourcer. So if your company has considerable management expertise at managing contracting, process redesign and relocation, and remote coordination, you also have a potentially larger set of non-core processes that could be considered for outsourcing. Since the converse is also true, this also warns against blindly imitating your peer companies in the industry as to what to outsource.

Note

1. Puranam, P. and Kannan, S. (2007) Seven myths about outsourcing, *Wall Street Journal*, June 16.

Further reading

Coase (1937) and Williamson (1975) are useful background reading for a reader with a deeper interest in transaction costs:

Coase, R. H. (1937). The nature of the firm. *Economica*, 4(16), 386–405.
Williamson, O. E. (1975). *Markets and Hierarchies: Analysis and Anti-Trust Implications*. New York: The Free Press.

For more on the importance of ongoing relationships for aligning interests, see:

Vanneste, B. S. and Frank, D. H. (2014). Forgiveness in vertical relationships: incentive and termination effects. *Organization Science*, 25(6), 1807–1822.

For more details on the sources of transaction costs in the outsourcing/offshoring of services, see:

Kotha, S. and Srikanth, K. (2013). Managing a global partnership model: lessons from the Boeing 787 "Dreamliner" program. *Global Strategy Journal*, 3(1), 41–66.
Srikanth, K. and Puranam, P. (2011). Integrating distributed work: comparing task design, communication, and tacit coordination mechanisms. *Strategic Management Journal*, 32(8), 849–875.

Srikanth, K. and Puranam, P. (2014). The firm as a coordination system: evidence from software services offshoring. *Organization Science*, 25(4), 1253–1271.

For meta-analyses related to outsourcing issues, see:
Geyskens, I., Steenkamp, J. B. E. M., and Kumar, N. (2006). Make, buy, or ally: a transaction cost theory meta-analysis. *Academy of Management Journal*, 49(3), 519–543.
Hawkins, T., Knipper, M. G., and Strutton, D. (2009). Opportunism in buyer–supplier relations: new insights from quantitative synthesis. *Journal of Marketing Channels*, 16(1), 43–75.

PART IV

Decisions about portfolio organization

9

Designing the multi-business corporation

MultiDevice, a maker of PC peripherals who used to be organized by function – marketing, manufacturing, R&D departments – recently undertook a dramatic re-organization towards a matrix organization with the two dimensions being product and customer. Polyton, a rival of MultiDevice which is also organized by function, has hired you to help them understand why MultiDevice made this change, and whether they should follow suit. How would you proceed?

Corporations that comprise multiple businesses ultimately compete with actors in the capital markets who can put together similar portfolios of businesses through stock ownership. The central issues in corporate strategy therefore pertain to how managers can create the most value from the portfolio of businesses they can stitch together with organizational and governance linkages (in a way that investors and mutual fund managers cannot). The overlap between issues in corporate strategy and organization design is thus naturally very high.

In previous chapters we considered which businesses should be in the corporate portfolio (Parts II and III, Chapters 4–8). This chapter provides a framework for thinking about the choices we face in organizing this portfolio of businesses, their relative merits, and the circumstances for changing from one to another. Our focus here is on "organizational macro-structures," by which we mean the stable pattern of interactions between groups of individuals specified at high levels of aggregation – for instance, as seen in organization charts. We will refer to these macro-structures simply as "structures." This sets the stage for more fine grained decisions about organization design pertaining to how individuals within the same group or across groups interact (or the "micro-structure").

Understanding the structure of the multi-business firm is critical for corporate strategists and those analyzing corporate strategies; in fact, we will show how to read the corporate strategy of the firm in its structure. Yet, it can seem hard to know where to begin, given the wide variations and complexities in organizational structures. Those complexities arise even within a single country. MNCs have added layers of complexity relative to one-country firms because they operate across geographies. With the simple ideas presented here, we hope to help you see why organizational structures are, to paraphrase the organizational economist Bob Gibbons, sometimes a mess, but seldom a mystery.[1]

We will structure our discussion around three key points: (1) the multi-business firm as a collection of value chain activities, (2) three basic principles for grouping activities within organizational structure, and (3) the basic alternatives for grouping the multiple value chains in a multi-business firm.

Corporations as collections of value chain activities

The first conceptual step to take is to think about the multi-business corporation as a collection of value chain activities.[2] The various economic activities conducted by a business have, either explicitly or implicitly, a series of value chain activities underlying them. A single business firm has only one value chain; a multi-business firm has many. In other words, each business a company operates may be thought to have a distinctive value chain.

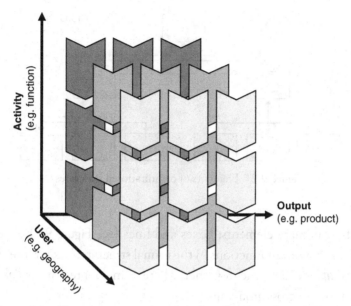

Figure 9.1 Corporations as value chain bundles along three dimensions

A value chain has three dimensions (see Figure 9.1). First, it comprises a set of (sequential) *activities*, e.g., R&D, manufacturing, or sales. Second, it results it some *output*, e.g., cars, motors, or lawn mowers. Third, the goal is to serve *users*. Two value chains may be largely identical in terms of activities and outputs, but may supply two different categories of *users* of the output – for instance, Unilever's Dove Soap business in India and the UK. We could think of different users by geography, as in the example above, or by segment within a geography, for instance small and medium sized businesses vs. Fortune 500 companies.

Three basic principles for designing organizational structure

The pioneering work of Nadler and Tushman (1997) provides the basis for much of our modern thinking about organizational struc-tures. As their work highlights, organization charts contain two

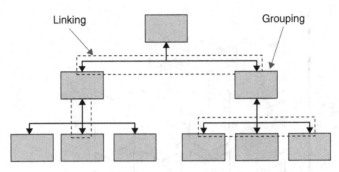

Figure 9.2 Elements of organizational structures

kinds of primary elements: boxes and lines (see Figure 9.2). These perform important functions in the formal structure; boxes represent the *grouping* of activities together, whereas lines represent the *linking* of activities across groupings.

Boxes correspond to sub-units within an organization. A box is a shorthand way of saying "the activities within this box are subject to common authority, goals, performance measurement, incentives, and procedures." Departments and divisions are common instances of boxes in an organization. Putting a set of activities into a box is an attempt to ensure high levels of integration across all the activities within the box, by aligning incentives, aiding coordination by using standard procedures, subjecting them to common oversight and authority, and formulating common goals and performance measures. This effect is enhanced through collocation when the grouping is within a geography.

However, boxes cannot be infinitely large, otherwise we would solve all the problems of integration across activities by putting them into one big box. As we include more activities in a box, monitoring, communications, and incentives can all grow weaker. There are *organizational scale diseconomies* in increasing the size of the boxes.

This leads to a few basic principles about the design of organizational structures.

Principle 1 ("Nesting"): Organizations beyond some size are bound to run into the limits of organizing within a single box, which necessitates boxes within boxes.

This nested structure implies that ultimately the firm can be seen as one big grouping, but as one looks at the next layer, one sees large divisions that are linked to each other, and at the next layer (within each division), departments that are linked to each other, and so on. Activities grouped together at one layer are linked to each other at the next higher layer, and so on (see Figure 9.2).[3]

Because activities can either lie within or outside a box, there is an inescapable discreteness to organizational structures; designers face some hard choices as to which activities they would like to prioritize for integration by placing them together within a box (and, by extension, which activities are not deemed a priority to be integrated). This is captured in the second principle.

Principle 2 ("Silos"): Boxes enhance the integration of activities within them, but also impede integration across activities in different boxes.

Thus integration benefits (within units) and the "silo syndrome" (between units) are really two sides of the same coin, and are both consequences of the grouping decision. In MNCs this problem is made worse when grouping boundaries coincide with geographic boundaries. That brings us to the lines, the linking mechanisms. These include horizontal (or lateral) relationships, such as committees, dedicated integrators, task forces, teams, and incentives. Some of these may be temporary and specific to a particular project, as in project based organizations.

While linking mechanisms help to integrate activities, grouping is the more powerful integration mechanism. Linking mechanisms are necessarily weaker because they cannot bundle common authority, incentives, and objectives (and often collocation) as powerfully as the grouping structures do. This suggests another principle.

Principle 3: The linking elements provide the "residual integration" that (i) cannot be provided by the grouping structures (boxes), (ii) but is still desirable, (iii) even if not fully achievable.

To the extent that organizations are designed with these principles in mind, one should be able to read the corporate strategy of a company in its organization chart: what kinds of activities does the top management feel are essential to integrate (and which ones are not seen as being as essential to integrate)? We will explain this point in detail by looking next at a number of common structural alternatives.

Prototypes of organizational structures

We can now look closely at a number of commonly occurring organizational structures, by combining the two concepts discussed above, (a) organizations as bundles of value chains in three dimensions (activity/output/user) and (b) grouping as the primary mechanism for achieving integration across activities. Figure 9.3 provides an overview.

Pure forms

These correspond to grouping activities along one of the three dimensions: by activity (e.g., put all R&D activities together), by output (group all the activities necessary to produce an output into one box), or by user (e.g., put all the activities needed to serve a particular user segment in one box).

The functional form ("F-form"), Figure 9.4, emphasizes integration across all similar value chain activities (e.g., integration across all R&D activities, or across all manufacturing activities). The product divisional or multi-divisional form ("M-form"), Figure 9.5, emphasizes integration across all the activities that are necessary to generate an outcome (e.g., the soaps division or the detergents division). The customer-centric form, Figure 9.6, emphasizes

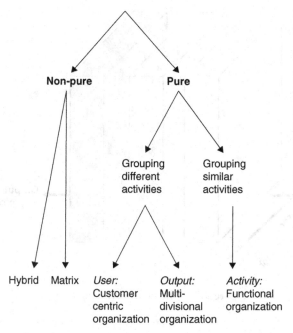

Figure 9.3 Prototypes of organizational structures

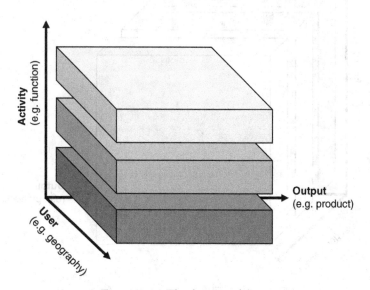

Figure 9.4 The functional form

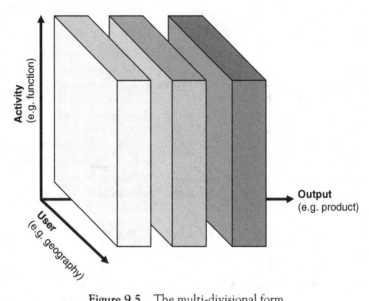

Figure 9.5 The multi-divisional form

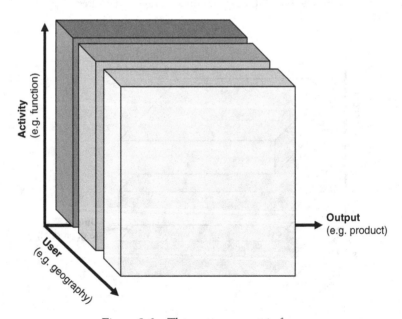

Figure 9.6 The customer-centric form

integration across all the value chain activities meant to cater to the needs of a particular user – in this case, customer segment (e.g., the Indian vs. UK subsidiaries of a fast-moving consumer goods company, or the government vs. banks, financial services, and insurance verticals in a technology company).

There is a fundamental difference between the functional form and the other two pure forms. The F-form has a grouping comprising similar activities (e.g., all R&D activities together or all sales activities together), whereas the M-form and the customer-centric form combine different types of activities inside the boxes (e.g., R&D, sales, or manufacturing mixed together). A consequence of Principle 2 is that these forms have different "footprints" in terms of costs and benefits, summarized in Table 9.1. **The essential idea is that grouping similar activities together (i.e., the F-form) emphasizes economies of scale at the expense of economies of scope; whereas grouping different activities together (i.e., the M-form and customer-centric form) does exactly the opposite.**

The difference between the M-form and customer-centric form arises primarily on the benefit side. By integrating across different sets of value chain activities, these two forms set different strategic emphases for the organization. Whereas the M-form focuses on collaboration across functions which

TABLE 9.1 *The benefits and costs of grouping similar vs. different activities*

Grouping	Similar activities	Different activities
Forms	Functional	Multi-divisional (e.g., product) or customer-centric
Benefits	Efficiency (lower costs, critical mass effects, scale economies)	Effectiveness (responsiveness, collaboration across functions, scope economies)
Costs	"Silo syndrome"	Duplication

improves time-to-market of the products and in general achieves high levels of integration across all the steps needed to sell a product, the customer-centric form focuses the organization on the breadth of a user's needs, which enhances its responsiveness. However, what is common to both is an emphasis on *inter-functional integration*, in which grouping is primarily around different value chain activities.

Looking at the pure forms exposes the stark trade-offs that confront organization designers: a choice between forms that emphasize *intra-functional integration* vs. those that emphasize *inter-functional integration*. If companies faced competitive environments in which it was obviously correct to emphasize one or the other (performance curve A in Figure 9.7), the designer could simply select one of the pure forms. It is much more common, however, to find companies struggling to achieve some degree of both (see performance curve B in Figure 9.7). This need to achieve a bit of both types of integration is a major source of variety in organizational structures that one sees in practice. Let's take a look at two important categories of how companies achieve this (within which there are lots of variations): the matrix form and the hybrid form, the so-called non-pure forms.

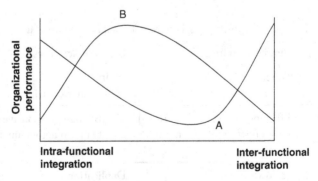

Figure 9.7   Performance implications of intra- vs. inter-functional integration

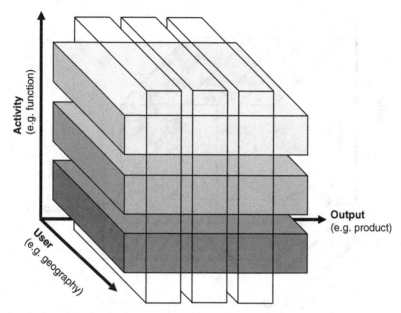

Figure 9.8 The product–function matrix

The matrix form

Matrix structures represent an ambitious attempt to circumvent Principles 2 and 3. In essence, the idea is that the same activity could belong to multiple groupings (boxes) at the same time. Figure 9.8 shows a two-dimensional matrix, but one can also imagine a three-dimensional one (with geography being the third, for instance). In practice, one of the dimensions of the matrix is often dominant, so that what might be an intended matrix form is actually a pure form with some linking mechanisms cutting across the boxes. Further, it is not an easy structure to manage. It is extremely coordination intensive, and requires managers who can manage and be managed around two or more dimensions of accountability (i.e., for each boss) simultaneously. Despite these challenges, the evidence indicates that the form has become very widespread among US corporations.

The hybrid form

In hybrid forms, or what are referred to somewhat inelegantly as "front end/back end" structures, the direction of grouping can be

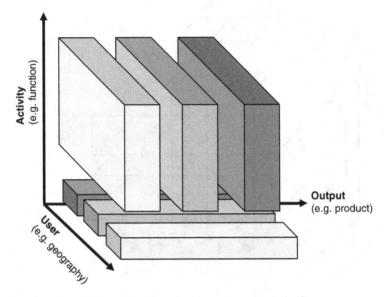

Figure 9.9 A technology–customer hybrid

different for different parts of the value chain. See Figure 9.9 for an example of a structure in which R&D is grouped by product line, but sales is grouped by customer segment. Many technology companies and investment banks have adopted such a structure, because it is conducive to the notion of bundling solution of products together for particular customer needs, while retaining the benefits of homogenous grouping (scale and cost efficiency) in technology development. As with all organizational structures, the problems arise "at the edges" of the boxes – getting sufficient integration across the boundaries of the groupings, which also effectively become "silos" (recall Principle 2). One approach features a dedicated integrating unit (often called the "Solutions" group) that sits between the technology and sales units.

Hybrid forms play a very important role in the structures of MNCs. The appendix to this chapter provides details about the basic archetypes of MNC structures.

When is it time to change the structure?

Broadly speaking, the need for structural change in organizations can arise from external factors and/or internal factors. It is useful to think of two broad categories of external factors. First, a **change in the competitive environment** could arise, such that the integration requirements for the firm shift from curve A to curve B in Figure 9.8. For instance, when the technology in an industry is mature and there is a well defined efficiency frontier, then curve A may be applicable: there are gains from focus. A classic example is Michael Porter's injunction to choose one of the generic strategies – differentiation or cost advantage[4] – but avoid being stuck in the middle. Second, **a shift in technology** could create periods in which it is better to pursue both differentiation and cost advantage simultaneously as the efficiency frontier moves. A less dramatic change could occur when external factors, such as a change in product demand, lead to a shift of the *inflection point* – i.e., a shift in the optimal balance between inter-functional and intra-functional integration.

There are also two important internal factors that could cause a re-organization, even in the absence of any external changes. First, as we have noted, every structure prioritizes certain activities to be integrated, and effectively de-emphasizes others. There are **opportunity costs** arising from those activities "left out" of the formal groupings. For instance, there are redundancies and cost inefficiencies in product divisions, and bottlenecks and delays in product development in functional structures. At some stage management may find these opportunity costs to be past a tolerance level and initiate a re-organization. In this view, managers pay sequential attention to problems, and re-organize to solve one problem, which gives rise to secondary problems, which in turn are solved by a future re-organization, and so on.

Second, a more subtle effect has to do with the **informal organization** – the off-the-chart pattern of linkages and connections between individuals and the culture of an organization. A shift towards one particular form directly realigns the formal structure, whereas the informal organization, the channels of communication and cooperation in the organization, will only adapt with a time lag. The analogy is to moving home: you will still retain some connections to your old neighbors for a while, though these will decline over time. Under certain conditions this **delayed adjustment of the informal organization** can actually be beneficial for the firm, in the sense that the formal incentives reward the employees for one course of action, whereas the informal organization is still geared towards a different set of activities. This generates a useful form of "compensatory fit" when doing some combination of activities is superior to doing either alone (curve B in Figure 9.8). However, this beneficial effect will wear off over time, so that a re-organization may again be necessary to achieve such a state of compensatory fit. Thus, even in the absence of any external changes, there may be an internal driver for organizational change that arises from the gradual adjustment of the informal organization towards the formal organization.

Application: MultiDevice

MultiDevice used to be organized into three departments, R&D, manufacturing, and distribution and sales. Recently it abandoned this functional structure in favor of a matrix of products (printers, monitors, and input devices) and customers (government, business-to-business or B2B, and business-to-consumer or B2C), see Figure 9.10.

Armed with the concepts from this chapter, you could tell your client Polyton that functional structures are good for cost efficiencies and bad for cross-functional integration. This re-organization by MultiDevice suggests that the need for cross-functional integration had either become, or recognized to have become, important. In particular, the need for rapid product development, as well as the need for meeting customer needs by bundling different

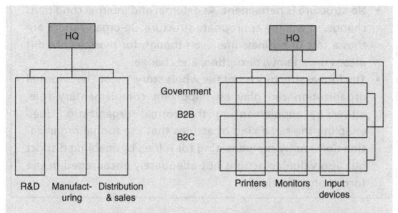

Figure 9.10 MultiDevice's re-organization from a functional structure to a matrix structure of products and customers

products together (into solutions) must have become critical. The first would have registered in the form of bottlenecks and delays in time-to-market. The second would have registered in the form of customer demand for one-stop shopping or "solutions." Both these could have been driven by changes in the external environment, or because of a recognition of these issues as they crossed a threshold level. It is unlikely that the change was motivated by the decay of a possible older informal structure that helped to achieve cross-functional integration, as both firms have historically been organized by function. It is therefore highly likely that these changes are also relevant to Polyton, so it should investigate a re-organization for itself.

Basic facts about organizational structures

- **Many different structures exist**: Companies adopt different structures based on the external and the internal conditions they face. Thus, we observe differences both between and within industries, and there is no one best structure for all.
- **No structure is perfect**: Every grouping arrangement emphasizes certain interactions but excludes others, which show up as opportunity costs and bottlenecks.

- **No structure is permanent**: As external and internal conditions change, so will the appropriate structure. Re-organizations are thus a fact of business life, even though for those involved it means uncertainty, disruption, and change.
- **The formal structure is not the whole story**: Is not The informal organization can play an important complementary role, either by supplementing the formal organization (i.e., enabling the same kind of actions that the formal organization does) or by compensating for it (i.e., by enabling distinct but also valuable actions not adequately encouraged in the formal organization).

Common mistakes to avoid

- **Do not forget to combine activities.** There is evidence that managers (particularly inexperienced ones) put more emphasis on thinking about the *partitioning up* of the activities within the organization than on how to *integrate* them. For instance, creating discrete specialized units to emphasize "clear measurement and accountability" without thinking about how these different activities will need to be integrated (i.e., how to group and link them) seems to be an error that novice organization designers make, but not experts.
- **Do not avoid re-organizations just because they are painful.** Re-organizations can have visible and painful negative consequences for employees, but to *rule out re-organizations* is not the solution. Explaining why they are necessary (and often seem to cycle between structures) may help to overcome employee skepticism and fatigue.
- **Do not blindly follow your competitors.** While you and your competitors may share external conditions (e.g., technological changes or demand characteristics), a structure should also take into account the factors that are internal, and possibly unique, to the organization (e.g., strategy, location, synergies, informal organization, and history).
- **Do not focus exclusively or primarily on the informal structure.** The informal structure is important but also hard to change directly. Instead, the formal structure offers a powerful set of

levers directly accessible to the top management; and one that will impact the informal structure indirectly. The trick is to use the levers of the formal structure with a sophisticated under-standing of their strengths and limitations.

- **Do not ignore location.** Organizational structures facilitate collaboration between some people at the cost of making it harder with others. Physical location does the same. So when (re-)designing an organization, take into account how the geographical location will reinforce or undermine the new structure.

Frequently asked questions

1. **You say little about the culture and social networks within the organization. Is that not more important than the boxes and arrows of the organizational chart?**

Ultimately what people do in an organization is shaped by what the formal structure asks them to do as well as the culture and social networks they find themselves embedded in. The latter may well diverge significantly from the former. However, our emphasis on the formal organization is driven by two considerations: first, that is what senior managers can directly control and, second, it is known to have an effect on shaping the informal organization. Thus, because the formal structure can be controlled and has direct and indirect (through the informal organization) effects on employee behavior, it is a key lever of managerial influence that we focus on.

2. **How does the ownership structure of a multi-business firm relate to its organizational structure?**

Organizational structure is not the same as ownership structure. Let's first consider the legal structure of ownership for a multi-business firm. As we noted in Chapter 1, it is useful to distinguish

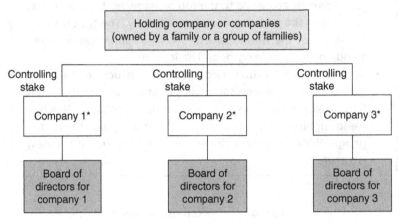

Figure 9.11 Typical ownership structure of a business group

*Some of the companies 1, 2, and 3 can be public companies
listed on a stock exchange, while others are private companies not
listed on any stock exchange.

between divisionalized and holding company legal structures for
managing multi-business portfolios. In a divisionalized structure,
the different businesses within the portfolio are units of a single
legal entity within a country. In a *holding company* structure, each
business is a legally distinct firm, and the parent holding company
owns controlling shares in each of the firms. Business groups
that dominate many emerging economies have a particular kind of
holding company structure, in which it is common for at least some
of the firms in the portfolio to be publicly listed on capital markets
(see Figure 9.11). This legal form has some unique properties arising
from the fact the governance of a firm in the portfolio is shared
between the holding company and the investors in the capital
markets; the joint effects of both can be different from the effects
of either acting alone.

Our focus in this chapter was on the variety of organizational
structures – functional, divisional, customer-centric, matrix, and
hybrid structures – by which units within the portfolio are grouped.

The ownership structure may limit the extent to which businesses can be arranged into a structure, particularly if the businesses are publicly listed. It is worth noting that the holding company structure from an organizational (not legal) point of view has the same structure as a multi-divisional firm; the major groupings in the portfolio are self-contained businesses.

Notes

1. Gibbons, R. (1999). Taking Coase seriously. *Administrative Science Quarterly*, 44(1), 145–157.
2. This section draws on Puranam, P. and Raveendran, M., "Note on organizational macro-structures."
3. For the interested reader, this is formally known as a "nested containment hierarchy," which is the precise kind of hierarchy that large formal organizations typically are.
4. Porter, M. E. (1985). *Competitive Advantage: Creating and Sustaining Superior Performance*. New York: The Free Press.

Further reading

For more on organizational structures, see:

Chittoor, R., Kale, P., and Puranam, P. (2014). Business groups in developing capital markets: towards a complementarity perspective. *Strategic Management Journal*, 36(9), 1277–1296.

Foss, N. J. (2003). Selective intervention and internal hybrids: interpreting and learning from the rise and decline of the Oticon spaghetti organization. *Organization Science*, 14(3), 331–349.

Galbraith, J. R. (2008). *Designing Matrix Organizations that Actually Work: How IBM, Proctor & Gamble and Others Design For Success*. San Francisco, CA: Jossey-Bass.

Gulati, R. (2010). *Reorganize for Resilience: Putting Customers at the Center of Your Business*. Boston, MA: Harvard Business School Press.

Gulati, R. and Puranam, P. (2009). Renewal through reorganization: the value of inconsistencies between formal and informal organization. *Organization Science*, 20(2), 422–440.

Kumar, N. and Puranam, P. (2011). Have you restructured for global success? *Harvard Business Review*, 89(10), 123–128.

Nadler, D. A. and Tushman, M. L. (1997). *Competing by Design: The Power of Organizational Architecture*. New York: Oxford University Press.

Nickerson, J. A. and Zenger, T. R. (2002). Being efficiently fickle: a dynamic theory of organizational choice. *Organization Science*, 13(5), 547–566.

Raveendran, M. (2014). Why re-organize? A test of three theories. *Working Paper*.

Sy, T. and Côté, S. (2004). Emotional intelligence: a key ability to succeed in the matrix organization. *Journal of Management Development*, 23(5), 437–455.

Vermeulen, F., Puranam, P., and Gulati, R. (2010). Change for change's sake. *Harvard Business Review*, 88(6), 70–76.

For more on global structures to compete, see:

Bartlett, C. A., Ghoshal, S., and Birkinshaw, J. (2003). *Transnational Management: Text, Cases and Readings in Cross-Border Management*, 4th edn. Burr Ridge, IL: McGraw-Hill.

Ghemawat, P. (2007). *Redefining Global Strategy: Crossing Borders in a World Where Differences Still Matter*. Boston, MA: Harvard Business School Press.

Lee, E. and Puranam, P. (2015). The nature of expertise in organization design: evidence from an expert–novice comparison. *Advances in Strategic Management*, 32, 181–209.

Appendix: MNCs and their structures

In this Appendix, we consider different organizational structures for MNCs. Figure A9.1 shows a simplified structure for a single-product MNC; it suppresses consideration of other products to keep the exposition simple.

The MNC operates in three geographies (G1–G3) and has a front end (F2) set of functions – customer facing activities like sales and distribution – as well as a back end (F1) set of functions – R&D, manufacturing – in its value chain. In principle, the company could replicate the value chain for each product in each geography. In practice, this is rare.

A key premise in the design of multi-national organizations is that the closer we get to the customer in the front end facing activities in each geography, the smaller the opportunities for achieving synergies with other parts of the company – the "last mile" is always localized by definition. However, the further

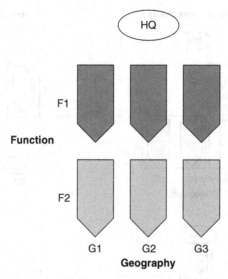

Figure A9.1 A single-product MNC

upstream we travel in a value chain, the greater the possibility of potential synergies across geographies. Within a value chain the synergies are always potentially high across succeeding stages, as each is a necessary input to the next.

The key point we make here is that where horizontal and vertical edges arise through grouping structures overlaid on Figure A9.1 – **and whether they coincide with geographic boundaries** – tells us a lot of about the advantages as well as the disadvantages of different structures to manage MNCs.

International sales division

For MNCs where the bulk of their business lies in their country of origin, the *international sales division* is often the structure that initiates their MNC status (Figure A9.2). By grouping all international activities together, the foreign operations of the firm get their requisite focus. In international divisions, with sub-units dedicated

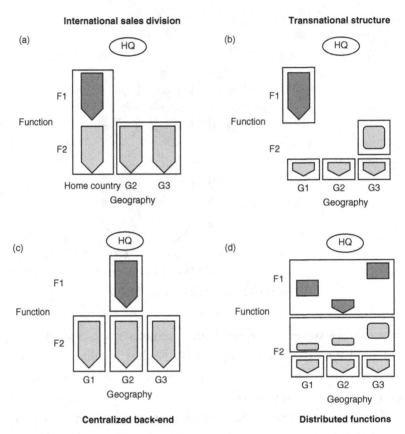

Figure A9.2 MNC structures

to individual countries, often only the front end (customer facing) parts of the value chain are located in the different geographies the MNC operates in. For instance, Sharp did most of its R&D and manufacturing in Japan and only had sales units abroad in the early stages of its international expansion.

The common friction points are between the front and back ends of the value chain as well as between the HQ in the home country and the international country units – where the "boxes" have edges – which also happen to coincide with geographic boundaries. Ikea, for instance, when it expanded to the US, initially struggled to pay attention to the feedback from its country managers that the US customers had some unique requirements. It was only after a Swedish manager was deputed from HQ to the US unit that the message finally received some attention (Galbraith, 2000).

Transnational structure

The *transnational structure* (Bartlett, Ghoshal, and Birkinshaw, 2003) allows particular geographies to specialize in particular parts of the value chain (Figure A9.2b) (for instance, manufacturing in Asia, R&D in the US), or in some cases product lines (develop CT scanners in Japan, X-ray machines in Europe). The benefits of integration arise mostly through global mandates in each geography that specialize in a particular part of the value chain. Frictions predictably arise both within as well as across more upstream parts of value chains.

Centralized back end

An alternative is a structure that does not privilege the country of origin in terms of the front of the value chain, though all back end operations are grouped in the home country (Figure A9.2c). Centralized global R&D based structures – often in the home country – in the pharmaceutical or tobacco industry illustrate this. In a multi-product company, this basic structure may also have a matrix structure grouped simultaneously along products as well as geographies, the classic example being ASEA Brown Boveri (ABB) under CEO Percy Barnevik. Alternately, the centralization of back end functions may be by product lines – what are known as "front end/back end" structures. However the key feature of this structure is the grouping of back end activities – possibly by product in a multi-product firm – while leaving the front end grouped by country. Common friction points are between the front and back ends of the value chain as this boundary coincides with geographic boundaries, which may coexist with frictions between the axes of the geography–product matrix structure if one is used.

Distributed functions

The novelty in an MNC's organizational structure created by intra-functional specialization – in particular, through the use of India and China as platforms for globally segmented innovation – can be seen in Figure A9.2d. Unlike either the transnational or the front end/back end organization, individual functions may be grouped organizationally **but distributed geographically**. This creates a need for **horizontal integration across geographies that is unprecedented in any of the prior structures**, as Figure A9.2 makes obvious. The level of coordination required exceeds the need to avoid duplication across geographies or the "good to have" horizontal exchange of best practices and ideas that are generally sufficient in the other structures; here, coordination may often be required within the project. In addition, there are the usual within value chain (vertical) integration challenges across geographies common to all structures.

Designing the corporate HQ

> A2G, Inc. is a multi-business corporation with seven business divisions. These vary in size and range from relatively small (fewer than 100 employees, $50 million in annual sales) to quite large (10,000 employees, $2 billion in annual sales). The businesses span a range of industries, some of which are related (e.g., heavy earth moving equipment, construction) and others which are not (e.g., publishing services). The corporate HQ currently has 20 employees. The newly appointed CEO of A2G has asked you to analyze the role of corporate HQ and recommend what changes, if any, you would make to how it is organized. Where would you start?

Recall from Chapter 1 that the goal of the corporate strategist is to exploit synergies through administrative control that cannot be replicated by mere investors. The HQ, where the corporate strategists reside, is ultimately the custodian of corporate advantage. Its goal is to ask (and help answer) the question of why the collection of businesses they administer is worth more than what they would be worth if operated independently.

We will use "HQ" to refer not only to the corporate HQ in a multi-divisional corporation but in fact to any administrative unit making strategic decisions that cut across multiple businesses. These could be regional, national, or divisional HQ, or indeed the holding company of a portfolio of companies (as in a business group). To the extent that any of these entities is responsible for ensuring that the set of businesses they administer creates more value than what they would if operated independently, they are in effect pursuing corporate advantage. In addition, the HQ may also be the organizational or physical location of shared service units.

This chapter focuses on the mechanisms of influence, or the **influence models**, available to the HQ to achieve this objective, *given a fixed portfolio composition*. This focus is critical in order to understand each component of corporate advantage clearly; HQs create corporate advantage through the decisions they make about portfolio composition (the topics of Chapters 4–8), but also about how they manage the businesses that exist in the portfolio (this chapter and Chapter 9, which focuses on the organizational structures used to manage the portfolio), as well as how they manage the process of bringing businesses into the portfolio (Chapters 11 and 12). Of course, there are complementarities between the decisions about what value chains go into the portfolio (i.e., the scope of the multi-business organization, deriving from the diversification and refocusing choices covered in Chapters 4–8), the organizational structure (Chapter 9) and the influence model that the HQ uses to derive synergies and generate corporate advantage (this chapter). We will elaborate on these linkages at the end of the chapter. To begin with, we focus on the models of HQ influence on a portfolio of businesses, *given* its scope and organizational structure.

In Chapter 1, we said that corporate advantage comes broadly from either portfolio assembly ("selection") or portfolio modification ("synergy"). We defined "synergy" as an umbrella term to describe the various ways in which the cash flows and discount rates of businesses in a portfolio can be **modified** through administrative influence. Synergy is the means through which corporate advantage is created relative to a typical investor who can

assemble the same portfolio of investments (without exercising administrative influence over them, as she lacks the decision rights to do so).

In this chapter we explain how **the appropriate influence model for HQ – defined as the way HQ influences individual businesses in the portfolio – is contingent on the choice of how corporate advantage is being pursued.**

HQ influence in portfolio assembly (selection)

A corporate strategy based on pure portfolio assembly (without any modification of businesses in the portfolio) requires being able to systematically spot and access under-valued opportunities, as well as exit businesses when good opportunities to do so arise. The strategic capabilities needed for such an approach include:

- **Environment scanning for new opportunities:** This primarily involves business strategy expertise, such as understanding sources of competitive advantage, industry structure, regulatory environment, technological and demand changes.
- **Expertise at M&A and alliances:** While these are important vehicles for broadening the scope of the multi-business organization (as discussed in Chapters 5 and 6 in this book), they are also useful within businesses to build them out or strengthen them. As such the insights from Chapters 5 and 6, and 11 and 12, are all relevant for M&A and alliances conducted within an industry to strengthen an existing business.
- **Expertise at refocusing:** Chapters 8 and 9 describe the logic of refocusing through various forms of divestiture and outsourcing, and these should actively be under consideration by a HQ with a pure portfolio assembly approach to corporate advantage.

These strategic capabilities could either be embedded among explicitly designated roles/units, or performed informally by a team with multiple responsibilities.

Even if there was no modification of businesses after entry into the portfolio, nonetheless a multi-business corporation, by virtue of being a corporation (and particularly if it is a publicly listed one), requires some **corporate management functions** (CMF), such as treasury, risk management, taxation, financial reporting, company secretary and legal counsel, government relations, and investor relations. Details on these CMFs can be found in the appendix to this chapter. They represent what are sometimes known as the "obligatory staffing" of the HQ. If there are any benefits in consolidating and combining these functions across businesses, then there may be some (almost inadvertent) synergy effects. In a holding company structure, most of these CMFs are not strictly necessary at the HQ as they would most likely exist at the individual company level (and definitely so if the individual company is listed, as in business groups), so one could in principle have a very lean corporate HQ in these cases.

HQ influence in business modification (synergy)

Everything we have said above about the influence of the HQ in pure portfolio assembly models is also applicable to cases where corporate advantage is being pursued through business modification (synergy). Furthermore, there is a whole variety of additional means of influence to consider when the HQ is pursuing a synergy approach to corporate advantage.

Much of current thinking on how HQs "parent" their businesses owes its origins to the pioneering work of Goold, Campbell, and Alexander (1994). A distillation of their work suggests two critical dimensions of influence of the HQ on businesses in the portfolio of the multi-business organization – standalone vs. linkage influence, and evaluative vs. directive influence (see Figure 10.1).

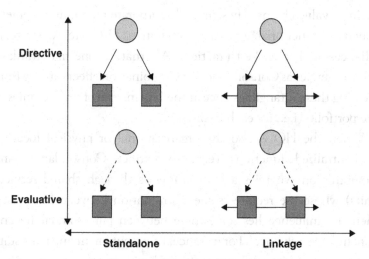

Figure 10.1 HQ influence has two dimensions

Horizontal dimension: standalone vs. linkage

This dimension indicates the nature of the **horizontal** relationships in the portfolio – those between the businesses in a portfolio. Under **standalone** influence, the HQ does not encourage any meaningful B2B relationships. The HQ influence is felt solely through a vertical HQ-to-business relationship. The businesses independently benefit from, or use a valuable resource or capability that is located at, the HQ. Under **linkage influence**, the HQ encourages businesses to work together in alliance-like fashion. The HQ influence is felt through the B2B relationship fostered and administered under the supervision of the HQ (in addition to any vertical influence that the HQ may employ).

Note that synergies play a role in **both** models of influence. In linkage influence, the HQ exerts authority to enable the extraction of synergies of all kinds (Consolidation, Combination, Customization, and Connection) between businesses. In standalone influence, the HQ is the locus of intangible resources and capabilities that have Connection/Customization synergies with the business value chains. These include corporate brand; management expertise; functional expertise in finance, HR, M&A, strategic alliances; and other best practices. Alternately, one may think of these synergies as Consolidation or Combination effects arising from creating these intangibles once at the HQ instead of several times in the portfolio (i.e., for each business).

When the HQ is also the organizational or physical location of centralized functions (e.g., to extract Consolidation and Combination synergies across businesses through shared services units) whose use requires some coordination between businesses, then the influence lies somewhere between pure standalone and pure linkage influences. For instance, IT procurement and real estate management functions across different businesses may be centralized at HQ; in all other matters, the businesses may operate independently from each other.

Vertical dimension: directive vs. evaluative

This dimension indicates the nature of the **vertical** relationships in the portfolio – those between businesses and the HQ. **Directive influence** refers to the control that the HQ exerts on businesses by directly influencing their strategic decisions and actions through approving, vetoing, or ordering them. When the HQ uses directive influence, resource allocation (e.g., capital budgeting) tends to be a rigorous process with a lot of scrutiny and vetting by the HQ before budget approvals. Capital budgeting becomes the key process through which the strategic decisions at the business level are overseen and controlled by the HQ in this model of influence. This is accompanied by close monitoring of the implementation of decisions via operational targets. In contrast, **evaluative influence** refers to control by the HQ of businesses, primarily through setting financial performance targets and evaluating outcomes; the business units may, however, have a high degree of autonomy in terms of their decisions. The analogy is to incentivizing behavior (directive control) vs. outcomes (evaluative control). Essentially, the locus of strategy-making and implementation in each business remains at the business level for evaluative control and moves to the HQ for directive control.

These are, of course, extreme cases, with intermediate points possibly being much more common (e.g., the HQ decides, business leadership implements, the HQ evaluates outcomes as a measure of implementation success). The HQ, for instance, may be actively involved both in guiding and approving business unit strategy as well as managing performance through targets and incentives. GE under Jack Welch was famous for a rigorous capital budgeting *and* performance evaluation process. Note that synergies play a critical role in both the directive and evaluative models of influence, and that both are consistent with a "strong" (influential) HQ.

Models of HQ influence: the four prototypes

The role and composition of the HQ will naturally look different in these different models. Directive influence models tend to rely on strategic planning capabilities concentrated at the HQ. Further, **directive approaches can more easily pursue one-sided synergies (in which one business gains more than the other loses, leaving the aggregate portfolio better off).** Evaluative influence relies more on financial control and performance management, with high degrees of delegation and autonomy on strategic decision-making. One-sided synergies may be harder to achieve in such settings, and the focus may be mostly on two-sided synergies.

Further, standalone influence models tend to involve portfolios of businesses that look quite distinct from each other to the external observer (prompting the label "conglomerate") because the synergies across them mostly occur at the back end of the value chains and possibly in corporate management functions. In linkage models,

TABLE 10.1 *Prototypes of HQ influence*

	Standalone	Linkage
Directive	**Turnaround** • The HQ takes active role in BU level strategy making • Emphasis on operational targets • Connection/ Customization synergies between the HQ and BUs based on intangibles	**Sharing resources** • The HQ takes active role in BU level strategy-making • Emphasis on operational targets • Connection/Customization synergies between the HQ and BUs based on intangibles • One-sided or two-sided synergies from Consolidation/ Combination/Customization/ Connection across businesses
Evaluative	**Portfolio** • BUs have autonomy in strategic decision making • Emphasis on financial targets • Connection/ Customization synergies between the HQ and BUs based on intangibles	**Setting context** • BUs have autonomy in strategic decision-making • Emphasis on financial targets • Connection/Customization synergies between the HQ and BUs based on intangibles • Two-sided synergies from Combination/ Connection/ Customization across businesses

since the portfolio is such that it supports active management of inter-business synergies by the HQ (e.g., shared manufacturing, R&D, or sales and distribution), external observers often see such portfolios as being more "related."

Combining the two horizontal approaches (standalone vs. linkage) with the two vertical approaches (evaluative vs. directive) yields four prototypes of HQ influence (see Table 10.1). Note that these models of influence are just that – models. Reality involves hybrids and combinations. In Table 10.1, "BU" stands for "business unit."

Standalone, evaluative

The **standalone, evaluative (SE)** influence model comes closest to the pure portfolio assembly model, yet differs from it in the sense that there is some attempt at indirect modification of businesses through evaluative control. Financial target setting and performance management are key activities in the HQ in this case, besides any CMF that are necessary to meet regulatory requirements. The management capabilities that underlie evaluative control constitute the intangible assets that generate Connection/Customization synergies with the businesses; the cost of creating and hosting these are economized by hosting them once at the HQ (rather than replicating them across businesses). Berkshire Hathaway under Warren Buffett comes close to this model. "Portfolio planning" and "financial control" are terms often used to describe the activities of the HQ in this model of influence. The Chinese firm Fosun manages their portfolio in a broadly similar manner, and the businesses are globally distributed.

Standalone, directive

The **standalone, directive (SD)** influence model is associated with a restructuring orientation. Like pure portfolio assembly, the selection of businesses is an important part of HQ activity, but unlike pure portfolio assembly there is an active attempt at modifying businesses through directive control. "Restructuring" and the "PE model" are terms often used to describe the role of the HQ. The directive attempts can include changes in business model, business strategy, staffing, and compensation. Strategic planning and turnaround management are key HQ activities in this model, besides any CMF that are necessary to meet regulatory requirements.

The management capabilities that underlie directive control constitute the intangible assets that generate Connection/Customization synergies with the businesses; the cost of creating and hosting these are economized by hosting them once at the HQ (rather than replicating them across businesses). The HQ may also be the physical or organizational location of tangible assets in the form of shared services functions that create Consolidation/ Combination synergies across businesses in back office and IT functions. While this prototype bears some similarity to the private equity/LBO model of business improvement, there is a significant difference; eventual exit from the business is not presumed and indeed may be difficult if shared service functions have been created (in fact, a joke often told about unsuccessful conglomerates is that they were private equity firms that forgot to exit). Conglomerates such as Hanson and Tyco were formerly famous for following this model. Danaher Corporation, the US equipment manufacturer, is an instance of this approach in contemporary times, though its scope is less broad than what one would consider a typical conglomerate.

Linkage, directive

The **linkage, directive (LD)** influence model explicitly focuses on actively managing operational synergies through linkages between businesses by directive control. Besides the CMF, the HQ in organizations following this model is likely to have strategic planning teams, corporate development functions (M&A and/or alliance teams), and centers of expertise (in areas like best practices, procurement, etc.). The HQ may also be the physical or organizational location of shared services functions that create Consolidation/Combination synergies across businesses in back office and IT functions. "Sharing tangible and intangible assets" and "corporate development capabilities" are labels often associated with such a model. An organizational culture that allows linkages to be exploited across businesses is often seen as a critical ingredient for success within this model, because even in a directive approach there are limits to what the HQ can formally force the businesses to do in terms of collaboration. Technology and fast-moving consumer goods companies like Cisco Systems and Procter & Gamble (P&G) illustrate this model of influence.

Linkage, evaluative
Finally, the **linkage, evaluative (LE)** influence model explicitly focuses on managing operational synergies through linkages between businesses, but does so passively rather than actively. Rather than direct businesses to realize synergies between them, the goal instead is to create a context that allows businesses to collaborate on synergy realization. While the HQ will still host corporate development functions (M&A and/or alliance teams), and centers of expertise (in areas like best practices, procurement, etc.), their use by business units is more likely to be **elective rather than imposed**. Instead, a strong corporate HR function with an emphasis on building the informal organization that glues the businesses together may be prominent. "Setting context," "cultural engineering," and "special projects" are terms often associated with this model of HQ operation. It would seem somewhat more difficult for this influence model to work across geographies because of the cultural and time zone differences.

Resource allocation by the HQ

The influence of the HQ is ultimately exerted on the basis of its resource allocation decisions, regardless of which HQ influence model is adopted; ultimately the HQ has the power to allocate resources to the businesses, not the other way round.

Resource allocation in *directive control* takes the form that major capital expenditure commitments (and therefore strategic investments) cannot be made without approval and rigorous screen-ing, regardless of the need for capital rationing. In *evaluative control*, capital expenditure requests are granted semi-automatically if they clear hurdles, but individual performance related incentives depend on past performance.

Resource allocation by the HQ may do better or worse than resource allocation by individual investors via the capital markets. The HQ ostensibly has access to better information about each business and the decisions rights to enforce actions by their subordinates that enhance the value of these investments. At the same time, it has access to a smaller set of alternatives and is prone to conflicts of interest between the HQ and shareholders. We focus on providing guidelines for HQ decision-making about resource allocation under the assumption that the decisions are motivated by a desire to enhance the value of the firm.

Resource allocation in multi-business organizations involves decisions about how to spread investment across a portfolio of businesses, and not only whether or not to invest in a particular business. This raises two challenges: **synergy** and **uncertainty**. First the businesses in a multi-business organization are not independent of each other; there are *interactions* between them. These could be in the form of synergies or dis-synergies. How should one take these into account when allocating resources across the portfolio? Second, from the field of finance we have well developed theories for resource allocation under risk (i.e., the future is uncertain but we can describe the possible outcomes and the probability of each of these outcomes occurring). These produce heuristics such as investing in projects only if their internal rate of return (IRR) exceeds their weighted average cost of capital (WACC), or to only invest in positive NPV projects. Under fundamental uncertainty (i.e., the future is uncertain but we do not know all the possible outcomes nor

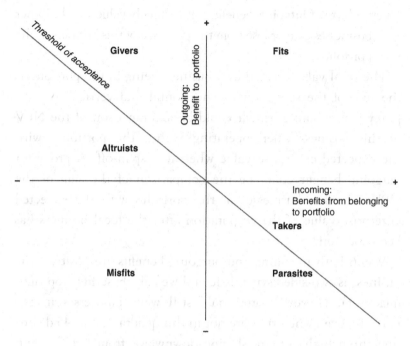

Figure 10.2 Synergistic portfolio framework

their probabilities of occurring), organizations' researchers have recognized that the problem is one of managing the well known exploration–exploitation trade-off: how to balance investment in businesses likely to do well (exploitation) vs. investment in businesses with uncertain outcomes (exploration), which may turn out to be the "next big thing." If the only way in which one can learn about the value of a business opportunity is by trying it, then some degree of exploratory investment is optimal. But how much?

The **synergistic portfolio framework** tackles both synergies and uncertainty in resource allocation decisions (see Figure 10.2). The two axes correspond respectively to:

Horizontal axis: **Incoming** benefit – how much does this business gain or lose in value from belonging to this portfolio?

Vertical axis: **Outgoing** benefit – how much value do the other businesses gain or lose from the presence of this business in the portfolio?

The total value created by a business being in the portfolio is the sum of the scores on the horizontal and vertical axes. A proxy for incoming benefit could be a comparison of the NPV of this business when operating within the portfolio, with the expected enterprise value when it is spun-off. A proxy for outgoing benefit could be the comparison of the sum of the NPVs of other businesses in the portfolio with the expected enterprise value of the corporation after the focal business has been spun-off.

When both incoming and outgoing benefits are positive, the business is two-sided synergistic and we call these **fits** (top right quadrant). However, one could still want businesses in the portfolio even when they are not in this quadrant. The 45 degree line through the origin, sloping downwards from left to right, shows the **threshold of acceptance** for investment opportunities in the portfolio; if they are above it to the right, it is worth investing in them. This is because both **givers** (high outgoing benefit, low but negative incoming benefit) and **takers** (high incoming benefit, low but negative outgoing benefit) improve the overall value of the portfolio. However, **altruists** (high and negative incoming benefit, low and positive outgoing benefit), **misfits** (negative incoming and outgoing benefit), and **parasites** (high and negative outgoing benefit, low and positive incoming benefit) do not, and should receive little investment or consideration for divestment.

The goal of resource allocation in the portfolio is thus to push businesses further away from the origin toward the top and right, away from the investment threshold. The movement of each business in the portfolio over time can be traced through this diagram.

However, we must still account for the uncertainty of investment opportunities. We classify each business as best as we can but because such classification depends on assumptions about an uncertain future and we are bound to make errors. A tractable way to think about this involves distinguishing errors of *omission* (believing an opportunity was below the threshold when in fact it was above) from those of *commission* (believing an opportunity was above the threshold when in fact it was not).

First, you should try to minimize both errors by obtaining good information, making sensible assumptions, and following a structured decision process. However, completely eliminating both errors is impossible. To avoid commission errors, you would invest only if you were fully convinced that the business would do well but that would imply plenty of omission errors (i.e., missing out investments in businesses that would have been worthy of investments). To avoid omission errors, you would invest even if you were unsure about the viability of a business but that would imply plenty of commission errors (i.e., money wasted on businesses that turn out to go nowhere). Second, therefore, you should try to minimize the more costly of the two errors. Omission costs increase relative to commission costs if there is a unique opportunity to acquire, a decline in the availability of alternatives, a temporary regulatory loophole, or a technology with increasing returns or network externalities. Higher costs of omission (relative to costs of commission) stimulate exploration. Figure 10.3 shows how the threshold of acceptance should change location as the costs of omission and commission rise.

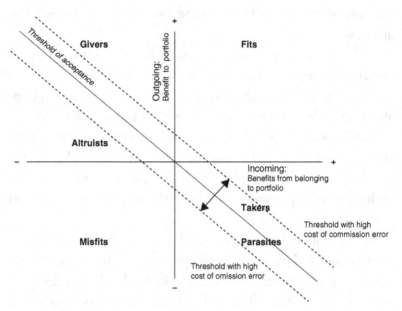

Figure 10.3 The cost of omission and commission errors
influences the threshold of acceptance

Application: A2G

A2G has seven business divisions, four of which are in related
industries ((A) heavy earth moving, (B) construction, (C) building
materials, and (D) infrastructure) and three that are not ((E) publishing services, (F) textile manufacturing, and (G) casinos).

The role of the corporate HQ can be analyzed along two dimensions. The first dimension is *horizontal*, i.e., whether the corporate HQ
influences the standalone improvements or linkage benefits of the
businesses. For divisions A, B, C, and D the linkage benefits are
plausible because they operate in related industries. For divisions E,
F, and G, standalone improvements are the best that can be hoped for
because of the lack of apparent operational synergies between the
divisions.

The second dimension is *vertical*, i.e., directive vs. evaluative control. For divisions A, B, C, and D (active in related industries) the

linkage benefits mostly arise from bundling products and services in order to sell complete projects to customers (i.e., Connection synergies). These synergies are mostly two-sided because everyone benefits. Hence, there is no need for the corporate HQ to be actively involved. Furthermore, because the upstream value chains of A, B, C, and D are quite different, there is no benefit consolidating them at the corporate HQ level. An evaluative approach seems sufficient for A, B, C, and D. This is also the more logical approach for E, F, and G because of the diversity in industries – the corporate HQ is unlikely to be able to add much value.

Accordingly, a cluster approach in which A–D are in one cluster, with E, F, and G operating more or less autonomously seems indicated. Further, this suggests that an evaluative approach focusing on standalone improvements for all divisions and linkage benefits for some is appropriate for A2G.

In terms of resource allocation, you seek information on how much each division gains from being part of A2G (incoming benefit) and how much the rest of A2G gains from having that division in the portfolio (outgoing benefit). The CEO provides you with the data in Table 10.2, which shows for each business the enterprise value computed in two ways: current value within the portfolio (NPV of the going concern), and value of a spin-off (NPV, multiples of comparable standalone firms, IPO pricing, or other techniques used to compute standalone value, see also Chapter 11 on M&A valuation).

You calculate the incoming and outgoing benefit for each division (see Table 10.3) and plot these in an expanding horizons framework (see Figure 10.4). You realize that the portfolio of A2G consists of one misfit (textile manufacturing), one parasite (casinos), one giver (infrastructure), two takers (publishing services and building materials), and two fits (heavy earth moving and construction). As expected, the related divisions within the cluster benefit more from and provide benefits to the portfolio than the unrelated divisions do.

In terms of capital allocation for the next year, recall that A2G follows an evaluative not a directive approach, and is not particularly cash constrained, but investors have been pushing for higher dividends. Furthermore, most businesses are relatively

TABLE 10.2 *Enterprise values before and after hypothetical spin-off (in million dollars)*

	Enterprise value			
	Division		Rest of corporation	
Division	Before a spin-off	After a spin-off	Before a spin-off	After a spin-off
(A) Heavy earth moving	150	100	830	600
(B) Construction	230	200	750	500
(C) Building materials	180	160	800	810
(D) Infrastructure	80	90	890	840
(E) Publishing services	120	80	860	865
(F) Textile manufacturing	110	160	870	890
(G) Casinos	110	100	870	950

mature (so that reasonably good information is available about their prospects) and stable (so that it might be possible, though not necessary, to reallocate resources from one business to another). Further, there is no obvious gain from exploration, as the costs of commission (i.e., making a bad investment) are probably larger than the costs of omission (i.e., ignoring a good business opportunity).

With these ideas in mind, we can now turn to investment decisions by business. Textile manufacturing stands out in a negative sense: it does not benefit from the portfolio and reduces its value. You can suggest minimizing funding and consider a divestiture for this business. While casinos is a thriving business, the rest suffers from casinos due to the negative reputation from gambling. You can again suggest cutting funding and to consider removing casinos from the portfolio altogether. Next, publishing services gains significantly

TABLE 10.3 *Benefits from and to A2G for each division (in million dollars)*

Division	Enterprise value of business		Incoming benefit	Enterprise value of rest of corporation		Outgoing benefit	Classification
	Before a spin-off	After a spin-off		Before a spin-off	After a spin-off		
(A) Heavy earth moving	150	100	50	640	600	230	Fit
(B) Construction	230	200	30	750	500	250	Fit
(C) Building materials	180	160	20	800	810	−10	Taker
(D) Infrastructure	80	90	−10	890	840	50	Giver
(E) Publishing services	120	80	40	860	865	−5	Taker
(F) Textile manufacturing	110	160	−50	870	890	−20	Misfit
(G) Casinos	110	100	0	870	950	−80	Parasite

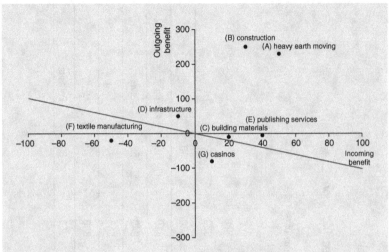

Figure 10.4 Synergistic portfolio framework for A2G

from the portfolio at a small cost to it. You maintain funding at last year's level but flag that their success depends on other divisions in the portfolio. You leave it to them to decide how to do it. On balance, the related businesses are doing well so you maintain funding, though you make additional funds available for projects that increase outgoing benefits (e.g., for building materials) or incoming benefits (e.g., infrastructure).

There are thus two divisions that appear to be struggling in the sense that they would be worth more after spin-off than in the portfolio: textile manufacturing (misfit) and infrastructure (giver). The former you suggest restructuring or divesting, though the latter should continue to receive funds because it is adding value to the corporation. In contrast, on the face of it, casinos (a parasite) is doing well but it is unclear why it should remain in this corporate portfolio, and you would consider divesting it too. Note that these decisions are uniquely driven by the synergistic portfolio framework; an approach that ignored the interactions within the portfolio would (erroneously) recommend divesting textile and infrastructure, and keeping casinos.

Basic facts about the corporate HQ

- Studies decomposing the variance in profitability to business unit, corporate parent, and industry level factors have found that the corporate parent factor represents around 10 to 20 percent of total variance (and 20 to 25 percent of explained variance), using the most recent techniques (McGahan and Porter, 2002). This is in between that for industry and that for business unit. However, it is now understood that this may be a significant under-estimate of the impact of the corporate HQ because of data limitations and the methodology, which mainly has to do with the fact that many business unit specific factors actually originate through HQ decisions.
- The size of the corporate HQ relative to the total size of the corporation varies enormously across sectors and geographies. Primary drivers of differences in HQ size are the scale of shared service functions provided to the businesses in the portfolio, as well as the extent of linkage influence exercised by the HQ.
- The cost of the corporate HQ in large multi-business corporations can range from 2 percent to 7 percent of sales (Roland Berger, 2013) but may be much higher in terms of operating profit.[1] Holding company HQs are relatively cheaper than other kinds of HQs.
- Most multi-business companies use some form of corporate portfolio management frameworks. However, their use in actual capital allocation decisions seems limited, and the missing role of portfolio levels effects (i.e., synergies and dis-synergies between businesses) in most existing frameworks is recognized.

Common mistakes to avoid

- Directive control will only work if the HQ has sufficient competence to understand the specifics of each business. It is unlikely to work in highly diverse portfolios.
- Over-estimating the value of a linkage approach can occur if the HQ has a poor understanding of the value chains of the respective businesses and the sources of potential synergies between

them. The linkage approach, like the directive approach, is thus less likely to work in portfolios with high diversity.

- The flip side to the previous point is that the HQ may overlook the fact that one-sided synergies will not materialize unless there is directive control. Left to their own devices, business units will only pursue two-sided synergies, but the loser in a one-sided synergy project will have little incentive to collaborate unless the HQ intervenes to force a re-distribution of gains.
- The pressures towards uniformity of influence models across businesses are quite high. They arise from the need to maintain perceptions of equity across businesses as well as limits on managerial capacity at the HQ to entertain different and possibly conflicting dominant logics within it. However, it is useful to recognize that these pressures can lead to inappropriate levels of uniformity, and can be dealt with through portfolio restructuring (e.g., divestment) or re-organization (e.g., clustering into homogenous clusters within which a single influence model can be applied).
- Offering centralized shared functions at the HQ is value adding only when there are synergies from consolidating across businesses and significant transaction costs if these functions are outsourced; otherwise, the HQ may end up forcing business to procure internally from it what can be procured more cheaply through external providers.

Frequently asked questions

1. How is the synergistic portfolio framework different from the Boston Consulting Group's portfolio allocation framework?

Corporate portfolio management frameworks such as the Boston Consulting Group's (BCG) growth-share matrix (famous for its "Stars / Cash Cows / Question Marks / Dogs"), the GE–McKinsey framework, or the Business Attractiveness Matrix of Campbell, Whitehead, Alexander, and Goold (2014) are all driven by the same basic idea: the businesses in a corporate portfolio can be compared to each other on two basic dimensions, namely the attractiveness of the industry the business is in, and the competitive advantage of the business within that industry. These frameworks identify the conjunction of high industry attractiveness and high competitive advantage as the "sweet-spot" for investment, while also recognizing the challenge of balancing exploration and exploitation; they encourage investment in businesses that are in attractive industries but have not yet established a strong competitive advantage. For instance, in the BCG framework, the injunction is to do some exploration (the Question Marks), but to curtail losses by divesting the Dogs, and to exploit the Stars by investing in them again. The Cash Cows provide the cash flows for these investments (a somewhat archaic view of the source of funds, as it ignores capital flows from outside the corporation). However, the approach is very much anchored in business strategy; the axes of the matrix represent competitive advantage within an industry and industry attractiveness, respectively, **but ignore the most important element of corporate strategy: synergies. Indeed none of the popular corporate portfolio management frameworks accounts properly for synergies in the sense of a business benefiting from belonging to a portfolio, and of the portfolio benefiting from the inclusion of a business.** The synergistic portfolio framework tackles both: synergies and the trade-off between exploitation and exploration.

2. **How disciplined are corporate HQs at actually allocating resources? Don't politics and power play an important role?**

The evidence on capital allocation within multi-business corporations suggests:
(1) High levels of stability over time: What a division got last year and what it will get this year is highly correlated (> 0.90).

(2) A strong tendency towards "corporate socialism": The number of divisions in the firm is negatively correlated with capital allocation to a division.

Many reasons have been suggested for these results, including the possibility that investment opportunities across the portfolio change slowly, cognitive biases, political pressures, and fairness concerns. A key point to bear in mind is that with organizational resource allocation (as opposed to an individual's resource allocation, say over a portfolio of investments) the information needed to make these allocation decisions is distributed across individuals whose interests diverge from the organization's as well as from each other's interests; unanimity over the appropriate allocation of resources may not exist (Kang, Burton, and Mitchell, 2011).[2]

There is no simple solution to these issues besides recognizing that discriminating allocations may matter most when there are stable and large differences across investment opportunities and in situations of standalone influence. In linkage influence models, particularly if differences in investment opportunities are smaller, it may be acceptable to invest more equally rather than equitably, in order to preserve collaboration and harmony within the portfolio.

3. Don't the choices of influence model and organizational structure (Chapter 9) have to be made jointly?

Yes. The complementarities between these choices are driven by one core factor: organizing the businesses into units with measurable profit and loss is useful when (a) adopting an evaluative control approach (because evaluation is easier for units that have measurable profits or losses), as well as (b) when the influence is primarily standalone rather than linkage (because each unit's profits are not directly influenced by others). These links between organizational structure and influence models are summarized in Table 10.4, where "P&L" is profit and loss.

TABLE 10.4 *The link between organizational structure and influence model*

Corporate advantage based on	Organizational structure	Influence model
Selection	Autonomous business units/ companies	Standalone, evaluative
Selection and synergies	P&L units organized by business, geography; or functional units (cost centers); hybrid and matrix organization	Standalone or linkage; directive or evaluative.

4. How does the synergistic portfolio framework relate to the HQ influence models?

In general, the synergistic portfolio framework is applicable under all influence models. Regardless of which influence model is used, the HQ ultimately has to decide how to allocate resources across the businesses. Furthermore, each of the influence models is consistent with synergies in the portfolio, which is what the synergistic portfolio framework aims to exploit. More specifically, we do not anticipate that the acceptance threshold or the distribution of businesses across different categories varies systematically by influence model.

5. Is it necessary for the same influence model to be used for every business in the portfolio? What if the portfolio is highly varied?

An implicit premise in the discussion of influence models we presented above is that the same influence model is used for the entire portfolio. However, this may not be a reasonable premise in multi-business organizations with significant diversity in portfolio composition. A solution to this problem of large diversity is to partition the portfolio into clusters (or "segments," or "domains") with greater homogeneity within than between clusters. This allows different influence models to be applied to different clusters. For instance a cluster of businesses could be defined on the basis of:

- **Stronger synergies within clusters than between**; these could include synergies that require linkage (e.g, knowledge sharing or cross-selling between businesses), or standalone approaches (e.g., common brands).
- **Greater scope for application of common management techniques and models within a cluster,** which is the case when there are similarities across businesses within a cluster in terms of:
  (a) Sizes of capital investment projects
  (b) Time spans of investment projects
  (c) Sources of risk
  (d) Management capabilities required by different businesses
  (e) Key success factors
  (f) Stages in industry life cycles
  (g) Competitive positions occupied by each business within its industry
  (h) Performance goals and measures
  (i) Time horizons for measuring performance.

When such similarities exist, they create what is known as a "dominant general management logic," which binds the businesses together and makes it easier to administer them jointly. The challenge is that the HQ may still be constrained in terms of how many different dominant logics can be simultaneously accommodated by it. A strategy of clustering the portfolio is thus likely to require some division of labor within the HQ in terms of cluster specific responsibility, and consequently at least a two-tiered reporting structure within it.

It is useful to document the influence model as it applies to each business within the portfolio in terms of a "responsibility chart" or "delegation contract". This document explicitly states what decisions are to be taken by the business management, which ones are the prerogative of the HQ, and which ones require approval by (or informing of) the HQ but are ultimately taken at the business level.

Notes

1. Zimmermann, T. and Huhle, F. (2013). *Corporate Headquarters Study 2012 – Developing Value Adding Capabilities to Overcome the Parenting Advantage Paradox,* www.rolandberger.com/expertise/functional_issues/organization/corporate_headquarters; www.rolandberger.com/media.pdf/Roland_Berger_Headquarters_Short_version_20130502.pdf.
2. Kang, H.-G., Burton, R.M., and Mitchell, W. (2009). How potential knowledge spillovers between venture capitalists' entrepreneurial projects affect the specialization and diversification of VC funds when VC effort has value. *Strategic Enterprise Journal,* 5(3), 227–246.

Further reading

For more on variance decomposition studies, see:

Bowman, E. H. and Helfat, C. E. (2001). Does corporate strategy matter? *Strategic Management Journal,* 22(1), 1–23.
McGahan, A. M. and Porter, M. E. (2002). What do we know about variance in accounting profitability? *Management Science,* 48(7), 834–851.

On the size and location of HQs, see:

Birkinshaw, J., Braunerhjelm, P., Holm, U., and Terjesen, S. (2006). Why do some multinational corporations relocate their headquarters overseas? *Strategic Management Journal,* 27(7), 681–700.
Collis, D., Young, D., and Goold, M. (2007). The size, structure, and performance of corporate headquarters. *Strategic Management Journal,* 28(4), 383–405.

For more on corporate portfolio management tools, see:

Campbell, A., Goold, M., Alexander, M., and Whitehead, J. (2014). *Strategy for the Corporate Level: Where to Invest, What to Cut Back and How to Grow Organisations With Multiple Divisions,* 2nd edn. San Francisco, CA: Jossey-Bass.

Goold, M., Campbell, A., and Alexander, M. (1994). *Corporate Level Strategy: Creating Value in the Multi-Business Company*. New York: John Wiley.

Nippa, M., Pidun, U., and Rubner, H. (2011). Corporate portfolio management: appraising four decades of academic research. *Academy of Management Perspectives*, 25(4), 50–66.

Pidun, U., Rubner, H., Krühler, M., Untiedt, R., and Nippa, M. (2011). Corporate portfolio management: theory and practice. *Journal of Applied Corporate Finance*, 23(1), 63–76.

For more on internal capital markets, see:
Maksimovic, V. and Phillips, G. M. (2007). Conglomerate firms and internal capital markets. In B. E. Eckbo (ed.), *Handbook of Corporate Finance*. Amsterdam: Elsevier, 423–479.

Stein, J. C. (1997). Internal capital markets and the competition for corporate resources. *Journal of Finance*, 52(1), 111–133.

CMF has the following key components: treasury, risk management, taxation, financial reporting, company secretary and legal counsel, government relations, and investor relations. For details on these, see:
Treasury: Bragg, S. M. (2010). *Treasury Management: The Practitioner's Guide*. Hoboken, NJ: John Wiley.

Risk management: Hopkin, B. (2014). *Fundamentals of Risk Management – Understanding, Evaluating and Implementing Effective Risk Management*. 3rd edn. London: Kogan Page.

Taxation: Schreiber, U. (2013). *International Company Taxation: An Introduction to the Legal and Economic Principles*. London: Springer.

Financial reporting: Melville, A. (2015). *International Financial Reporting – A Practical Guide*. 5th edn. Harlow: Pearson.

Company secretary: Armour, D. (2012). *The ICSA Company Secretary's Handbook*. London: ICSA Publishing.

Legal counsel: Veasy, E. N. and Di Gugliemo, C. T. (2012). *Indispensable Counsel: The Chief Legal Officer in the New Reality*: Oxford University Press.

Government relations: Lee, M., Neeley, G., and Stewart, K.(2011). *The Practice of Government Public Relations*. Boca Raton, FL: CRC Press.

11

Managing the M&A process

> TechnoSystems Plc is a successful software company that specializes in operating systems. It sees an opportunity to expand into a new niche software sector, productivity applications. LittleCo. is a small unlisted company that has developed award winning products in the productivity applications domain, but does not have much of a brand name or customer base yet. It has emerged as a candidate for acquisition by TechnoSystems. How would you value the firm? How would you plan the post-merger integration?

An **acquisition** occurs when one company buys another company, or a business of that other company. A **merger** occurs when a new company is formed and the acquirer and target companies are dissolved.[1] **Mergers and acquisitions** (M&As) are different for tax purposes and similar for many strategic purposes. We focus on their communalities rather than differences and will mostly use the term "acquisitions" to talk about both.

There are several stages in an M&A process involving people and experts from within and outside the acquirer–target firms: target selection, valuation and negotiation, due diligence, integration, and post-deal evaluation (see Figure 11.1).

227

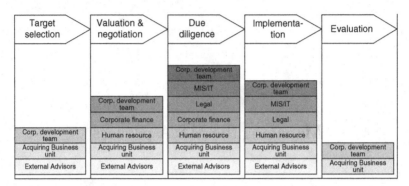

Target selection	Valuation & negotiation	Due diligence	Implementation	Evaluation
		Corp. development team		
		MIS/IT	Corp. development team	
	Corp. development team	Legal	MIS/IT	
	Corporate finance	Corporate finance	Legal	
Corp. development team	Human resource	Human resource	Human resource	
Acquiring Business unit	Acquiring Business unit	Acquiring Business unit	Acquiring Business unit	Corp. development team
External Advisors	External Advisors	External Advisors	External Advisors	Acquiring Business unit

Figure 11.1   Stages and people in an M&A process

Much of the strategic thinking on when to do an M&A (as opposed to an alliance or organic growth), described in Chapters 4, 5, and 6, must be completed before beginning the first step of the M&A process, *target selection*. During the *valuation and negotiation* phase, the acquirer estimates how much the target is worth and finds a price that is acceptable to both. *Due diligence* refers to a period in which the acquirer, having made an offer, is granted access to private data by the target to verify its valuation. *Implementation* refers to the process of achieving the desired level of integration of activities across acquirer and target in order to extract synergies. *Evaluation* refers to a post-transaction review of what went right and wrong. This is particularly useful for serial acquirers, whose transactions tend to be similar enough to apply learning from prior transactions to future ones.

There are enormous technical complexities at each stage, and in all likelihood professional outside advisors (investment bankers, consultants, lawyers, and technical experts) will be involved. Our aim is to give the reader a map of the terrain, and a broad framework to bound and manage this complexity.[2]

Both the valuation and negotiation as well as post-merger integration (PMI) activities in a corporate acquisition depend on the underlying synergies in the transaction, which is why we focus on these. Ideally, these two activities should also depend on each other – the valuation must take into account the anticipated PMI challenges, and the PMI activities must be mindful of the value drivers in the valuation.

Valuation and negotiation: how much should you pay for a company?

Valuing a company, particularly for the purposes of acquiring it, is a quantitative exercise. At the same time it is quite subjective (because it depends critically on assumptions about an uncertain future based on limited information). In this section we offer several guidelines to help navigate the uncertainties of valuation. **We cannot significantly reduce the uncertainties in valuation, but we can develop a disciplined way of taking these into account, of documenting the assumptions we make in dealing with uncertainty, and of engaging in a reasonable bargaining process, to ultimately lead to a price to which both parties agree.**

The first point to realize is that valuation is an *iterative* process. In arriving at the decision to acquire, a systematic approach such as we recommended in Chapters 4, 5, and 6, would already have made at least some approximate estimates of the value to the company from acquiring vs. allying vs. organic growth. Once the acquisition alternative has been finalized and a target has been shortlisted, we may use those estimates as a starting point and refine them.

Second, valuation – as a process for figuring out how much the target is worth to the acquirer – is different from the process of deciding what to pay for the target, which typically involves a process of bargaining and negotiation. **Valuation helps to set the upper and lower bounds on what the acquirer should be willing to pay (and the target should be willing to accept).** What an acquirer finally pays will be also be determined by the relative bargaining power and skill of the target (see Figure 11.2).

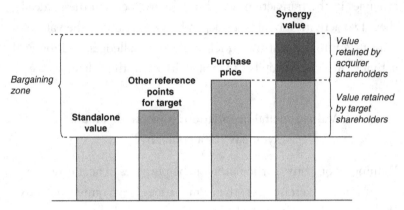

Figure 11.2 Valuation sets the lower and upper bound for negotiation

The **lower bound** in a valuation process is determined by the standalone value of the target firm. This is what the target firm would be valued at by an acquirer with zero synergies of acquiring the target (and effectively ignores the costs of integration that are synergy independent: more on this below). It represents a hypothetical benchmark, and any offer below this would be rejected by the target firm unless the acquirer spots a bargain that even the target firm management cannot see or is unwilling to see.

If the target firm is listed in an efficient capital market (and it is not yet widely known that the target firm may be in play), the current market capitalization of the firm is a good indicator of the equity value. Equity plus the firm's debt (minus cash balances) gives the **standalone enterprise value**. If there is no market price, or the price does not reflect well the underlying value, some other commonly used techniques include:

- **Intrinsic valuation**: Analyze what a firm is worth by considering what assets it has or will have in the future. Measures include:
  - **NPV of future cash flows**: Estimate the cash flows that the target company would generate if operated on a standalone basis. Next, discount those cash flows to take into account the

riskiness and the timing of those cash flows. Often cash flows are detailed for only a limited period (say, the next five or seven years) and any subsequent cash flows are grouped together in a terminal value based on some blanket assumptions on growth and investment requirements.

- **Balance sheet metrics**: Use book value, i.e., what is given on the balance sheet. This works better if a company's most valuable assets are indeed on the balance sheet, e.g., physical capital but not human capital. This method is not forward looking. Alternatively, liquidation value of the target company could be used. This is the expected price of physical assets in a quick sell.

- **Relative valuation**: Analyze what a firm is worth by comparing with other firms.

  - **Earnings multiples**: From the income statement, obtain the target's EBITDA and multiply by the ratio of enterprise value to EBITDA for a comparable, standalone listed company. This assumes that the target company and peer firm have similar expected growth rates and risk. It is better to use enterprise value than equity value to eliminate differences in capital structure (i.e., debt vs. equity).

  - **Revenue multiples**: Use the target's revenue and multiply by the enterprise value/revenue ratio for a comparable, standalone listed company.

  - **Other multiples**: Sometimes using earnings multiples is not feasible (e.g., loss-making companies), nor are revenue multiples (e.g., young companies). Other multiples could include those on book value or the number of customers.

The **upper bound** for the valuation of the target company is its **synergistic value**, or standalone value + the value of synergies with the acquirer. To estimate this synergistic value of the target, we can use the NPV of future cash flows of both the target + the acquirer after taking into account the effects of synergies between them as well as the costs of extracting them. The appendix to Chapter 2 provides details on how to value synergies using value drivers and NPV.

As an *additional reference point* to estimate the value of synergies, one may also compute the premium over standalone value offered in prior acquisitions between similar acquirers and targets (also called deal multiples), and apply this to the standalone value of the target firm. Two points are worth emphasizing here: first, EBITDA or revenue multiples help estimate standalone value, whereas deal multiples help to estimate synergistic value. Second, these multiple based valuation methods are approximate; no pair of acquirer and target firms is identical. **Nothing beats NPV with good information but good information about an uncertain future is difficult, if not impossible, to obtain.** Hence, it is useful to also look at deal multiples. They may also serve as a bargaining tactic: more on this below.

The synergistic value of the target can be broken down in a few different ways, which allow one to be more conservative by ignoring certain parts of the synergistic valuation when setting the upper bound. These include:

• Synergistic value of target = Standalone value of target + NPV(Synergy impact on target) + NPV(Synergy impact on acquirer)
• Synergistic value of target = Standalone value of target + NPV(Synergy from Consolidation) + NPV(Synergy from Combination) + NPV(Synergy from Connection) + NPV(Synergy from Customization).

These breakdowns help us to be conservative in the actual bidding and deal closing stage, as the upper bound can be set not at the Synergistic value of the target, but instead at the Standalone value of the target + Some portion of the synergy value (e.g., ignoring the synergy impact on the acquirer, ignoring all synergies other than Consolidation, or discounting the more uncertain synergies at a higher discount rate than the target's weighted average cost of capital (WACC)). No matter which synergies are prioritized, integration costs should be taken into account. These refer to the costs of making the organizational changes in the target and the acquirer to create a new combined organization and to help extract synergies.

Integration costs can be separated into **synergy dependent** and **synergy independent** integration costs. The synergy independent costs of integration do not depend on the type or value of the synergy being extracted through integration, but instead depend on the scale and age of the target organization. All else being equal, larger and older organizations, regardless of the nature of the synergies involved in the deal, will require greater integration efforts to convert their systems and processes to be compatible with the acquirer, and to separate and divest unwanted assets. The synergy dependent costs of integration depend on the kind of synergies being extracted; they may be thought of as a variable tax that eats into the value of the synergy. If no synergy is extracted, then there are no integration costs of this kind. As we noted in Chapter 2, we can make some informed conjectures about the differences between the integration costs (as a percentage of synergy value) as well as the uncertainty associated with each type of synergy.

Between the upper bound (synergistic value) and lower bound (standalone value) of the target firm lies a bargaining zone, within which acquirers and targets may hope to find a point of agreement. Each side may of course use bargaining tactics, such as the use of other valuation benchmarks, to push the price in their respective favor. For instance:

- Targets can use (potential) offers from alternative bidders to get acquirers to raise the offer price
- Acquirers and targets may use historical transactions of broadly comparable targets, or standalone value of broadly comparable

targets to justify their preferred value of premium over standalone value

- Acquirers may estimate the cost of organic growth – what it would cost them to build internally – to set a ceiling on what they are willing to pay
- If the target is unlisted, the estimated valuation of the target firm on the IPO may be another benchmark the target can use to improve its bargaining position
- Listed target firms may use their historically higher share prices to argue that their current share price does not accurately reflect its standalone value.

There are many financial complexities to valuation, including estimating the cost of capital and financing the transaction, for which we refer readers to other sources.[3] The key points about valuation that a corporate strategist must know are what we have covered. The essence is simple – valuation is not about finding the "true" value of the target firm, it is about finding a number that all sides are happy with. It is (sophisticated) guesswork, it is negotiated, and it is about a range rather than a point estimate. This does not mean that the quantitative analysis serves no purpose; it does. It offers a disciplined language for the negotiation to take place in.

PMI: how much should you integrate both companies?

At a fundamental level, the problem of PMI is essentially an **organization design problem**. A new common organizational structure must be designed and implemented that brings the acquirer and target organization together. It involves going from two organizations with distinct structures (both formal and informal) to a new common organization, and one that enables the exploitation of the synergies that motivated the acquisition in the first place. It is also, interestingly, an organization redesign problem largely free of the baggage (or benefits) of an informal organization; except in the case of an alliance converting into an acquisition, the two organizations are often strangers to each other before the deal.

PMI planning ideally commences at the stage of valuation (as the synergies that are being valued must be the ones that are extracted through PMI) and is completed before the formal completion of the deal, at which point the PMI plans are implemented. A separate program management office may then be created to oversee the PMI process, with a host of PMI projects targeted at the extraction of particular synergies. We focus on the planning of the PMI process, the key decisions to be made, and the trade-offs to be considered.

There are several known challenges to PMI that researchers and managers are aware of. These include:

- **Complexity**: This is a function of the number of inter-related decisions on the trade-offs to be made and implemented, which increase with the size of the target as well as the type of synergy (higher for synergies requiring significant modification to resources, such as Customization and Consolidation).

- **Limited information**: Many of the decisions that are premises in the PMI planning phase are made without accurate information. These include decisions about synergies and valuation. It is only when PMI commences that more detailed information emerges, which may sometimes invalidate the assumptions and decisions made earlier in the process of the acquisition.

- **Functioning while integrating**: A PMI expert once remarked in our class that post-merger integration was a bit like trying to change the engine in a plane while it was flying. Keeping business running as usual while engaging in a complex integration process can be extremely difficult, and may lead to a lack of attention by the senior management towards pressing issues of competition.

- **Uncertainty and change**: PMI implies uncertainty and change for employees. Independent of whether the new circumstances leave them better or worse off, the period during which they do not know about their new circumstances can be very stressful. This lowers productivity and may lead to turnover. Assuming job mobility is higher for more talented and qualified employees, a period of uncertainty can actually leave the acquirer with a target organization from which the best human capital has departed.

- **Cultural differences**: The acquirer and the target typically differ not only in their formal structures, but also in their organizational and possibly national cultures. These differences can impede collaboration across organizations and create conflict.

Choosing the level of integration involves balancing the benefits from collaboration with the costs of disruption

In PMI we need to balance two consequences when deciding on organizational integration levels – the need for collaboration, and the need for minimizing disruption (see Figure 11.3). There is considerable evidence from research on the existence of this trade-off.

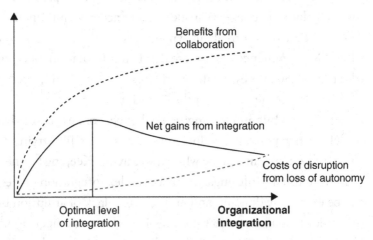

Figure 11.3 The fundamental trade-off in PMI between collaboration and disruption

Note that we are interested in reducing disruption not only because we care about how employees feel after being acquired, but also because we care about the impact of the disruption on their productivity – a case of enlightened self-interest. Thus choosing an optimal level of integration requires trading off the benefits from collaboration against the costs of disruption.

In general, some degree of integration is necessary to get synergies in acquisitions (and it is precisely the ability the extract synergies that distinguishes a corporate strategist from pure investors, see Chapter 1), though how much will vary from case to case as a function of the benefits from collaboration, and the implementation competence of the acquirer at managing the costs of disruption. For instance, the benefits of integration may rise and peak faster for some types of synergies – particularly those that require limited modification of resources across value chains (e.g., Connection, Combination). These types of synergies may, all else being equal, require lower levels of integration than synergies involving Consolidation or Customization. It may also be the case that the costs of disruption for the same level of integration may vary with the similarity of cultures between acquirer and target, or the ability of the acquirer to implement a given level of integration smoothly.

Grouping and linking are the key integration choices

We can think about the PMI decision regarding the combined organizational structure in terms of two sequential choices: one about *grouping* (into organizational units such as departments with a common boss, incentives, and procedures – i.e., the boxes in an organization chart) and the other about *linking* activities across groupings (such as vertical reporting, dedicated liaisons, and temporary task forces – i.e., the lines in organization charts). This follows from Chapter 9, in which we explained that grouping and linking were the two key choices for organizational design (see Figure 11.4).

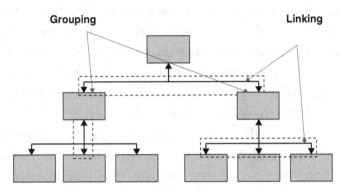

Figure 11.4 Grouping and linking

1. Grouping choices Consider two organizational units, one from the target, T, one from the acquirer, A. What are the different levels to which these two could be organizationally integrated after an acquisition? The first integration choice is about *grouping* these units together with the following options:

0. **Autonomy:** Both units exist within the merged company but operate completely independent of each other, but for the fact that ultimately both units report to the same CEO.

1. **Peer:** The two units work together as peers; almost like an alliance within the company, but power is symmetric.

2. **Report:** One unit (typically T) reports to the other (typically A).

3. **Absorption:** One unit is completely absorbed into another.

Two things happen as we go from 0 to 3 above. First, the number of mechanisms by which one could foster collaboration between the individuals in the two units increases. Reporting to the same boss, being part of the same organizational unit, and being rewarded on the same performance metric fosters a greater degree of collaboration than is feasible for individuals working in different organizational units, even if the unit's goals are ostensibly to collaborate. Second, increases in the degree of integration mean progressively greater levels of changes in roles, status, identity, job security, authority, and autonomy. This change is typically disruptive, and demotivating.

2. **Linking choices** The second integration choice is about *linking* units, or how the target and acquirer unit's employees' (a) incentives, (b) information channels, and (c) work practices are changed – to either keep them operating autonomously (towards the left–low scores on the scales) or collaboratively (towards the right–high scores on the scales), see Figure 11.5. As with grouping, a move to the high end of the scale improves collaboration by aligning interests and information, but also potentially induces disruptive changes.

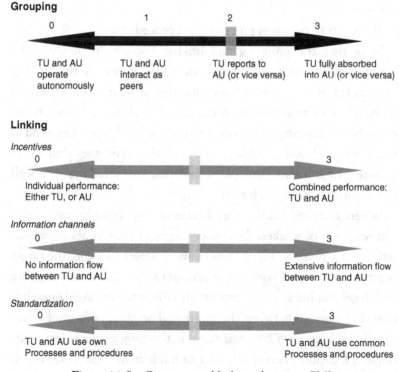

Figure 11.5 Grouping and linking choices in PMI

To consider these linking choices in more detail, think of them as lying on this spectrum:

(a) **Incentives**:

0: Continue to reward on individual unit's performance, i.e., either target or acquirer

←⟶

3: Reward on combined target/acquirer unit performance

(b) **Information channels**:

0: No information flows between target and acquirer unit

←⟶

3: Extensive information flows between target and acquirer unit

(c) **Standardization of work procedures**:

0: Let target and acquirer continue to use own processes and procedures

←⟶

3: Switch to common processes and procedures

Note that the grouping and linking choices are likely to be *complements* – the value of choosing low scores on the linking choices (incentives, information, and standardization) is enhanced when a low score is chosen on the grouping choice and vice versa; conversely, choosing high scores on the linking choices goes hand in hand with choosing high scores on the grouping dimension (Figure 11.6). If this principle is violated, you should have a well thought through reason for this.

Where relevant and feasible, choices of *geographic/physical location* can reinforce or weaken the consequences of choices about organizational integration. These choices about where to locate the target organizational units within the acquirer's organizational structure and in geographic space eventually also shape the informal organization that emerges between the target and acquirer personnel. They thus have long-term consequences. If the target unit is left in its original location, then it is harder to implement high scores on all dimensions of linking and grouping. In contrast, relocating the

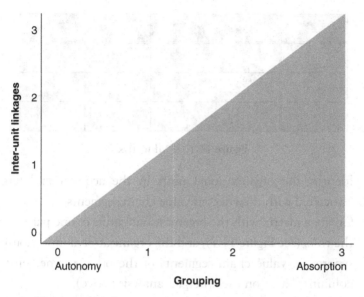

Figure 11.6   Grouping choices constrain linking choices

target unit to the acquirer unit location facilitates the implementation of higher scores and may indeed make high levels of integration less necessary (as informal interactions may suffice).

A framework for PMI planning

Armed with these principles, we can introduce the basic framework for integration planning. **The key principle behind this framework is that in every acquisition, each pair of organizational units from the acquirer and target could have a different optimal level of integration between them, based on the synergy operators that link them.** The analysis has the following steps:

1. Start with a clear statement of potential synergies between the acquirer and target (preferably the same one used to value the target). Understand exactly where and how the value chains of the two companies will join up. Chapter 2 and the synergy operators are useful in this process.

	A1	A2	A3	A4
T1				
T2				
T3				

Figure 11.7   PMI matrix

2. Identify the organizational units in the acquirer and target associated with the affected value chain segments.

3. Create a matrix with the organizational units of one partner on the rows (see Figure 11.7), and the organizational units housing synergistic value chain segments of the other partner on the columns (based on the synergies analysis above).

4. In this acquirer–target matrix, for each cell, note the value of the synergies to be realized as estimated in the valuation phase.

5. Finally, for each cell consider the first order (i.e., grouping) choices about organizational design, as well as the second order (i.e., linking) choices. Bear in mind the collaboration–disruption trade-off when selecting the degree of integration.

6. For each target unit (row), the integration level should not be more than that determined by the **cell for which the synergies are greatest**.

7. You can choose to do the integration in **phases**. You can decide on a desired level of integration for Phase 1, achieve it, and then plan for the next level of integration in Phase 2. This is not the same as slow vs. fast implementation, in which the desired end state is known and we only vary the time taken to get there. Phase-wise integration can be very useful if you expect new information to emerge that may materially alter your plan for extracting synergies.

The guiding principle for these choices may be stated as follows. In general, lower levels of integration (i.e., low scores on grouping and linking choices) are sufficient for low modification and dissimilar underlying resources. Thus the synergies requiring least and most integration, in that order, are likely to be Connection, [Combination, Customization], Consolidation.

Application: TechnoSystems buys LittleCo

Consider the example of TechnoSystems acquiring the start-up software firm LittleCo at the beginning of this chapter. At this stage, we assume that the relevant synergies have been identified (see Chapter 2 for guidance) and that the preferred growth mode is acquisition rather than alliance or organic growth (see Chapters 4, 5, and 6). TechnoSystems wants to buy LittleCo primarily for Customization and Connection synergies; the technology must be made inter-operable with the acquirer's suite of technologies, and will be sold by the acquirer's sales force.

For the negotiation, we prepare a lower bound based on LittleCo's standalone value and an upper bound based on the synergistic value between TechnoSystems and LittleCo Because LittleCo is not listed, we cannot use a stock price as starting point. Instead, we could use a discounted cash flow (DCF) approach (if sufficient information is available) and additionally, as a sanity check, we could rely on the EBITDA multiple of peers (if LittleCo makes a profit) or their revenue multiple. Let's say the valuation process leads to an estimate of standalone value at $100 million.

For the synergies, we rely on a DCF approach that suggests synergies (net of integration costs and appropriately discounted for risk and timeliness) of $60 million. These come mostly from revenue enhancements: selling the target's products through the acquirer's sales force ($43 million), from enhancing inter-operability of technologies ($15 million), and a modest cost

TechnoSystems		
LittleCo	*R&D*	*Sales*
R&D	Customization ($15 million) Grouping level: 2	Connection ($43 million) Grouping level: 1
Sales	0	Consolidation ($2 million) Grouping level: 3

Figure 11.8 PMI matrix for TechnoSystems and LittleCo

saving from eliminating redundancy in sales force ($2 million). Thus, the bargaining zone lies between $100 and $160 million.

Without revealing the figure of $160 million during the negotiations, TechnoSystems uses past data on similar acquisition deals and IPO transactions to convince LittleCo. that they should be taken over for $110 million.

This is a simple enough deal that we do not need a multi-phase integration approach. The integration matrix might look as in Figure 11.8 (scores are for the structural grouping decision and range from degree 0 = autonomy to degree 3 = full absorption).

In this case, the gains from inter-operability are less important than the gains from the acquirer's sales force cross-selling the target's products. Therefore, it may suffice for the target R&D unit to be integrated to degree 1 with the acquirer's sales force and also with the acquirer's R&D unit. Choosing a higher level of integration (e.g., degree 2) with the acquirer's R&D unit may create so much disruption that the synergy with the acquirer's sales unit is not realizable. In contrast, it is clear that the target's sales force can be completely integrated into the acquirer's sales unit.

Basic facts about M&As

- **On average, acquirers do not benefit from an acquisition:** Hundreds of studies have analyzed hundreds of thousands of acquisitions and found no noticeable effect (i.e., either positive or negative) on share price (short or long term), ROA, ROE, or ROS, *on average*. There is of course wide variance in outcomes.
- **Most target's shareholders benefit from an acquisition:** Typically, a takeover announcement is accompanied by a 30 percent increase in the share price. This means that the price the acquirer pays is much higher than what the target's share price was before.
- **On average, acquisitions generate value:** the combined market capitalization of the acquirer and the target go up. The increase is about 2 percent (reflecting the fact that acquirers tend to be bigger than targets).[4] So whether M&As on average are beneficial depends on the perspective taken: acquirer, target, or society.
- In their meta-analysis on the effect of cultural differences on several outcome variables, Stahl and Voight (2008) report findings that show no systematic effect of culture on outcomes. One explanation lies in the selection of targets. Perhaps culturally different partners are only chosen when synergy extraction does not require intense collaboration. If so, then both culturally similar and dissimilar acquisitions may end up with comparable performance.

Common mistakes to avoid

- **Do not go after just one target, but have alternatives:** Alternatives include alliances and organic growth. But even if you have decided on an M&A, keep in mind the need to work with a short list of candidates. Treating a partner as unique may lead you to missing out on other valuable partners or to over-paying.
- **When estimating the standalone value of the target, use the target's discount rate, not the acquirer's:** A discount rate takes

into account that cash flows are risky. The right risk level is that of the target not of the acquirer. Two implications of using the acquirer's, and hence wrong, discount rate are: (1) the standalone value of the target would depend on the perspective taken (e.g., potential acquirer A would conclude a different standalone value than potential acquirer B), and (2) it would lead to over-estimation of the standalone (and likely over-payment) value if the acquirer's discount rate is lower than the acquirer's (most acquirers are bigger than their targets, and discount rates tend to be lower for bigger firms).

- **Do not treat PMI as all or nothing:** Because integration involves a trade-off between the benefits from collaboration and the costs of disruption, typical integrations are rarely full integration or no integration at all. Further, an integration will look different for different parts of the organization.
- **Do not wait with planning PMI until after a deal has been struck:** Unless you are chasing an under-valued target, PMI is the justification for an acquisition. When considering whether the deal is worth it, you need to know what synergies are present and how those can be extracted. Furthermore, because implementation requires a lot of planning, it is better to start early rather than later.
- **PMI in more complex deals does not have to happen all at once:** A multi-phase integration process, in which new information is expected to arise and is taken into account before formulating the next round of PMI plans, can be very useful in complex transactions.

Frequently asked questions

1. What is the difference between integration and implementation?

Integration is the extent to which the different organizations are combined. Low integration, for instance, means keeping the acquired organization as an autonomous entity, often with its own profit and loss responsibility. High integration means that it literally disappears off the organization chart. Intermediate levels of integration, with dense linkages between distinct organizational units (through integrating managers, committees, teams, processes, incentives) are also possible, and indeed are typical.

Thus the "integration level" is the extent to which units across the two organizations will be put together. It could vary from "very little" to "very much." And it could be different for different parts of the target organization.

Implementation is the process by which one gets to the desired level of integration. Implementation refers to the project management activities necessary to get to the desired level of integration. It includes linking IT, back office, payroll, HR, etc. Communication is a key element as well.

There are arguments for both fast and slow (i.e., multi-phase) implementation. Faster implementation may be better in terms of removing uncertainty about the steady state conditions that the acquired employees face, and in generating the quick wins that lend confidence to both organizations that the merger can create value. However, there are also good reasons to implement more slowly: if the acquirer is yet to understand the target firm's organization and sources of synergy, or if the key assets of the target firm are embedded in human capital, it may be better to postpone any potential disruption until at least some of these have been transferred to the acquirer. Thus, the speed of implementation must balance the benefit of waiting for more information and postponing disruption effects with the cost of uncertainty imposed on the organization and missed opportunities for extracting synergies in a gradual, multi-phase approach.

In this usage of the terms "integration" and "implementation," "partial implementation" makes no sense, but "partial integration" may indeed be the optimal solution for a particular target. On the other hand "slow integration" does not make much sense with this usage, but "slow implementation" may be a sensible approach if it is valuable to delay the disruption effects for any desired level of integration, or collect additional information about the sources of value.

2. You have not mentioned culture much. Is this not important?

Culture is (very) important. We did not say much about planning for "cultural integration" because our view is that this is best achieved by selection rather than change.

To expand on this: first, clearly cultural differences matter in impeding effective collaboration between acquirer and target personnel. Differences in culture can create in-group/out-group suspicions and misunderstandings. Second, these are likely to be most salient when the synergies require close collaboration between partners – for instance, more in the case of Customization and Consolidation than in the case of Connection or Combination. Third, while robust methods to assess cultural differences between acquirer and target exist, and can be useful for anticipating cultural clashes, there are few robust techniques to engineer a desired culture. To assess differences in culture, a number of techniques including simple observation of how things get done, as well as more elaborate surveys or interviewing based methods to measure the differences in culture between organizations, can be used. However, to create a desired culture, while we know that retention, socialization, incentives, symbols, and leadership matter, these play out over larger time scales and feature a large degree of uncertainty.

For these reasons, we recommend that selecting targets that are culturally compatible (particularly for synergies requiring high levels of collaboration), may be more useful than attempting to merge cultures after the deal has been done.

3. Are cross-border M&As different from M&As within a single country?

Yes and no. No, because the basic decisions and trade-offs described in this chapter still apply: valuation provides a bargaining zone for negotiations, the grouping of organizational units depends on the synergies, and linking works in line with grouping.

Yes, because many of the problems we highlighted are exacerbated in an international context. Beginning with valuation, we have seen that a basic problem is obtaining reliable information and making reasonable assumptions. Our ability to do so may be lower for another country. Likewise, many companies struggle with PMI in a single country and the complexities of PMI are only compounded in an international context: cultures will be more different, geographical and time distances will lead to more misunderstandings, uncertainty will be higher, and regulation may be more restrictive.

4. In terms of share price, why does an acquirer typically not benefit from an acquisition but a target does?

First, acquiring is less painful for an acquirer than for a target. If given a choice, most managers would prefer being an acquirer to being a target. Hence, you would need to pay (heavily) for someone to take on the role of target.

Second, a target often has a strong alternative, giving it the upper hand in negotiations. The synergies between an acquirer and a target can often be replicated between the target and a *different* acquirer. If so, then the target can either implicitly or explicitly create a bidding contest for the company, resulting in a high price. Hence, this is more a question of value capture than value creation.

5. If acquisitions provide little benefit for an acquirer, why do companies keep doing them?

To start with a caveat: precisely measuring M&A performance is difficult, and the high rates of failure of an M&A may be somewhat exaggerated. But that said, if the failure rate is very likely at or above the 50 percent mark, what could be some reasons?

First, people make predictable errors when making decisions. For example, one well known behavioral bias is that we are over-confident. So a CEO may acknowledge that many acquisitions fail, but not her own that she is about to do!

Second, many people are involved in the acquisition decision. It may not be a great outcome for shareholders, but it surely is for investment bankers, lawyers, and often too for acquiring CEOs (e.g., higher pay and more prestige).

Third, what's the alternative? If companies want to grow, acquisitions do not necessarily perform well, but alliances and organic growth are also fraught with difficulties.

6. I am familiar with the integration framework of Haspeslagh and Jemison (1991): holding, preservation, symbiosis, and absorption. How is your approach different?

We too are familiar and inspired by their foundational work. We emphasize two additional points. First, the unit of analysis for the integration decision is the unit (e.g., department) rather than the firm. Thus, you can decide to integrate some departments and not others. Second, we make explicit that the timing of integration (e.g., in a multi-phase process) is a decision distinct from the degree of integration.

7. I understand how to calculate a price for an acquisition when I pay in cash, but what if I pay in stock?

Conceptually, there is no difference. As with a payment in cash, you begin with a valuation of the synergies. Here we consider that company A acquires company B using the example of the appendix to Chapter 2. Assumptions are as before and, in addition, net debt is 90 for company A and 30 for company B, the value of net debt remains the same after the acquisition, prior to the acquisition each company has 10 million shares outstanding, and company A will pay company B in newly issued shares. Table 11.1 shows the equity value (= NPV − net debt) for each company with and without synergies. We assume that the calculated equity values per share equals the price the shares are trading for at the announcement of the acquisition.

TABLE 11.1 *Valuation of synergies (all in million dollars except where noted otherwise)*

	A	B	Total
Without synergies			
NPV	448.33	115.29	563.62
Net debt	90.00	30.00	120.00
Equity value	358.33	85.29	443.62
Number of shares (million)	10	10	
Equity value ($ per share)	35.83	8.53	
With synergies			
NPV	503.67	139.82	643.49
Net debt	90.00	30.00	120.00
Equity value	413.67	109.82	523.49
Impact of synergies	55.34	24.53	79.87

Next, you will have to decide on a price – i.e., how the total expected synergies of 79.87 will be divided between company A and company B. Let's say you represent the shareholders of company A. At a minimum, you do not want to be worse off than before. The top row of Table 11.2 shows the situation where company A gets nothing and company B gets all the synergies. This would increase company B's equity value from 85.29 to 165.16, which translates into a 94 percent premium on equity value for company B (and 0 percent for company A). Thus, the price offered for a share in company B would be 94 percent more than the current value of the share – i.e., 16.52 (from 8.53). The currency used is company A's share, which is worth 35.83 (0 percent premium). Thus, each share of company B is converted to almost half a share of company A (16.52/35.83 = 0.46).

Likewise, company B's shareholders do not want to be worse off than before. The numbers are reversed, see the bottom row of Table 11.2: company A would get 100 percent of the synergies and company B nothing. This implies a 22 percent premium per share for company A and 0 percent for company B. Thus, the price offered for a share in company B is 8.53. The currency used is company A's share, which would be worth 43.82 (22 percent premium). Therefore, each share of company B is converted to 0.19 share of company A.

The bargaining zone is between these two extremes. You will prefer fewer shares offered for a share of company B and use your bargaining skills to drive down the premium for company B (e.g., by claiming that company A will create more synergies than company B, or pointing to a possible difference between actual share price and calculated equity value per share (without synergies)).

TABLE 11.2 *Division of synergies*

Share of synergies (percent)			Equity value (million $)			Premium (percent)		Equity value ($ per share)		Shares offered	
A	B	Total	A	B	Total	A	B	A	B	A	B
0	100	100	358.33	165.16	523.49	0	94	35.83	16.52	0.46	1
10	90	100	366.32	157.17	523.49	2	84	36.63	15.72	0.43	1
20	80	100	374.30	149.19	523.49	4	75	37.43	14.92	0.40	1
30	70	100	382.29	141.20	523.49	7	66	38.23	14.12	0.37	1
40	60	100	390.28	133.21	523.49	9	56	39.03	13.32	0.34	1
50	50	100	398.27	125.23	523.49	11	47	39.83	12.52	0.31	1
60	40	100	406.25	117.24	523.49	13	37	40.63	11.72	0.29	1
70	30	100	414.24	109.25	523.49	16	28	41.42	10.93	0.26	1
80	20	100	422.23	101.26	523.49	18	19	42.22	10.13	0.24	1
90	10	100	430.21	93.28	523.49	20	9	43.02	9.33	0.22	1
100	0	100	438.20	85.29	523.49	22	0	43.82	8.53	0.19	1

Notes

1. A merger of equals is the term used when two companies in a merger, or an acquisition, have similar ownership and control. Post-merger integration occurs in both mergers and acquisitions.
2. For more technical details about the various stages of the M&A process refer, for instance, to Bruner, R. 2004. *Applied Mergers and Acquisitions*. Hoboken, NJ: John Wiley.
3. For instance, see Hawawini, G. and Viallet, C. (2011). *Finance for Executives: Managing for Value Creation*, 4th edn. Mason, WI: South-Western, Cengage Learning.
   Narayanan, M. P. and Nanda, V. K. (2004). *Finance for Strategic Decision-Making: What Non-Financial Managers Need to Know*. Boston, MA: Jossey-Bass.
4. Andrade, G., Mitchell, M., and Stafford, E. (2001). New evidence and perspectives on mergers. *Journal of Economic Perspectives*, 15(2), 103–120.

Further reading

For more on PMI, see:

Capron, L., Dussauge, P., and Mitchell, W. (1998). Resource redeployment following horizontal acquisitions in Europe and North America, 1988–1992. *Strategic Management Journal*, 19(7), 631–662.

Capron, L. and Guillén, M. (2009). National corporate governance institutions and post-acquisition target reorganization. *Strategic Management Journal*, 30(8), 803–833.

Haspeslagh, P. C. and Jemison, D. B. (1991). *Managing Acquisitions: Creating Value through Corporate Renewal*. New York: The Free Press.

For a further discussion on the trade-off between collaboration and disruption in PMI, see:

Puranam, P., Singh, H., and Zollo, M. (2006). Organizing for innovation: managing the coordination–autonomy dilemma in technology acquisitions. *Academy of Management Journal*, 49(2), 263–280.

Puranam, P. and Srikanth, K. (2007). What they know vs. what they do: how acquirers leverage technology acquisitions. *Strategic Management Journal*, 28(8), 805–825.

For meta-analyses on M&A, see:

Haleblian, J., Devers, C. E., McNamara, G., Carpenter, M. A., and Davison, R. B. (2009). Taking stock of what we know about mergers and acquisitions: a review and research agenda. *Journal of Management*, 35(3), 469–502.

King, D. R., Dalton, D. R., Daily, C. M., and Covin, J. G. (2004). Meta-analyses of post-acquisition performance: indications of unidentified moderators. *Strategic Management Journal*, 25(2), 187–200.
Stahl, G. K. and Voigt, A. (2008). Do cultural differences matter in mergers and acquisitions? A tentative model and examination. *Organization Science*, 19(1), 160–176.

Managing the alliance process

*Burger Behemoth Plc has decided that the best way for it to diver-
sify into the theme park business is to form a non-equity alliance
with Mighty Monkey. Burger Behemoth is a successful chain of fast-
food restaurants, with a large network of restaurants around the
country, some of which are franchised and others fully owned. Its
brand has come to stand for standard, tasty, convenient, and quick
meals, and it has enormous customer loyalty among families with
young children below 12, and also among busy executives on the
road. Mighty Monkey is an experienced player in the theme park
business. How should this alliance be implemented?*

Strategic alliances are **temporary, lateral** forms of collaboration
between organizations. They are temporary because the alliance
typically has a finite life (after which it may or may not be renewed).
They are lateral because neither partner has final authority over the
other (unlike in an acquisition, when the acquirer's managers effectively have authority over the target firm's employees after the deal is
completed). Alliances lie between simple arm's-length market relationships and a merger or acquisition. Unlike in M&As, in alliances
the parties remain legally independent and both sides know that the
relationship is not necessarily permanent. Unlike in simple market

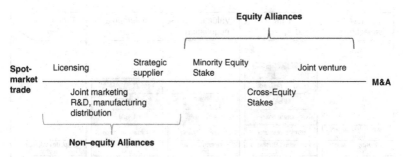

Figure 12.1 A continuum of governance forms

relationships, in alliances intensive collaboration between partners is essential, and a contract alone does not suffice. Something additional is needed in the form of **organizational linkages** between partners, which may be based on prior or expected interactions between the partners, or equity stakes of one (or both) in the other. The term "alliance" thus covers a wide spectrum of non-equity and equity based relationships (including joint ventures), as shown in Figure 12.1. This chapter covers the general principles that apply to all of them.

There are several stages in the process of setting up an alliance involving several people from within and outside the partner firms (see Figure 12.2). Much of the strategic thinking on diversification described in Chapters 4, 5, and 6 must be completed before and overlaps partly with Step 1 (*partner selection*) of the alliance process. In the remainder of the chapter we assume that this thinking has been done – i.e., there's an understanding of the potential synergies (Chapter 2) and transaction costs (Chapter 3), and an alliance is deemed a superior alternative to an M&A or organic growth (Chapters 4–6).

Due diligence in an alliance process refers to a period in which the partners may exchange more information (beyond what was available in the public domain) with each other to confirm that the partnership is based on valid assumptions. The key decision

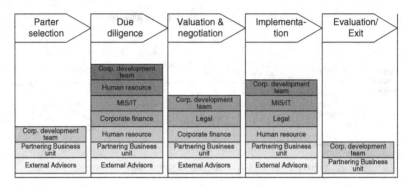

Parter selection	Due diligence	Valuation & negotiation	Implementa-tion	Evaluation/ Exit
	Corp. development team			
	Human resource		Corp. development team	
	MIS/IT	Corp. development team	MIS/IT	
	Corporate finance	Legal	Legal	
Corp. development team	Human resource	Corporate finance	Human resource	
Partnering Business unit	Partnering Business unit	Partnering Business unit	Partnering Business unit	Corp. development team
External Advisors	External Advisors	External Advisors	External Advisors	Partnering Business unit

Figure 12.2   Stages and stakeholders in an alliance process

here is whether to proceed with the alliance with the selected partner, or not. Unlike in an M&A, this step typically precedes the valuation and negotiation of alliance terms. The key decisions in *valuation and negotiation* pertain to the structuring of the alliance and how to split the gains between partners. *Implementation* refers to the process of achieving the desired level of integration of activities across partners in order to extract synergies. Which activities to integrate, and to what extent, are the key decisions at this stage. The valuation and negotiation of the terms of the alliance, as well as implementation activities, depend on the underlying synergies in the partnership. Ideally, these activities should also depend on each other – the terms of the alliance must take into account the anticipated implementation challenges, and the implementation activities must be mindful of the value drivers assumed in the valuation and alliance terms. *Evaluation* refers to a periodic review of whether the alliance is meeting its objectives, and may lead to decisions to terminate the alliance. This is also particularly useful for companies that do a lot of alliances that tend to be similar enough to apply learning from prior alliances to future ones. Uniquely, the evaluation phase in an alliance is not just about learning to do better in the future (as is the case in the

TABLE 12.1 *Differences between M&A and alliances*

	M&A	Alliances
Partner / target selection	Binary and one-time decision	Continuous and ongoing decision (scale up or down the relationship, exit, or continue)
Due diligence	Heavy emphasis on financials to justify price for target	Less focused on financials (because you invest less and take on less risk), more focused on competitive landscape and cultural issues (because collaboration is key)
Valuation and negotiation	Distribution of gains: at the beginning of the transaction	Distribution of gains: during the life of the alliance; may change over the course of the relationship
Implementation	• Ability to handle one-sided synergies: high • Trade-off is between collaboration and disruption created by PMI • Transfer of capabilities: often explicit goal	• Ability to handle one-sided synergies: low • Trade-off between collaboration and competition (even if in a different industry, the partner may use the alliance to enter the industry independently) • Transfer of capabilities: (sometimes the hidden goal of the alliance)
Evaluation	Continuation of the relationship is the default (the alternative is divestiture)	Continuation is an explicit criterion (the alternative is termination of the alliance)

M&A process), but also a decision on whether to continue or terminate the focal alliance itself. While the basic steps for an alliance resemble those for an M&A, the emphasis in each is different (see Table 12.1).

There are many complexities at each stage of an alliance, and in all likelihood, professional advisors (consultants, lawyers, and technical experts) will be involved. The complexity increases if equity shares or a joint venture is involved. This is because the valuation of the partner who is being invested in becomes a much more serious exercise and, in the case of a joint venture, a new legal entity must be created. Our aim is to give the reader a map of the terrain, and a broad framework to bound and manage this complexity from the perspective of a corporate strategist. Our focus in this chapter will therefore be on the key decisions involved in partner selection, valuation and negotiation, and implementation.

Partner selection: should we work with this partner?

While synergies between their value chains may attract partners to each other, how to share these can be extremely contentious in alliances. In an M&A context, this sharing of synergy value between target and acquirer happens upfront, through payment of the acquisition premium. This is not so in the case of an alliance, as both partners continue to operate as autonomous entities pursuing their own goals. Because unity of interests cannot be presumed (i.e., one partner typically has no authority over the other) and the relationship itself is temporary (i.e., it has a finite life, and interim reviews can lead to termination) several problems related to synergy valuation and distribution between partners become significant:

1. **Managing one-sided synergies**: Recall from Chapter 2 that synergies between businesses may be *one-sided* (one business benefits but not the other) or *two-sided* (both businesses benefit). One-sided synergies, particularly, those that require ongoing efforts to extract, are particularly difficult to manage in alliances. This is because it is difficult to force the partner who must make these efforts to do so because the benefit to themselves is minimal.

2. **Ongoing competition between alliance partners:** Alliances between competitors are common (and may evoke scrutiny by anti-trust regulators when the partners jointly have significant market share). Partners may compete in the same business as the alliance or may have other businesses that are in competition with each other. Because each partner remains independent and has its own goals, conflict may be unavoidable within an alliance. This can negatively impact partners' willingness to collaborate, without which alliances are typically doomed.

3. **Learning races:** Partners in an alliance sometimes have hidden agendas. In particular, each side may have an incentive to copy the capabilities of the other through the alliance. This is more relevant for synergies involving dissimilar resources (i.e., Connection and Customization) than those involving similar resources (i.e., Consolidation or Combination). Such "learning races" may occur behind the veneer of collaboration, where the goal of each partner is in reality to make the other party redundant as quickly as possible.

Thus, collaboration between partners in an alliance may often be difficult to achieve, even if there are clearly synergies from doing so. This is because collaboration cannot be enforced, and incentives may not be aligned. Perhaps just as significant as misaligned incentives, though, may be the *suspicion* of misaligned incentives. In any case, when we are uncertain about the partner's likelihood of collaborating, what should we do?[1]

Assessing the robustness or fragility of collaboration in an alliance

We describe a simple analytical framework that helps you understand whether collaboration by each side may be expected to arise in a robust manner (i.e., collaboration is not sensitive to the private motivations of the partner), and offers some suggestions on what to do if it does not. To be clear, by collaboration, we mean the actions each partner takes towards working together that **cannot** be commanded by contracts or authority. Take the example of an alliance between two companies set up to develop new products. Successful new product development requires that both parties make available the necessary funds and people to do research. If a party provides all essential inputs, then in this case it is said to *collaborate*. If a party withholds the required resources (e.g., not putting the best people at the disposal of the partner), then it does *not collaborate*. Contractually, this may be hard to do anything about. Checking the collaboration conditions involves three steps.

Step I: Define and compare scenarios. The first step in this analysis is to define collaboration – what you or the partner would do if you/they were to deliver the spirit and not just the letter of the agreement. Given that each party has two options (collaborating or not collaborating), four scenarios are possible for a given relationship: (A) both parties do not collaborate, (B) only you collaborate, (C) only the other party collaborates, and (D) both parties collaborate. In this step you estimate how attractive each scenario is for yourself. These payoffs will help to assess which choices are optimal for you.

Although hard numbers are ideal, even subjective assessments of payoffs can be useful because what matters is the relative, not absolute magnitude of these payoffs. With a subjective assessment it is helpful to pick one base scenario that is assigned a score of zero (e.g. scenario A). The other scenarios are rated on a scale of –10 to 10. A positive number for a scenario indicates how much it is preferred over scenario A. A negative number implies by how much a scenario is less preferred than scenario A (see Figure 12.3).

Step II: Analyze scenarios. The second step is to calculate two measures from your payoff matrix: your gains from free-riding and your costs for one-sided collaboration. Free-riding means not collaborating when the other does. In our initial alliance example this

You collaborate	B You:_____	D You:_____
You do not collaborate	A You:_____	C You:_____
You Other	Other does not collaborate	Other collaborates

Figure 12.3 Determining the attractiveness of each scenario

happens when one party decides not to contribute resources to new product development, while the other does. *Gains from free-riding* (written as "F") occur if a party does not make any investments, yet is still able to take some or most of the benefits. Losses from free-riding may occur because any benefits from the relationship can only be claimed if a party collaborates. Whether free-riding results in gains or losses for you, follows directly from the payoff matrix in Figure 12.3. Scenario C is the scenario in which you free-ride: the other collaborates but you do not. Scenario D is the scenario in which you do not free-ride, because you collaborate (just like the other party). If your payoff in scenario C is higher than in D, then you have gains from free-riding. If your payoff is higher in scenario D than C, you lose from free-riding. In our framework, we calculate your gains from free-riding as $F = C - D$. If this is positive, then you gain. If this is negative then you lose from free-riding. For example, in the new product development alliance, you gain from free-riding if new products are successfully developed based on the other's contribution even without much of your own. You lose from free-riding if no new products get developed because you refuse to contribute (even if the other does).

The second measure is the *cost of unilateral collaboration* (written as "U"). Unilateral collaboration means collaborating, while the other does not. This is the exact opposite of free-riding. When only one party collaborates, that party is said to unilaterally collaborate and the other is said to free-ride. Unilateral collaboration can be costly or beneficial. It is costly if both party's investments are necessary to generate any benefits, for example in the presence of strong synergies. Unilateral collaboration can be valuable if, for example, committing resources to new product development generates valuable insights that may be applied elsewhere, or if there are "crowding out" effects where gains are smaller if both collaborate.

Whether one-sided collaboration results in gains or losses is again easily determined from the previous step's estimates. From your perspective, you unilaterally collaborate in scenario B. We use your payoffs in scenario A (in which neither party collaborates) to understand the impact of your one-sided collaboration. If your payoffs in scenario A are higher than in scenario B, one-sided collaboration is costly for you. If, on the other hand, your payoffs in scenario B outweigh those of scenario A, you benefit from one-sided collaboration. In our framework we express the outcome of unilateral collaboration as a cost and calculate it as $U = B - A$. A negative number implies a cost, a positive number a gain. In an alliance for new product development, for instance, unilateral collaboration is costly if your efforts are wasted if the other does not contribute. You gain from unilateral collaboration if you can successfully develop new products even without much input from the other, or when working on new products you learn something that is useful in other markets.

Step III: Assess the importance of your partner's collaboration. This involves determining the dependence of your choice on the *partner's probability of collaborating* (written as "p"). The extent of this dependence varies dramatically for different combinations of the gains of free-riding (F) and costs to unilateral collaboration (U). Based on the two measures F and U, and whether their values are positive or negative, we have four possible situations (see Figure 12.4).

Gains from unilateral collaboration (U>0)	Situation 4: Pure free-riding problem	Situation 1: Bliss
Costs to unilateral collaboration (U<0)	Situation 2: Prisoner's dilemma	Situation 3: Pure coordination problem
	Gains from free-riding (F>0)	Costs to free-riding (F<0)

Figure 12.4 Four alliance situations

Situation 1: Costs of free-riding and gains from unilateral collaboration (F < 0, U > 0). In this situation you have no incentive to free-ride, as that will incur costs to you. Also in this situation you are not penalized if you unilaterally collaborate as unilateral collaboration is beneficial. From this it follows that you should always collaborate regardless of what the other does or regardless of what you think the other will do. Any belief you hold about the other is acceptable for you to collaborate. Thus, the partner's probability of collaborating (p) can be between 0 and 1 inclusive. This is a *blissful* situation of robust collaboration! In the new product development alliance example, you would always contribute fully.

Situation 2: Gains from free-riding and costs of unilateral collaboration (F > 0, U < 0). This situation is the exact opposite of the previous one. No belief is sufficient for you to collaborate. To see why, consider your best actions when the other collaborates and when the other does not. If the other collaborates, it is optimal for you not to collaborate due to gains from free-riding. If the other does not collaborate, you prefer no collaboration because you would incur costs for unilateral collaboration. Thus, no value of p will inspire you to collaborate. This type of payoff structure is often referred to as a *prisoner's dilemma*. This is a case of robust non-collaboration: you would not collaborate for any value of p, i.e., for any belief about the other partner's intentions. In the alliance for new product development, you would always be reluctant to invest in the alliance.

Situation 3: Costs of free-riding and costs of unilateral collaboration (F < 0, U < 0). The belief you hold about the other collaborating influences whether you will collaborate. Because there are costs of free-riding, you have no incentive to free-ride if the other collaborates. Yet, if you do not know for certain that the other will collaborate, you are also worried about the costs of one-sided collaboration should the other not collaborate. Only with a sufficiently strong belief will the rewards from joint collaboration outweigh the risk of losses from unilateral collaboration. The belief about the partner's probability of collaboration, p required for you to collaborate can be shown to be $p > \frac{U}{U+F}$. This type of payoff structure is known as a *pure coordination* game. The danger in this class of games does not come from greed – the tendency to take advantage of the other for short-term gains. Rather, the issue is fear – the avoidance of mutually beneficial outcomes due to uncertainty about the other's actions. In the new product development alliance, you would contribute if you are sufficiently sure the other does too.

Situation 4: Gains from free-riding and gains from unilateral collaboration (F > 0, U < 0). Like the previous situation, collaboration is only optimal for some beliefs. Unlike the previous situation, not fear but greed is the main obstacle to joint collaboration. Because there are benefits of unilateral collaboration, you would collaborate if the other does not. Fear is absent. However, if the other collaborates you are tempted not to collaborate. If greedy, one will take the gains from free-riding at the expense of the other. Interestingly, you will collaborate if the other does not, and not collaborate if the other does. This is a *pure free-riding* game. Therefore, you will collaborate only below some probability that the other will collaborate. The formula for the exact cutoff probability is given by $p < \frac{U}{U+F}$. In the new product development alliance, you would only contribute if paradoxically the other does not. This would be the case if it is beneficial that new products are developed but it is best if the other does most of the work.

So how does this analysis inform partner selection? *Situation 1* (costs of free-riding and gains from unilateral collaboration) is the most attractive because you would collaborate and benefit from the alliance regardless of the motivations of the other partner. More generally, if there is a choice among multiple potential alliances, you should prioritize those that seem to belong to situation 1.

Situation 3 (costs of free-riding and of unilateral collaboration) and *situation 4* (gains from free-riding and from unilateral collaboration) are more complicated. In these pure coordination or pure free-riding situations, the partner's probability of collaboration influences your own willingness to collaborate. Hence, **partner selection and communication with the partner are crucial in these situations**. A good starting point is to analyze the payoffs per scenario for each potential partner, just as you did for yourself. While the alliance may look like a situation 3 (or 4) to you, for the other side it may look like bliss (situation 1) or a prisoner's dilemma (situation 2).

Working through the alliance from the other side's perspective should give you some indication of how likely the other is to collaborate. Consider multiple partners because for some it will be more attractive to collaborate than for others. If both of you face situation 3, joint discussions and communication may suffice to solve the problem. Furthermore, you may have good information about how a partner has behaved in similar situations in the past. If doubts about a partner's probability to collaborate remain, you could ask for the alliance to be implemented gradually. You can start with smaller initiatives and when these are successful, progress to bigger projects. Alternatively, you could try to jointly alter the payoffs by restructuring incentives, and trying to make collaboration less dependent on the partner's actions (and vice versa – the partner may have similar concerns about you). There are limits to doing this, though, as contracts cannot be used to manage all aspects of collaborative behavior (which is why we have alliances in the first place).

Situation 2 (gains from free-riding and costs of unilateral collaboration) is potentially the hardest situation. First, you need to analyze whether the problem appears on just your side or on both sides. For example, you may be reluctant to collaborate (because of temptation for free-riding or fear of unilateral collaboration) but the other side may consider it a bliss situation and would be glad to collaborate. If the problem is really on your side (i.e., the other is likely to collaborate), then you need not worry about costs to unilateral collaboration. For the gains from free-riding you have to ask yourself whether this temptation is worth more than a potential future alliance with the same partner (which would be put in jeopardy) or alliance with other partners (if your bad reputation spreads).

If the problem is on both sides, then it might be useful to flag the situation in the valuation and negotiation stage and ask for contractual assurance or bonuses/ penalties, though one should be aware that ultimately such approaches are limited. Second, if the interaction between partners is likely to recur a large number of times in the future and if non-collaboration in any iteration is likely to be easily detected, then the two partners could agree to adopt a strategy of "collaborate as long as the other does." However, these conditions are more likely to hold for a buyer–supplier relationship than, say, a one-off technology development partnership. Finally, abandoning this alliance partner is also an option at this stage.

Trust and partner selection

Because a contract is insufficient, trust is important in alliances. Based on the above classification, we can predict where trust will be higher and where lower. It is crucial to distinguish trust from *perceived trustworthiness*. Trust is your willingness to be vulnerable to a partner's actions based on a belief that the partner will not harm you. Perceived trustworthiness is your belief that the partner will indeed not harm you.

We distinguish the same four situations from your perspective: bliss, pure coordination, pure free-riding, and prisoner's dilemma. Based on the above discussion, you will be most keen to engage in alliance in a bliss situation than in a pure coordination or pure free-riding situation, and least in a prisoner's dilemma situation. Thus, your trust will be highest in bliss, intermediate in pure coordination or pure free-riding, and lowest in prisoner's dilemma. In fact, one could argue that trust is irrelevant in a bliss situation because there is no risk involved and vulnerability is absent. Thus, trust depends on the situation (i.e., payoffs).

Because trust also depends on the other (i.e., perceived trustworthiness), you can increase trust through careful partner selection. In pure coordination, you would like to find a partner whom you think is trustworthy. Obtaining information about past behavior (e.g., references) is useful as are steps to increase trustworthiness (e.g., transparency, reliability). For pure free-riding, it is about your trustworthiness rather than about your partner's. Here the "danger" is that you will exploit the other's collaboration, not that the other will exploit your collaboration. Thus, the question is whether you can keep your greed in check. The other's trustworthiness is not relevant (because there are gains from unilateral collaboration). The prisoner's dilemma is a combination of both these considerations, finding a trustworthy partner and resisting the urge to exploit the other. Finally, in "bliss" situations, the partner's trustworthiness is irrelevant.

Valuation and negotiation: how should we share the effort and rewards?

Valuing the benefits of an alliance is an iterative process. In arriving at the decision to ally, a systematic approach, such as we recommended in Chapters 5 and 6, would already have made at least some approximate estimates of the value to the company from acquiring vs. allying vs. organic growth. Once the alliance alternative has been finalized and a target has been shortlisted, we may use those estimates as a starting point and refine them.

Synergies in alliances fall into the usual 4C's: Consolidation, Combination, Customization, and Connection. A rigorous method to estimate the value of these synergies is through the NPV of future cash flows of both the partners after taking into account the effects of synergies between them (as well as the costs of extracting them). The appendix to Chapter 2 provides details on how to value synergies using value drivers and DCFs.

Integration costs refer to the costs of making the organizational changes across the partners to integrate activities and extract synergies. In alliances, these costs are likely to be, for the most part, dependent on the kind of synergies being extracted; they may be thought of as a tax that eats into the value of the synergy. As we noted in Chapter 2, we can make some informed conjectures about the *differences* between the integration costs (as a percentage of synergy value) as well as the uncertainty associated with each type of synergy.

In Chapter 5 we described how the anticipated costs of restructuring and ensuring compatibility influence the choice between acquisition and alliance. These costs are independent of the magnitude of synergies in the relationship. Unlike in M&As, there are fewer synergy *independent* integration costs in an alliance. Synergy independent costs of integration depend on the scale and age of the target organization. All else being equal, larger and older organizations, regardless of the nature of the synergies involved in the deal, will require greater efforts to convert their systems and processes to be compatible with the acquirer, and to separate and divest unwanted assets. These costs are largely avoided in a strategic alliance, so that valuing an alliance is largely restricted to valuing synergies and integration costs (as a fraction of the former).

When negotiating an M&A, how the value of synergies (net of integration costs) is to be split between the partners in the form of an acquisition premium is often the most important point of negotiation, as the acquirer can unilaterally decide how to organize the combined entity. In contrast, when negotiating an alliance, the parties also need to jointly decide how to organize it. This is because an alliance is a *temporary, lateral* organization. Finally, the negotiation process also shapes expectations about the partner's likelihood of collaboration. We examine these ideas in detail below.

Design elements of an alliance

Organization scientists recognize that any organization, even a temporary, lateral one, features the division of labor and the integration of effort. The division of labor in organizations refers to dissecting the organization's goals into contributory tasks and the allocation of these tasks to individual members within the organization. The integration of effort within an organization requires mechanisms to incentivize the effort to cooperate as well as to provide the necessary information to do so. Seen as an organization, an alliance must thus have solutions to four basic problems of organizing:

1. *Task division* (a.k.a. "What needs to be done"): This refers to the goals and scope of the alliance, and what its value chain will look like. Essentially, one can think of the alliance as a new business, and specify its business model (who are the customers, what is the value proposition and how will it be delivered), value chain, and underlying resources needed to operate.

2. *Task allocation* (a.k.a. "Who does what"): This is the division of the roles and responsibilities among the partners: which partner will contribute which pieces of the alliance's value chain. While

conceptually task allocation is a distinct step from task division, in practice the two will go together; indeed, the task division will reflect what the two partners can uniquely bring to the table to create synergies.

3. *Value sharing* (a.k.a. "Who gets what"): This refers to how the value created by the two partners will be shared between them. Shares can be expressed contractually in terms of profits or sales (e.g., through a royalty), in terms of the share of equity of one firm in another, or in a jointly owned new firm (e.g., as in a joint venture), or as fixed fees paid by one partner to another (e.g., licensing fees take this form).

4. *Interface* (a.k.a. "Who talks to whom"): This specifies the channels of communication and structures of coordination (e.g., task forces, committees, integrator roles) between the alliance partners. It is effectively the organizational structure of the alliance.

Because alliances, like most organizations, do not solve the problems above perfectly, a fifth design element is also important:

5. *Dispute resolution* (a.k.a. "Who is the tie-breaker"): When disputes arise, who has the final say on which issues? If the partners must go to court, which jurisdiction will they be under? What if any is the possible arbitration process?

These correspond to the key design elements of an alliance agreement, and most contracts between partners will have clauses that specifically reflect these elements. The partners must negotiate on and agree on these design elements in order to extract the most value they can from the alliance. The challenge lies in the fact that these negotiations simultaneously determine:

(a) The "size of the pie," i.e., how much value from synergy can be created by linking the appropriate value chain activities across partners, which is determined by choices about task division, task allocation, and interface.

(b) The "share of the pie," i.e., how much each gets, which is determined by the choices about value sharing.

What typically matters to each side ultimately is neither the size of the pie nor the share of the pie, but the "size of the bite" they can get. An important exception is the class of situations in which the perceived fairness of the "share of the pie" each gets influences the future willingness to collaborate in the alliance; when collaboration is not robust in an alliance, this factor must be weighed carefully, and may require the partners to settle for "smaller bites" to preserve perceptions of equity.

Joint ventures are complicated relative to other forms of alliances because the share of equity reflects not only the distribution of profits between parents, but also the relative control they exercise on the decisions of the joint venture, because board representation is usually proportional to equity share. A critical part of the value sharing issue is an agreement on the conditions under which the partnership will be terminated, and how the assets will be shared at that point.

Another challenge that surfaces frequently in alliance negotiation is the handling of one-sided synergies. For instance, gains from Consolidation (e.g., both partners have factories, one of the factories can be shut down) also represent significant opportunity costs – each player essentially gives up that part of the value chain. In a hierarchical arrangement, like an M&A, the distribution of these gains is easier as a single decision-maker buys control of both sets of resources to be consolidated.

Integration in alliances: what and how much to integrate?

To extract the synergies in an alliance requires setting up the organization to do so. This will connect activities across the partners, in order to coordinate them. Integration is thus an elaboration and implementation of the decisions about the alliance interface reached during the negotiations about the key design elements of the alliance structure.

Integration planning ideally commences at the stage of valuation (as the synergies that are being valued must be the ones that are extracted) and is completed before the formal announcement of the alliance, at which point the integration plans can be implemented. A separate program management office may then be created to oversee the integration process, with a host of integration projects targeted at the extraction of particular synergies. We focus here on the planning of the integration process, the key decisions to be made, and the trade-offs to be considered.

Integration in alliances is typically not as complicated as it in the case of acquisitions. This is because of the (relatively) limited scope of activities involved across partners, as well as the lower incidence of Consolidation synergies in alliances (partners are typically unlikely to give up an in-house activity for a temporary lateral arrangement). However, partners typically differ not only in their formal structures, but also in their organizational and possibly national cultures. These differences can impede collaboration across organizations and create conflict.

Organizational structure decisions consist of two sequential choices: one about *grouping* (into organizational units) and the other about *linking* activities across groupings (i.e., the boxes and arrows in organization charts, see Figure 12.5).

Given the lateral, temporary nature of alliance organizations, grouping decisions are unlikely to be involved in the integration of activities; rather the focus is on linking mechanisms. This also implies that the trade-off between collaboration and disruption, which is so central in M&A integration (see Chapter 11), does not play as important a role in alliances, and that the range of linking choices is limited in alliances relative to M&A; extremely high levels of linking are ruled out because grouping is ruled out.

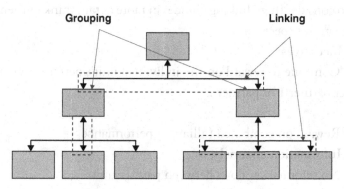

Figure 12.5 Grouping and linking

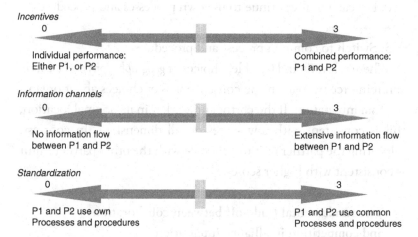

Figure 12.6 Linking choices in alliance integration

Linking choices

The key integration choice in an alliance is about *linking* units or how (a) incentives, (b) information channels, and (c) work practices are changed across units from the two partner organizations (P1 and P2) to either keep them operating autonomously (towards the left–low scores on the scales) or collaboratively (towards the right–high scores on the scales), see Figure 12.6.

To consider these linking choices in more detail, think of them as lying on this spectrum:

(a) **Incentives**:

0: Continue to reward on the individual unit's performance, i.e., either partner 1 or partner 2

←—→

3: Reward on combined (alliance) performance

(b) **Information channels**:

0: No information flows between partner units

←—→

3: Extensive information flows between units across partners

(c) **Standardization of work procedures**:

0: Let each unit continue to use own processes and procedures

←—→

3: Switch to common process and procedures.

Where relevant and feasible, choices of *geographic/physical location* can reinforce or weaken the consequences of choices about organizational integration. If the partner unit is left in its original location, this is consistent with low scores on all dimensions. In contrast, relocating the partner unit to collocate with the other partner's unit is consistent with higher scores.

The fundamental trade-off between collaboration and competition in alliance integration

As one goes from the left to the right of these scales, two things happen. First the degree of collaboration between the individuals in the units involved across partners increases. Common incentives, free flow of information, and smooth operating procedures all enable the employees of partner firms to collaborate effectively to extract the synergies that motivated the alliance. Second, precisely for the same reasons, the exposure of each partner to the other, in terms of possible leakage of knowledge and talent, also increases. In an M&A context this would not have been a problem, as the two units ultimately belong to the same firm. In an alliance this is not the case, as the partners may (implicitly) compete.

This competition has its roots in the temporary nature of an alliance; eventually each partner can foresee a future in which the other partner does not exist. There can thus exist situations in which each partner is essentially aiming to make the other redundant to themselves; they have an incentive to "copy" the capabilities of the other. This is especially relevant when synergies between partners are from Customization or from Connection, as these involve dissimilar resources. Note that this "hidden agenda" would not be a problem in a permanent relationship like an acquisition. To the extent this hidden agenda is suspected to exist, integration decisions must balance the need for coordination between the partners, while minimizing the size of the "window" through which the partners can observe, learn from, and copy each other's capabilities.

A framework for alliance integration planning

Armed with these principles, we can introduce the basic framework for integration planning in alliances. **The key principle behind this framework is that, in every alliance, each pair of organizational units from the partner firms could have a different optimal level of integration between them, based on the synergy operators that link them.** Take the following steps:

1. Start with a clear statement of potential synergies between the partners (preferably the same one used to value the alliance): Understand exactly where and how the value chains of the two companies will join up. Chapter 2 and the synergy operators provide insight into this process.

2. Identify the organizational units in the partner firms associated with the affected value chain segments.

3. Create a matrix with the organizational units of one partner on the rows (see Figure 12.7), and the organizational units housing synergistic value chain segments of the other partner on the columns (based on the synergies analysis above).

4. In this partner–partner matrix, for each cell, note the value of the synergies to be realized as estimated in the valuation phase. In addition, also put down the impact of risk of leakage of capability (and possibly any implicit learning benefits for yourself).

5. Finally, for each cell, consider the linking choices: Bear in mind the Collaboration–Competition trade-off when selecting the degree of integration.

6. For each unit (row), the integration level should be such as to avoid conflict with the cell for which the synergies are greatest.

7. You can choose to do the integration in phases: You can decide on a desired level of integration for **phase 1**, achieve it, and then plan for the next level of integration in **phase 2**. This is not the same as slow vs. fast implementation, in which the desired end state is known and we only vary the time taken to get there. Phase-wise integration can be very useful if you expect new information to emerge that may materially alter your plan for extracting synergies (e.g., on how trustworthy the partner really is).

	A1	A2	A3	A4
B1				
B2				
B3				

Figure 12.7   Alliance integration matrix

The guiding principle for these choices may be stated as follows: in general, lower levels of integration (i.e., low scores on linking choices) are sufficient for low modification and dissimilar underlying resources. Thus the synergies requiring least and most integration, in that order, are likely to be Connection, [Combination, Customization], Consolidation. At the same time, you will want to avoid high integration across units in which you see significant dangers of leakage of knowledge and skills to the partner (i.e., in Connection and Customization synergies).

Application: the Burger Behemoth–Mighty Monkey alliance

In the case of the planned alliance between Burger Behemoth and Mighty Monkey, the goal is for Burger Behemoth to access the physical infrastructure, content development, and service delivery capabilities needed to operate in this business via this alliance. In return, Mighty Monkey sees value in being able to access the brand and customer loyalty of Burger Behemoth, particularly in the segment of families with children below 12. *A priori*, there are benefits from collaborating.

Partner selection: While the partner has been identified, Burger Behemoth might benefit from considering the robustness or fragility of collaboration in this alliance. Collaboration for Burger Behemoth could involve making efforts at cross-selling the theme park through its restaurants, and accommodating requests from Mighty Monkey for co-branding, and resisting from trying to "copy" the capabilities at theme park management from Mighty Monkey. Collaboration for Mighty Monkey might mean making sure that its infrastructure and services are at the best possible level to prevent any dilution of Burger Behemoth's brand, and to avoid "copying" Burger Behemoth's capabilities at managing customer loyalty in the families with young children segment. It is likely that in a situation such as this, neither party gains from holding back on collaboration when the other collaborates (i.e., there are no gains from free-riding), though both parties may suffer if they unilaterally collaborate. If we assume it is unlikely that Burger Behemoth would want to copy Mighty Monkey's capabilities with the intention of eventual entry on their own, and we also assume a symmetric reasoning process for Mighty Monkey, then this situation looks like a pure coordination problem. Communicating their concerns to each other and setting up a transparent system for mutual verification of collaboration efforts could be useful in this context.

If, on the other hand, there is some private gain for each side to try to copy the capabilities of the other, then we could be looking at a situation that seems like a prisoner's dilemma. In this situation, it is unlikely that either side would collaborate. Modifying the payoffs by explicitly agreeing non-compete conditions, widening the scope of the relationship to gradually increase more and more the theme park sites that Mighty Monkey has, or finding a different partner, are some of the options they have to choose from.

Valuation and negotiation: In this situation, the synergies are largely from Connection, and the effects are primarily on revenues. Therefore the two sides will have to agree on some form of revenue sharing agreement, which is able to estimate the incremental revenue produced by the alliance. The design of the alliance structure is quite straightforward: task division and task allocation must recognize the relative competencies of Burger Behemoth and Mighty Monkey, and the interface can be a relatively thin one (probably located within the marketing departments of the two firms).

Alliance integration: Given the nature of the synergies, there is a limited need for integration between partners, even if there were no concerns about "learning races." If such concerns exist, maintaining a thin interface becomes even more critical. In either case, this will be a fairly easy alliance to implement.

Basic facts about alliances

- **Alliances are difficult to manage**: When managers are asked to rate their alliance, about 50 percent get rated as unsuccessful. This is similar to reported baseline success rates for organic growth projects or M&As. In many ways, though, alliances are harder to manage than acquisitions, when there are significant one-sided synergies (some of which may be secret) and when partners are trying to "learn/copy" the dissimilar resources of others, even though alliances are cheaper to set up than acquisitions. This is because, in an acquisition, the control of one partner over the other is absolute but in an alliance it is not. Thus, unless the terms of the alliance are such as to induce effective collaboration, it is likely that in an alliance the relationship will revert to the letter rather than the spirit of the contract.

- **Alliances are not forever**: While the duration varies by type of alliance and by context, many alliances terminate within ten years of formation. This holds also for joint ventures, where typically one partner eventually buys out the other. Note that a terminated alliance is not the same as a failed alliance. Many alliances are set up precisely for a limited period, and sometimes as a reaction to regulatory requirements, which when changed may lead to termination.
- **Alliance negotiations must take into account concerns about fairness if ongoing collaboration between partners is critical to the success of the alliance**: Some common contentious issues in alliance negotiations include diverging views of the goal, jockeying for relative control, profit sharing, cannibalization of businesses not involved in the alliance, distribution of one-sided synergies, learning races, and exit conditions.

Common mistakes to avoid

- **Mistaking equality for equity**: Equity involves each partner getting a share that is proportional to its contribution; sometimes this may be very different from equality. Negotiations between prospective alliance partners may sometimes become mired in issues around perceived inequality. But because partners typically will make different sized contributions and have different bargaining power, expecting equal shares is unrealistic. There is an important exception to this: if the differences in contribution and bargaining power across partners is small, and ongoing collaboration between partners is critical to the future of the alliance, then ignoring equity and sharing equally may be sensible.

- **Mistaking value creation for value captured**: Remember, your goal in an alliance is to maximize total profits for yourself. The size of the bite is what matters, not the total size of the pie or the equality of the shares of the pie. To reiterate the important exception here: if ongoing collaboration between partners will be critical to the future of the alliance, then negotiating hard to win the last dollar of expected value may vitiate the relationship to the extent that the other partner does not collaborate as needed.
- **Ignoring the possibilities of learning races**: An alliance does not guarantee a permanent meeting of interests. You must therefore consider the possibility of learning races and how your bargaining power relative to the partner may evolve over time.
- **Ignoring exit conditions**: Alliances are temporary organizations. It is therefore important to agree, as part of the alliance design, the conditions under which the alliance can be terminated, and the distribution of assets between the parties at that point. This may seem like striking a discordant note in the negotiation and design phase where the rhetoric is all about partnership; nonetheless, it is necessary.

Frequently asked questions

1. **My company wants to become better at managing alliances. What should we do?**

Experience is a useful mentor, but only if lessons across alliances are actively integrated. Two hurdles need to be overcome. First, just doing multiple alliances will not necessarily lead to insight unless effort is made to distil the lessons learned. Second, alliances occur across the corporation so that lessons learned in one business are not automatically available to other businesses. A solution for both hurdles is to set up a dedicated alliance team, for example, at the corporate level. Give this group the responsibility for documenting the lessons learned from ongoing alliances and disseminating this information across the corporation. They should also be given a formal role in the initiation of new alliances and evaluation of ongoing ones.

> **2. I have heard that in alliances one has to avoid the challenge of the "prisoner's dilemma" where each side ends up not collaborating even though there are synergies from collaboration. How can I avoid this problem?**

In a prisoner's dilemma, there are no incentives to collaborate for each partner, regardless of what the other partner does. The only options are to try to restructure the payoffs, try to make the game a repeated one, or to find another partner for whom the alliance is not a prisoner's dilemma. Actually the prisoner's dilemma is only one of four possible situations in which you can find your alliance (see Figure 12.4); this particular structure has disproportionate mind-share among both students and managers. The more general issue is to understand to what extent the incentives to collaborate for one partner depend on the expected actions of the other. That's what the framework to assess the robustness or fragility of collaboration does.

> **3. How do international alliances differ from alliances between companies within a country?**

Many of the same issues are still relevant in international alliances as in domestic ones. However, new complications are introduced by the cross-border nature of these alliances. For instance, regulatory requirements sometimes force companies to enter a market through a joint venture (rather than a wholly owned subsidiary), so that in these cases the alliance structure is not the first best choice for the company. This has often been mandated in emerging markets. Second, differences in IP regimes across countries can accentuate the learning race problems of alliances. Finally, cultural differences are likely to be more pronounced in cross-border contexts, but the effect of cultural differences are most pronounced when the synergies between partners require close collaboration (i.e., in Consolidation or Customization synergies).

4. How are joint ventures different from other kinds of alliances?

Joint ventures are a particular form of equity alliance. Their uniqueness arises from the fact that a new legal entity, the joint venture company, is created, in which the parents own shares (see Figure 12.8). A common division is 50–50 percent ownership but other divisions are possible.

Joint ventures are preferred over acquisitions when the partners have diversified interests that have few points of overlap. There is

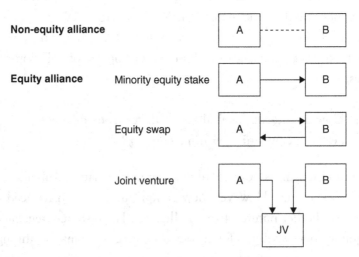

Figure 12.8 Non-equity and equity alliances

relatively low exposure to risk, and limited motivational consequences. Joint ventures are preferred over alliances when a high degree of coordination and incentive alignment for *relevant personnel* from the parent companies is important. However, joint ventures also open up each side to greater risk of knowledge leakage than other forms of alliance. Joint ventures are harder to negotiate than traditional alliances because relative control and profit sharing are often tied together in the equity shares of the parents. In addition, many of the traditional challenges of alliances remain relevant – such as cannibalization, learning races, and one-sided synergies.

5. I have multiple alliances. Does that matter? Would I do anything differently than if I had just a few?

Yes. There could be both benefits and costs. The benefits include an ability to broker between otherwise unconnected partners. For example, a new technology that you learn in one alliance might be fruitfully applied in one of your other alliances. Furthermore, by having multiple alliances within an industry, you might be better able to compete with others who are not in your network. On the cost side, your existing alliance could restrict the number of new alliances that you can enter. For example, others might be reluctant to share technology with you if there is a risk it could end up with their competitors. Possible solutions include taking an equity stake or structuring the alliance such that knowledge flows are limited.

Note

1. This section is a simplified presentation of the arguments in Puranam, P., Kretschmer, T., and Vanneste, B., "Note on Analyzing Fragility in Collaborative Relationships."

Further reading

On the importance of partnering to compete, see:

Dyer, J. H. and Singh, H. (1998). The relational view: cooperative strategy and sources of interorganizational competitive advantage. *Academy of Management Review*, 23(4), 660–679.

For meta-analysis on alliances, see:

Hawkins, T., Knipper, M. G., and Strutton, D. (2009). Opportunism in buyer–supplier relations: new insights from quantitative synthesis. *Journal of Marketing Channels*, 16(1), 43–75.

Reus, T. H. and Rottig, D. (2009). Meta-analyses of international joint venture performance determinants. *Management International Review*, 49(5), 607–640.

For the role of trust in alliances, see:

Gulati, R. (1995). Does familiarity breed trust? The implications of repeated ties for contractual choice in alliances. *Academy of Management Journal*, 38(1), 85–112.

Mayer, R. C., Davis, J. H., and Schoorman, F. D. (1995). An integrative model of organizational trust. *Academy of Management Review*, 20(3), 709–734.

Puranam, P. and Vanneste, B. S. (2009). Trust and governance: untangling a tangled web. *Academy of Management Review*, 34(1), 11–31.

Vanneste, B. S., Puranam, P., and Kretschmer, T. (2014). Trust over time in exchange relationships: meta-analysis and theory. *Strategic Management Journal*, 35(12), 1891–1902.

For the role of learning in alliances, see:

Kale, P., Dyer, J. H., and Singh, H. (2002). Alliance capability, stock market response, and long term alliance success: the role of the alliance function. *Strategic Management Journal*, 23(8), 747–767.

Kale, P. and Singh, H. (2007). Building firm capabilities through learning: the role of the alliance learning process in alliance capability and firm-level alliance success. *Strategic Management Journal*, 28(10), 981–1000.

Inkpen, A. C. and Tsang, E. W. K. (2007). Learning and strategic alliances. *Academy of Management Annals*, 1(1), 479–511.

Vanneste, B. S. and Puranam, P. (2010). Repeated interactions and contractual detail: identifying the learning effect. *Organization Science*, 21(1), 186–201.

For more on exiting from alliances, see:

Gulati, R., Sytch, M., and Mehrotra, P. (2008). Breaking up is never easy: planning for exit in a strategic alliance. *California Management Review*, 50(4), 147–163.

For more on networks of alliances, see:

Greve, H., Rowley, T., and Shipilov, A. (2014). *The Network Advantage: How to Unlock Value from Your Alliances and Partnerships*. New York/San Francisco, CA: Wiley/Jossey-Bass.

Lavie, D. (2007). Alliance portfolios and firm performance: a study of value creation and appropriation in the US software industry. *Strategic Management Journal*, 28(12), 1187–1212.

Index